D1544501

# ACTING WILDE

"I love acting – it is so much more real than life," Oscar Wilde famously wrote. *Acting Wilde* demonstrates that Wilde's plays, fiction, and critical theory are organized by the idea that all so-called "reality" is a mode of performance, and that the "meanings" of life are really the scripted elements of a dramatic spectacle. Wilde's real issue was whether one could become the author of his own script, the creator of the character and role he inhabits. It was a question he struggled to answer from the beginning of his career to the end, whether in his position as the pre-eminent dramatist in English or as the beleaguered defendant on trial for "gross indecency." Introducing important new evidence from Wilde's career-launching tour of America, the often tortured revisions of his plays, and the recently discovered written record of his first courtroom trial, this book reconstructs Wilde's strategic dramatizing of himself.

KERRY POWELL is Professor and Chair of English at Miami University. He is the editor of *The Cambridge Companion to Victorian and Edwardian Theatre* (2004), and the author of *Women and Victorian Theatre* (1997) and *Oscar Wilde and the Theatre of the 1890s* (1990).

# ACTING WILDE: VICTORIAN SEXUALITY, THEATRE, AND OSCAR WILDE

KERRY POWELL

*Miami University*

CAMBRIDGE
UNIVERSITY PRESS

CAMBRIDGE UNIVERSITY PRESS

Cambridge, New York, Melbourne, Madrid, Cape Town, Singapore, São Paulo, Delhi

Cambridge University Press
The Edinburgh Building, Cambridge CB2 8RU, UK

Published in the United States of America by Cambridge University Press, New York

www.cambridge.org
Information on this title: www.cambridge.org/9780521516921

First published 2009

Printed in the United Kingdom at the University Press, Cambridge

*A catalogue record for this publication is available from the British Library*

ISBN 978-0-521-51692-1 hardback

To Felice

*"The woman I love …"*

# Contents

# Illustrations

# Acknowledgments

I would like to thank Merlin Holland, grandson of Oscar Wilde, for sharing behind-the-scenes information about the recently discovered transcript of Wilde's first courtroom trial. Merlin's generosity and trust made it possible for me to characterize the origins and enormous importance of this document more fully than has been done before. I also appreciate permission to photograph pages from the "lost" trial transcript, granted by the anonymous donor who placed the manuscript on permanent loan at the British Library.

Three other distinguished critics of Wilde have had a major influence upon *Acting Wilde*: they are Joseph Bristow, Sos Eltis, and Peter Raby. I am glad to have this opportunity to express my appreciation for their own remarkable work as well as for their friendship and support in numerous ways. It is a pleasure also to acknowledge a great debt, both professional and personal, to John Kucich and Dianne Sadoff, who have helpfully consulted on this project and life in general over a period of time. I am grateful as well for the legal research and expertise that Barbara Morgenstern generously contributed to this project.

This book could never have been written without the assistance of archivists at the British Library, the Clark Memorial Library at UCLA, the Harry Ransom Humanities Research Center at the University of Texas, the special collections unit of the Texas Christian University library, the New York Public Library, the University of Cambridge library, and the Woman's Library, London. I am deeply grateful as well to the department of English and the faculty research committee of Miami University for making available the time and financial resources to make this book possible.

My greatest debt is to my partner, Felice Marcus, who makes everything possible.

# Introduction
## Acting Wilde

*"One's true character is what one wishes to be, more than what one is."*
– A line in an early autograph manuscript of *An Ideal Husband*,
unfortunately canceled in the process of revision.

"I love acting," says a character in Oscar Wilde's novel *The Picture of Dorian Gray*. "It is so much more real than life."[1] The proposition is striking in its anti-Victorian contention that dramatic artifice holds sway on *both* sides of the curtain, and that the conscious actor has a greater claim on "reality" than the unwitting performers beyond the footlights.

Wilde was among the first to discern that life is a continuum of performance, and everyone an actor – not metaphorically, as in Shakespeare's "All the world's a stage," but *really*. In his darkest hour, imprisoned at hard labor and recognizing himself as the unwilling principal of an all-too-real, grotesque puppet-play, Wilde maintained his belief in the power of the actor, even when thwarted and diminished, to shape reality through performance. "Puppets themselves have passions," he wrote from prison. "They will bring a new plot into what they are presenting, and twist the ordered issue of vicissitude to suit some whim or appetite of their own."[2] This freedom-in-bondage is "the eternal paradox of human life," Wilde goes on to reflect, and it is a paradox that determined his work as a playwright as well. It is most fully realized in *The Importance of Being Earnest*, a play in which personal identity is contingent on external forces – an array of textual, ritual, and theatrical practices – and yet is capable, within limits, of disrupting this "ordered issue of vicissitude" by means of an insurgent self-enactment to fulfill the desire left unsatisfied by one's assigned role. It is Wilde's visionary theatricality with which this book is concerned; and far more than has been acknowledged, it lies at the core of his importance in the realms of both theatre and thought.

This intertextuality of theatre and life took shape for Wilde as something much deeper and more complex than the dandified "posing" with which his contemporaries and later generations stigmatized or, in a few cases, valorized him.³ Wilde's theatricality was only coincidentally, and briefly, concerned with wearing his hair long, dressing in velvet and silk, and walking about London with a lily in his hand. Rather, it was, or became over time, a philosophy with revolutionary aims and high ideals, yet conflicted and compromised, and laboriously worked out in both his life and work. What began as the high-spirited and largely unreflective "posing" of a young aesthete in the early 1880s would turn deadly serious in time as Wilde grappled with the anxieties and difficulties of forming a new, performative interpretation of life. At issue were the dynamics of personal and gendered identity, and the shifting currents of Wilde's debates with his adversaries and with himself on these points can be detected in the still incomplete record of his life and in the much-revised writing he undertook for the actual theatre. Wilde's theatricality, however, cannot be adequately accounted for by postmodern theories of performance and subjectivity, although it is surprising to see how prophetically he anticipated them in the *fin de siècle*. To appreciate and understand Wilde's performative achievement, it is necessary above all to situate him in the controversies of his historical moment regarding gender and subjectivity, while at the same time attending to the archival record of his hesitations and second guesses as a playwright for the late-Victorian stage.

This book, therefore, will attempt to recover Wilde's theatre and theatricality in the web of historical circumstance in which they were formed. His developing ideas of gendered and sexual identity, I will argue, arise out of a contentious dialogue with late-nineteenth-century feminism and its struggle to disturb the settled meanings of such concepts as "masculine" and "feminine." Wilde's best-known plays, from *Lady Windermere's Fan* to *The Importance of Being Earnest*, were written to a considerable degree in response to the radical views that drove a militant and still widely misunderstood women's movement. Feminist political action of the time was informed by a vast outpouring of polemical journalism, books, and pamphlets – documents little-known today, yet historic in their challenge to established ideas of what it meant to be a "man" or "woman," setting up a field of tension in which Wilde's own attempts at self-fashioning took root. Wilde's theatricality was both revolutionary and historically specific, making for a significance that we cannot adequately appreciate outside the context of an under-historicized, late-Victorian feminism as well as a variety of related legal and other social texts of the time.

Within this crucible of conflict over personal and gendered identity, Wilde's dramas for the London stage were written and rewritten, his revisions providing a map of the intellectual ferment that underlay their changing form. The present study is the first, I believe, to base its analysis on first-hand examination of all surviving, pre-production manuscripts and typescripts of these plays – numerous drafts, scattered geographically, but crucial for their revelation of the advances, retreats, and dead-ends of Wilde's thinking about gender and subjectivity in his comedies of the early 1890s. No edition of Wilde's plays captures the full range and nuance of these revisions, and no criticism of Wilde, as far as I know, has taken them all into account. Nevertheless, this book owes a considerable debt to the ground-breaking work of Sos Eltis, whose *Revising Wilde* was the first and, until now, only book to focus on Wilde's rewriting of his own dramas. In addition to being based on the virtually complete archive of surviving play manuscripts, however, the "Oscar Wilde" who emerges from the present study is more contingent and conflicted, more "Victorian" and less consistently progressive in his sexual and political views, than the Wilde whom Eltis draws in her powerfully argued analysis.[4]

By 1895 Wilde's career as a playwright was effectively finished, brought to an end by his arrest and trials on charges of gross indecency, culminating in a sentence of two years in prison. But his trials and imprisonment were dramas in their own right, as perceived by Wilde as well as his tormentors, a view that is vividly communicated in the defendant's long letter from prison, *De Profundis*, and in the long-lost but recently discovered transcript of one of his trials. There was no known surviving transcript of any of Wilde's three trials until this one came to light only a few years ago, and this study, as far as I know, is the first to make use of it in any serious or detailed way. The transcript reveals a courtroom proceeding that was, in effect, a mosaic of competing dramatizations of "Oscar Wilde," performances enacted by Wilde himself and others that were staged by his adversaries in a contest to specify and define the celebrated principal of the case and the nature (if any) of masculinity itself. It is difficult to over-estimate the importance of the lost transcript to Wilde studies, and the impact it is sure to have on our understanding of the trial of the century and the man it was about.

Terry Eagleton has observed that Oscar Wilde lived and expressed, *avant la lettre*, the fundamental insights of contemporary cultural theory. Most notably, late-twentieth-century theories of performance can be seen as an elaborate footnote to Wilde, who produced art, including the art of life, in performative terms without the benefit of a theory of performance to guide him. What we now call performativity came to Wilde and his dramatic characters in the rush of events, as the expression of their own passions and musings rather than as a developed system of thought. Wilde's vaguely rebellious and exuberant "posing" in the early 1880s matured over time into tactical, urgent reflections on social performance in a world that, as he came to know it, was controlled by a dramatic script that preceded him. The directives of that controlling script were expressed in legal processes, social rituals, and the theatre itself, and the burning question – for Wilde, as for later theorists such as Victor Turner, Jacques Derrida, and Judith Butler – was whether the actors could exercise improvisational freedom and make the play their own, if only within limits. Especially in his last plays and in the courtroom trials and their aftermath, Wilde consciously sought to enact an alternative masculinity that would upset the foundations of Victorian social life – yet he was never able to work out, either for himself or others, precisely what would constitute this new kind of man. In both his life and drama Wilde's efforts to articulate a new vision of manhood stopped short of their destination; for the more he talked and wrote, the more he became enmeshed in the web of custom and power that he most wanted to break free of. Wilde's performativity was prophetic, but also of its time, shaped and limited by the late-Victorian conditions that framed it. Among those contextual conditions were historic disputes over gendered identity, controversies hugely influential at the time, but blurred, distorted, or overlooked entirely in our retrospective vision today.

Wilde, moreover, was a Victorian himself, inhabiting the world of Matthew Arnold while envisioning and to some degree actually living a postmodernity yet to be born. He stood at the crossroads where ideas of a "genuine self," in Matthew Arnold's nostalgic phrase, began to be superseded by an unstable, performance-based subjectivity. Arnold's poem "The Buried Life" (1852) laments the "disguises" behind which modern individuals present themselves to each other and even to themselves, disguises that estrange us, in Arnold's view, from the authenticity of a "hidden" self that constitutes our core being.[5] But the theatricality that Arnold, and Victorians generally, feared as deadening to the "soul" was embraced by Wilde precisely because it freed him from the structures of fixed truth, opening new worlds of possibility for the individual.

Nina Auerbach has speculated that the source of Victorian fears of theatricality was a historically new anxiety that the "true" self, and indeed all "truth," was performed rather than real; Victorians were haunted, in other words, by a dread of "the theatricality of sincerity itself."[6] But Oscar Wilde was not. "Is insincerity such a terrible thing?" he writes in *The Picture of Dorian Gray.* "I think not. It is merely a method by which we can multiply our personalities." And Lord Henry Wotton's paradoxical remark in the same novel – "I love acting. It is so much more real than life" – recognizes the theatricality of the "real" world and celebrates the power of the conscious actor to perform a superior "reality" of his or her own design. Yet the ugly ending of *The Picture of Dorian Gray*, and of Wilde's own life and career, suggests that these large and subversive claims for a performative interpretation of life do not tell the whole story, even for Wilde.

At the same time, it would be mistaken to construct a simplistic binary of the "performed" and the "real." For Wilde, as for a few recent critics of Victorian performativity, no such clear-cut distinction is possible, and all so-called authenticity has its performative dimension. Lynn Voskuil has recently demonstrated that in Victorian England, theatricality and authenticity were inseparably entangled in the construction of the "symbolic typologies by which the English knew themselves as individuals, as a public, and as a nation."[7] Theatricality, rather than subverting "reality," commingles with and potentially enhances it, as Lord Henry Wotton suggests in *The Picture of Dorian Gray* when he imagines the theatricality of authenticity – moments when "we are no longer the actors, but the spectators of the play ... Or rather we are both. We watch ourselves, and the mere wonder of the spectacle enthralls us."[8] James Eli Adams has argued persuasively that for the Victorians there was "the intractable element of theatricality in all masculine self-fashioning." There was not one regimen of Victorian masculinity, but many, as Adams reminds us – including "gentleman, dandy, priest, prophet, soldier, and professional," varied scripts of manhood that were inevitably performed for an audience.[9] Herbert Sussman, in an earlier analysis, makes a similar point, arguing that Victorian masculinity was "varied and multiform" (even though contrasting versions of manhood held in common some underlying features such as ascetic self-regulation and homosocial bonding).[10] Typically these discourses of Victorian masculinity were performed unselfconsciously, in resistance to the idea that masculinity, or any form of identity, is socially constructed or mediated. Wilde's revolutionary contribution was not only to conceive of gender, personal identity, and life itself as "performed," but to welcome this recognition with open arms and adopt, in both theory and practice, a calculated strategy of self-fashioning. The grand scale of his analysis and ambition was matched only by the catastrophe in which it engulfed him. In ensuing chapters this book will examine Wilde's success and failure in achieving the liberation that he sought through dramatic self-enactment, both in his plays and in his life. Chapter 1, "Posing and dis-posing: Oscar Wilde in America and beyond," sets the stage for this analysis by recalling Wilde's visit to America in 1882 to give a series of lectures promoting the new Gilbert and Sullivan comic opera, *Patience*

– a slashing satire of the new "aestheticism" of which Wilde himself was already the most notorious embodiment. In America, he appeared in lecture halls as the look-alike of Reginald Bunthorne, the effeminate, velvet- and lace-clad central character of *Patience* who had been conceived in the first place as a parody of Wilde. Posed as a caricature of himself, Wilde nevertheless aimed to undermine the Gilbert and Sullivan "Oscar Wilde" by simultaneously performing the tenets of an aestheticism in which he really believed, including opposition to the commercial and legal principles that accounted for his presence in America in the first place. The self-contradictions and limitations of such an undertaking were materialized dramatically one evening when Wilde and his entourage went to the theatre to see a performance of *Patience* in New York City. The real-life "Bunthorne" – i.e., the gorgeously accoutered Wilde himself – took a prominent seat where he attracted the fascinated gaze of the audience toward a counter-performance that he carried out in competition with the enactment of Bunthorne/Wilde on stage. Was Wilde *posing* in his theatre stall, or being *dis*-posed – confined in a role written, imposed, by someone or something else? This crucial question of agency in Wilde's flamboyant posing arose repeatedly in his American tour, and perhaps most notably with a famous photograph, "Oscar Wilde, No. 18," shot by the celebrity photographer Napoleon Sarony in his Manhattan studio and distributed widely by him for sale. This picture of Wilde – dressed in full Bunthorne regalia, with dreamy eyes, book in hand – would soon become the centerpiece of an important law case in intellectual property, the issue being one of "ownership" of this elaborately posed image of Wilde. Ultimately the U.S. Supreme Court determined that the photographer himself, Sarony, had so arranged and "disposed" his model, Wilde, that the photo was exclusively Sarony's in terms of property rights. It was a potent demonstration that one's pose or self-presentation is not a matter of pure personal agency, but rather implicated in the regulatory processes of the social world. In this sense Wilde's audacious posing in America was "owned" and "authored," in a legal and broadly social sense, by forces far beyond himself.

The first chapter argues further that Wilde's ruminations on posing and self-enactment became increasingly sophisticated, if never wholly successful, after the experience of his American tour as "Bunthorne." In his essay "London Models," for example, Wilde characterizes artist's models as professors of posing who vacate any identity of their own, becoming neutral surfaces upon which artists enact themselves and their desires. This analysis of the model as a pastiche of poses could have been applied, with at least some accuracy, to Wilde's own experience in America, and it was an analysis that complicated the issue of personal agency, his own and in general, to an extreme degree. "The Portrait of Mr. W.H.," a story first published in 1889, posits the allegedly antique portrait of a boy, really a forgery, as "proof" that the model was the W.H. to whom Shakespeare dedicated his love sonnets, thus providing a genealogy and a discourse for the homosexuality that Wilde sought fumblingly to express and legitimate. In the story, the search for the boy's identity becomes in fact the search for a homosexual identity, including Wilde's own, but the success of the project depends upon the complete erasure of the model himself. The boy in the painting is posed by Wilde, much as Sarony had posed Wilde himself a few years before, and each of these *dis-posings* produced, at best, ambivalent results as far as Wilde's own self-enactment was concerned.

In the late 1880s and early 1890s Wilde continued to develop his ideas on the self-fashioning of the artist through art, including the ambiguous role of the model in an effort to realize himself on his own terms. In Wilde's maturing analysis, all great art is a mode of acting, an attempt by the artist to realize himself outside the limitations of the social and material world. Thus, in "The Critic as Artist," the best playwrights actually *become* the dramatic characters they create, and in "The Decay of Lying" it is the business of the actor to *mis*-represent Nature, turning Hamlet's aesthetic of mimesis inside-out. These hopeful theoretical pronouncements are always compromised by the narrative structures in which Wilde seeks to embed them, however, whether in fiction, plays, or life itself. Chapter 1 concludes with a discussion of *The Picture of Dorian Gray*, demonstrating that self-enactment is inevitably, even fatally, contingent upon the constraints it seeks to elude. Dorian Gray merges his identity with the picture he posed for, as the result of a stunningly efficacious speech act early in the novel, and in so doing transcends for a time not only the laws of representation (making life imitate art, rather than the other way round), but the laws of morality and social convention as well. At the end of the novel, Dorian's suicide and the entry of the police signal the end of this subversive enactment. Loathing himself (his aestheticized self), Dorian lies dead from the knife-wound he inflicted on his own portrait, reclaimed by the moral and social codes that he had defied in life.

Chapter 2, "Pure Wilde: feminism and masculinity in *Lady Windermere's Fan*, *Salomé*, and *A Woman of No Importance*," begins by arguing that Wilde's first great stage comedy, *Lady Windermere's Fan* (1892), was originally conceived as a harsh attack on social-purity feminists who sought to achieve gender equality by applying the "law of purity," as they called it,

to men and women equally. Through a series of drastic manuscript revisions, however, Wilde modified this melodramatic opposition to a newly
powerful women's movement and in the process diminished his most
theatrical and unconventional characters, the ones most like him. They
either disappear from these plays prematurely or are severely chastened
if not actually reformed by the puritanical morality they had set out to
oppose. In this surprising accommodation with the feminist puritans
responsible for the law that would later send him to prison, Wilde allows
his most aesthetic, dandified, and effeminate characters to be silenced or
co-opted by the puritanical legislators of gender and morality that, in earlier drafts, the play had mocked and demonized. Lady Windermere, in
later drafts, embraces a flexible and compassionate feminism, but leaves
no room for the wits and dandies who loomed so large earlier in the play.
In effect, Wilde writes himself out of his own play in order to make way
for a West End fourth act in which Lady Windermere and her priggish,
conventional husband are reunited in perfect harmony. Although in the
end Lady Windermere has enlarged her understanding of what it means to
be "a good woman," the category of goodness itself remains intact as she
pronounces the moralizing final lines of the play in complete ignorance of
the key facts of her own history and of the drama which bears her name.
In important respects, then, the "new" Lady Windermere is as much in
the dark as ever, and her redefined "goodness," although generous and
forgiving, can never be compatible with a Wildean stylistics of living that
displaces all moral categories.

Chapter 2 also identifies a less compromising Wilde – the playwright
who wrote and nearly brought the one-act tragedy *Salomé* to the London
stage in 1891–92, at precisely the time when *Lady Windermere's Fan* was
the hit of the season. The play was barred from the stage by the Examiner
of Plays after rehearsals had already begun, and for many good reasons – good at the time, at least: its depiction, directly and indirectly, of
male–male desire; its violent, sexually predatory heroine; and its blasphemous, erotically charged characterization of John the Baptist. In fact, as
Richard Dellamora has argued, *Salomé* was "so sure to enrage English
philistines that its conception needed to be translated into – perhaps even
to be imagined in – French."[11] Its title character is a powerful woman who
aggressively expresses and murderously gratifies her sexual desire for John
the Baptist. Wilde's Salomé operates on the borderland of gender, com-
bining her feminine exterior with "masculine" authority, self-assertion,
and sexual passion to produce a kind of transvestism of the soul. Indeed,
she is the organizing center for the gender confusion and reversals that

structure Wilde's one-act tragedy; for example, her own "masculinity" figures in a homosexual relay between the young Syrian captain who is in love with her and the page who is suicidally in love with him. Her passion for Jokanaan is similarly complicated, for her passionate and poetic descriptions of his physical beauty are a reverse echo of the biblical Song of Solomon, where the desiring subject is male, and the beautiful desired is female. Not only is Wilde's heroine "like" a man, but in the same sense his men are like women, and in this reorganized landscape of gender and sexuality the illustrator of the play, Aubrey Beardsley, percipiently detected the presence of Wilde himself – incorporating his features into four images, drawing him as the "Woman in the Moon" looking down with a sensual gaze on an effeminate and nude male, variously interpreted to be Jokanaan, the Syrian captain, and/or the Page. These gender crossings, including Wilde's own, culminate when the severed head of John the Baptist is brought to Salomé on a silver charger, and she makes love to it in full view of the audience. This realization of desire by Wilde's aggressively masculine heroine puts a threatening edge on Wilde's play; her appropriation of the penis through the symbolic decapitation of John the Baptist is suggestive of the peril in which unmitigated female power and sexuality place men.

His next play would attempt once again, as in *Lady Windermere's Fan*, to accommodate revolutionary perceptions of gender and sexuality to the socially conservative medium of West End comedy and heterosexual romance. Although *A Woman of No Importance* began in its earliest drafts as a rhetorical and ideological confrontation with an emerging and radical feminist movement, it developed in its final version into a search for common ground, a hybridized performance of gender which, if not fully realized in the text of the play, lies just over the horizon, beyond the final curtain. The marriage of the once-puritanical Hester Worsley and the bastard son Gerald Arbuthnot will reconfigure traditional understandings of gender, a goal of "Puritan women" and Lord Illingworth alike. Their marriage will be an accommodation between the excesses of feminist social purity on one hand and of Wildean dandyism and aestheticism, as embodied in Lord Illingworth, on the other. In *A Woman of No Importance*, as earlier in *Lady Windermere's Fan*, Wilde was making conciliatory gestures toward the advocates of social purity even as he was resisting them, and in return the play was received with satisfaction in some quarters where a positive reaction to Wilde could not have been expected. As one religious journal, for example, remarked in its review, "A living sermon is being preached nightly at the Haymarket."[12]

Despite the existence of a "pure Wilde" who could find common ground in his early plays with social-purity feminists such as Josephine Butler, another Oscar Wilde was increasingly at risk as the result of a recently enacted law on gross indecency that Butler and her legion of supporters had successfully pushed through Parliament. Chapter 3, "Performance anxiety in *An Ideal Husband*," examines Wilde's next play, *An Ideal Husband* (1895), as an anxious self-enactment under threat of criminal prosecution stemming from his dealings with male prostitutes and blackmailers. Wilde, like his central character Sir Robert Chiltern, was under pressure from the austere morality of militant feminism on one side while on the other being threatened with blackmail and public exposure for criminal behavior. At the heart of *An Ideal Husband* is the question of gendered identity and related, urgent issues for Wilde at the time. How does being a man or a woman determine the meaning, opportunities, and responsibilities of one's life? Is a person irrevocably defined by circumstance – not only his or her gender, but past behavior, political and legal contexts, and a body of fixed truth – if there is such a thing – that marks each of us as one thing or another for all time? Wilde's tortured revisions and rewrites – some of which have rarely (if ever) been dealt with in scholarship on *An Ideal Husband* – provide a map of the second thoughts and self-doubting that stood in the way of bringing this play, not to mention his life, to a happy or at least artistic conclusion. *An Ideal Husband* asks potentially revolutionary questions without ever answering them, or sometimes, unable to decide, by answering them in more ways than one – for example, the question of whether gendered identity is real or a theatrical enactment, and whether truth itself is "real" or in its own way a social performance. The disappointing result is a play laced with contradictions, one that turns away from the innovative conclusions it had been driving toward and finally sinks into an anachronistic and self-serving representation of gender in relation to the social world.

In Chapter 4, "Performativity and history: *Oscar Wilde and The Importance of Being Earnest*," I argue that Wilde would not make the same mistakes in his next and last play, *The Importance of Being Earnest* (1895), although the same issues were at stake as in its predecessor. Shaw and others who attacked *Earnest* from the beginning as a play conveying no sense of authentic being or reality, either in its characters or language, entirely missed the point, for a profound disbelief in so-called reality is the radical idea that drives the play, making it a turning point of the Victorian stage and of what we have come to call modern drama. The central character, Jack Worthing, stands for the contingency of selfhood: lacking any characterological center of gravity, he makes and unmakes himself, exposing identity as anything but single and unitary – not an essence of the individual, and certainly not a soul, but rather the product of texts, rituals, and performance. In the end, after a long string of manuscript revisions, Jack capriciously becomes "Earnest" as well as "Ernest," allowing Wilde to demonstrate not only the attenuated reality of an individual man, but of masculinity itself as a social concept, one that the Victorians loaded with all the formidably moralizing synonyms for "earnest" that could be found in a dictionary. "Earnest" is just a word, finally, and like all words an empty quantity waiting to be invested with meaning by the people who use it. Shaw, more distant from the postmodern frontier than Wilde was, could make no sense of *Earnest* because he was blind to the possibility that words, like people, are invested with perpetually shifting and unstable content that makes it impossible to say what they really and fixedly "mean." This lack of certain truth may seem to offer freedom to the individual in terms of his becoming what he or she wants to be, and in a limited sense, for Wilde, it does. Yet *Earnest* ends with Jack reinventing himself within and through the terms of his historical and social context, and thereby discovering the limits of performativity and becoming to some significant degree the very thing he has resisted all along.

Chapter 5, "The 'lost' transcript, sexual acting, and the meaning of Wilde's trials," is concerned with the catastrophe that befell Wilde at the moment of his greatest success as a playwright. Only a couple of months into its run as the hit of the West End season in 1895, *The Importance of Being Earnest* was abruptly canceled at the St. James's Theatre in the wake of Wilde's arrest on charges of gross indecency. *Earnest* was followed, although not on stage, by what Wilde would later refer to as the "hideous tragedy" of his trials, a brutal drama-in-life in which every important element eluded his control. Although the trials in Wilde's retrospective view were an irredeemably coarse drama – not metaphorically, but really – they have come to be seen more positively in our own time as a painful yet valuable crisis of transition between the Victorian world and what came after. The cultural cachet that now attaches to Wilde's trials stems from their reinterpretation as events leading to a historic, Foucauldian "specification of individuals" – the invention, in effect, of homosexuality as a group identity. Wilde would have been surprised, because from his own point of view the tragic significance of his trials was the opposite – that is, that they failed to produce the revolution in male subjectivity that he clearly aimed at. Indeed, even when called on to testify about it, Wilde was unclear and even unoriginal in his own thinking about what this imagined new manhood would be composed of. To the extent that Wilde was an actor in the courtroom, he was performing a drama of uncertainty, evasion, and self-repression rather than identity-formation. The recent discovery of the long-lost transcript of one of the trials, along with some other overlooked archival evidence, makes clear that the prosecution of Wilde was organized around both texts and sex – novels, letters, and poems represented as theatrical sites, in effect, where Wilde could be seen performing or "posing" sodomy and gross indecency. This connectedness of sex, texts, and performance in Wilde's trials is scarcely present at all in the shamelessly censored, canonical histories written by H. Montgomery Hyde and others. The newly discovered trial transcript, however, enables us to see for the first time what really happened – how Wilde was brought down by lawyers who linked him with an array of texts that they represented as venues of criminal sexuality and, at the same time, sites of Wilde's own self-performance.

Chapter 6, "Prison performativity," discusses Wilde's reconstruction of his downfall as a form of theatre from the perspective of his two years in prison at hard labor. His long letter from prison, *De Profundis*, characterizes his experiences in court and afterward as a "revolting and repellent tragedy," brutal and inartistic, when his life should have been, as he expected it to be, a "brilliant comedy." He had become an unwilling actor, speaking and moving under the control of external forces – "a puppet worked by some secret and unseen hand to bring terrible events to an issue," as he writes in *De Profundis*.[13] He believed his speech and actions to have been imposed from the outside, already scripted, a striking premonition of the attenuated actors – that is, all of us – who take part in the obligatory social drama theorized by late-twentieth-century exponents of a constraining performativity. Wilde cannot identify the author of his own theatre of cruelty, except as a shadowy force, faceless and unseen in any specific form. For Wilde as for some who followed much later, that subject without a face, as he calls it, suggests a matrix of relations that conspire to limit and form the individual through the ritualized and regulatory drama of social life. "There is no power that acts," as Judith Butler has written, "but only a reiterated acting that is power."[14] From this point of view it was no single individual who authored Wilde's catastrophe, but the impersonal agency that Wilde, in prison, now called "Society," the faceless puppet-master and disciplinarian of his wrecked life. Wilde's life-drama had become, in the end, the "social drama" of postmodern performativity, and it was in just such terms that Wilde prophetically realized himself in his cramped cell, a prisoner in more ways than one.

*Acting Wilde* ends with an epilogue, "Wilde and modern drama," which argues that it was Wilde – not Ibsen, Shaw, and other so-called realists – who charted the path that serious theatre would ultimately take in the next century. In his plays and his life, from the beginning of his career to its end, what Wilde wrote and experienced would undermine any secure basis for what we call truth and cast into doubt the existence of a "real" self. At the same time Wilde aspired to invent and reinvent himself and the world through performance – as he came to believe in prison that Christ had done without limits, and as his own creation in a comic vein, Jack Worthing, was able to do within very strict limits in *The Importance of Being Earnest*. Writing and living a century ahead of his time, Wilde opened the door to the theatre of Beckett, Pinter, Stoppard, Sarah Kane, and a host of others. The trapped, alienated, and role-playing characters of twentieth-century drama would experience, as did Wilde, the shattering of all certainty about who we are and the world we live in, but also the sure knowledge, as Antonin Artaud has expressed it, that "We are not free. And the sky can still fall on our heads. And the theatre has been created to teach us that first of all."[15]

# *Posing and dis-posing*

## Oscar Wilde in America and beyond

In 1882, the author of one slim volume of poems and an unperformed play, Oscar Wilde was sent to America by Richard D'Oyly Carte to give a series of lectures promoting the new Gilbert and Sullivan comic opera, *Patience*, a satire on the aesthetic movement with which Wilde was already closely identified. As he patiently explained to newspaper reporters who interviewed him aboard the *Arizona* upon his arrival in the country, he and a clique of apostles were fomenting a revolution in English life and art: "aestheticism," he called it – which he defined for the press as the "science of the beautiful" and "search for the secret of life." But in the public mind, as a reporter for the *New York Sun* noted, aestheticism was associated not so much with artistic and social revolution as with "marked peculiarities in costume," and Wilde complacently agreed, wearing an open-necked white shirt with a turned-down collar "of extraordinary size" under his fur-lined ulster, his brown hair falling far down on his shoulders. "Yes," he said languidly, "the movement has brought out individualities, but it is because of its force."[1]

Wilde's own "marked peculiarities in costume," along with his gospel of art, had brought him notoriety in England well in advance of his tour of America. In pursuing the aims of aestheticism, he admitted to a reporter in the same shipboard interview, "There is no doubt but that we all purposely went to the wildest extremes in dress and expressions."[2] Such conscious, outrageous posing attracted attention to Wilde before he had yet written anything, and soon he had become the most obvious target of numerous satires on aestheticism. He achieved notoriety when he was caricatured in drawings for *Punch* by George Du Maurier beginning in 1880 as the self-appointed apostles of art, Maudle and Postlethwaite. Soon thereafter, everyone, including Wilde himself, assumed he was the real-life model, or at least the primary one, for two bogus aesthetic poets, Lambert Streyke in F.C. Burnand's farcical drama *The Colonel* (1881), and Reginald Bunthorne in the far more famous *Patience*, a comic opera by Gilbert and

Sullivan that opened in London in April 1881 and in September of the same year in New York. When *Patience* opened in New York, more than three months before Wilde would arrive in the city himself, the *New York Daily Tribune* recognized in Bunthorne the "aesthetic sham" of the new Gilbert and Sullivan extravaganza, a character created "after the fashion of Swinburne, and still more after that of Oscar Wilde."[3]

Wilde welcomed these satiric representations of himself with open arms. "My friends and I went to see the first night of *Patience*" and had "all manner of fun," he told reporters in New York on January 8, the day before his first lecture in the city. "If he [the true artist] is not a mere sham, he cannot be disturbed by any caricature or exaggeration." As for Du Maurier's drawings, of which Wilde said he "supposed" he was also the original, "I have never felt pained at all by his caricatures or those of anyone else, and I think I have enjoyed them fully as much as anyone."[4] But several days earlier, at the end of Wilde's arrival interview in New York harbor, the reporter for the *New York Sun* descended over the side of the *Arizona* and heard the other passengers chanting a line from *Patience* – "A pallid and lank young man" – and shouting "jibes about aestheticism" for good measure. This interesting moment set the frame for Wilde's experiences to come in America: he *was* Bunthorne, the "pallid and lank young man" in *Patience*, as far as his shipmates were concerned; he had been absorbed into the Gilbert and Sullivan script that caricatured him and aestheticism more generally. Wilde, on his side, performed the role willingly, with his usual, self-confessed "extremes in dress and expressions," yet with the expectation that this posing as "Oscar Wilde," a caricature of himself, would somehow propagate the radical views of a gospel of art in which he seriously believed.

The question to be determined, then, was who would control the pose that Wilde had agreed to adopt in America – Wilde himself, or Gilbert and Sullivan's satirical dramatization of Wilde that he had been brought over to publicize. Despite the equanimity with which he was wearing the "managerial collar" of Gilbert and Sullivan's agents, the *New York Herald* discerned some tension between the "real" Wilde and the comic-opera version of himself; indeed, by coming to America in the first place, the *Herald* observed, Wilde had "deferentially admitted the point to the caricature of Du Maurier and the broad satire of Gilbert." He had become part of the play that mocked and chastised his aestheticism, or rather he had become the star actor in a spectacle ancillary to it, by virtue of his "consenting to come to this country to act under the same management as a side show to *Patience*, a perpetual and magnificent advertisement."

The *Herald* concluded on a note of admiration for Richard D'Oyly Carte's managerial skill, mixed with something like sympathy for Wilde for being his pawn, albeit a willing and good-natured one:

Mr. Carte's scheme is a brilliant one, but it is rather hard on the aesthetic lion to snare him and bring him over to this country with the idea of an artistic mission – the propagation of aesthetic culture. This is but a pretext, and Mr. Wilde, besides being in for a paying thing, evidently much enjoys the attention he receives, even if there is a managerial collar around his neck and a slight suspicion of the circus about the whole affair.[5]

As the *Herald* commentary implied, Wilde's performance as a Bunthorne look-alike was saturated with the same commercial and anti-aesthetic biases that he most wished to oppose. In New York he had become, of all things, a quotation of a popular new Savoy opera based in large part on a mocking dramatization of himself and his aestheticism.

Carte's well-oiled publicity campaign for Wilde began with advance stories in the newspapers of his imminent arrival in America, followed by interviews, high-society receptions covered by the press, and a cleverly conceived visit by Wilde to the theatre where *Patience* had been playing as a smash hit since September 22 of the previous year. This marketing of a comic-opera Oscar Wilde produced the desired results. Carriages started arriving at Chickering Hall for Wilde's first lecture shortly after 7:00 p.m. on January 9, 1882; outside the auditorium, scalpers hawked tickets for $2, and by 8:00 p.m. every seat in the house was taken. The *New York Sun* framed the event, Wilde's first performance on any stage, in the context of the Gilbert and Sullivan extravaganza that he been hired to promote: "The first night of *Patience* could not have surpassed, if indeed, it equaled, last night's entertainment," the reporter gushed.[6] Wilde himself was dressed in the style of Reginald Bunthorne, his counterpart in *Patience*, and New York newspapers lavished attention on the details of that costume and his audience's reaction to it. The *New York Times* described Wilde's appearance in studious detail:

His long and bushy hair crowded in front of his ears and nearly to his eyes, but it was brushed well off his forehead. He wore a low-necked shirt with a turned-down collar and large white necktie, a black claw-hammer coat and white vest, knee-breeches, long black stockings, and low shoes with bows. A heavy gold seal hung to a watch-guard from a fob-pocket … He wore white kid gloves … the audience looked in wonder upon him.[7]

A man arrayed in satin and lace was wonder enough, but it was what Wilde wore below the waist that transfixed reporters as well as tickled their sense of humor. "His nether garments did not extend to his ankles, as those of modest men ought to do, but stopped at his knees," the *Daily Tribune* noted wryly. "In fact he wore knee breeches."[8] These reactions were stimulated to a great extent by Wilde's departure from a conventionally masculine appearance. As the *Tribune* commented later on, Wilde's "femininely disposed hair" and "redundancy of collar and cravat" made him look like "a great homely girl – one of those girls whose brother is sure to be good looking, and who would be good looking herself had she been born a boy."[9]

Wilde's appearance on the borderline of gender was funny, or seemed so – like the character in *Patience* whose style and manner he deliberately evoked – and so the crowd laughed when he made his entrance for the first lecture. As opera glasses turned on him throughout the crowded house, the *Times* noted, "Some one chuckled. This was followed by quiet laughter from the rear of the hall. Then the tittering and chuckling increased, and must have soon grown to the full strength of a general laugh had not Col. [W.F.] Morse arisen from his seat and stepped to the edge of the platform."[10] After a momentary hush during the introduction by Col. Morse, who was Richard D'Oyly Carte's associate, Wilde began to speak in somewhat sepulchral tones, reading from a script, and the *Sun* reported that "a rude giggle" rippled through the crowd, although the speaker's face retained its "placid expression."[11] But a perceptive writer for the *New York World* opined that Wilde was "well worth seeing," putting his emphasis on the visual dimension of the spectacle – "his short breeches and silk stockings showing to even better advantage upon the stage than in the gilded drawing rooms where the young apostle has heretofore been seen."

Then why did people laugh? Answering his own question, the *World* reporter cut quickly to the heart of the matter: "Laugh, … one may … one must at times, at the attempt to make an original out of a caricature (for the conclusion is irresistible that the real creation is Gilbert and Sullivan's and not Wilde's.)"[12] In a sentence, the reporter had crystallized what would be the problematic element of Wilde's theatricality from the beginning of his career to its disastrous end: his attempt, perhaps doomed at the outset, to create himself anew, on his own terms, while inhabiting a character in a script written by someone else with very different motives. The struggle for control of Wilde's New York pose was evident to the *World* reporter, who judged that whether on stage or in "gilded drawing rooms," Wilde operated within the confines of a Gilbert and Sullivan script. At the same time, however, another "Oscar Wilde" was engaged in the contradictory enterprise of trying to break out of merely "frivolous" play-acting. As the

Figure 1. Drawn in a "feminine" pose and surrounded by images
of femininity, Wilde was satirized as "The Bard of Beauty" in the
July 1880 edition of *Time*, well before being parodied by Gilbert
and Sullivan in *Patience* as well as before publishing anything of
significance himself. (British Library)

reporter wrote in his review of the lecture for the next day's *New York World*: "In spite of the frivolous that is, perhaps unfortunately, inseparable from the man, it is not every day that one can sit in the hearing of so keen a critic or catch such glimpses of so clear a revelation of art."[13]

In the conflicted position of inventing himself from a script written by others, Wilde inadvertently yet inevitably certified Gilbert and Sullivan's satirical creation as an authentic version of himself. Although his lecture extolled aestheticism as the dawn of a "new English Renaissance," Wilde presented his remarks in the persona of the effeminate, self-confessed "aesthetic sham" Reginald Bunthorne, his knee breeches and silk stockings echoing the play's ridicule of all deviation from conventional, bourgeois masculinity. It was Wilde's conscious strategy to subvert *Patience* – its anti-aestheticism, its mockery of himself – from *within*, and indeed he framed his lecture in precisely these terms, calling into question the thesis of the Gilbert and Sullivan play in which, to all appearances, he was the main character brought to life. Contextualizing this promotional event at the outset, Wilde offered good-natured references to aestheticism, sunflowers and lilies, and his "old friend, Arthur Sullivan," laughing along with his audience as he did so. On another level, however, he wanted to talk about, and *be*, himself, rather than publicize *Patience* in the garb and style of its ridiculous leading character.

And so he asked the audience to join him in breaking free of the script of that play:

> I am asking, as you have listened for three hundred nights to my friend Mr. Arthur Sullivan's charming opera *Patience* (laughter), that you will listen to me for one night (renewed laughter); and as you have had satire, you may make the satire a little more piquant by knowing a little more of the truth; and that, in any case, you will not take the very brilliant lines of Mr. Gilbert any more as a revelation of the movement, than you would judge of the splendor of the sun or the majesty of the sea, by the dust that dances in the beams of the bubble that breaks on the wave. (Applause.)[14]

Wilde was presenting himself in Chickering Hall as "the splendor of the sun, the majesty of the sea," and in the context of his lecture Bunthorne and *Patience* were merely "the bubble that breaks on the wave," the manifestation of a "commercial spirit" that, Wilde alleged, was nevertheless destroying all the beauty and nobility of life. At the end of Wilde's lecture, as the audience passed out of the auditorium, attendants distributed pamphlets illustrated with pen-and-ink sketches as a promotion of the Standard Theatre production of *Patience*. It was "the acme of advertising," said the *New York Herald*. Certainly it did not look like the "revolution" in art and life that Wilde claimed to be stirring up in New York under the banner of aestheticism.[15]

Exactly what, or rather *who*, had the audience seen and heard on that January night in 1882 – an autonomous, self-directed revolutionary of aestheticism, or a man trapped in a comic-opera costume who actually reinforced the "commercial spirit" and orthodoxy of gender that he meant to attack? This mix-up and layering of identities was an unwitting prognostication of what it would mean to "be" someone in Wilde's mature work as a playwright, especially in *The Importance of Being Earnest*, and in the courtroom trials in which his performance of gendered identity was centrally at issue. Was it Wilde, or Bunthorne, or somehow both at once who were holding forth on stage in New York?

This question with no simple answer – who was Wilde, what was behind the mask? – had been brought into sharp focus on the evening of January 5, several days before Wilde's first lecture, when with some companions he attended a performance of *Patience* at the Standard Theatre. A writer for the *New York Daily Tribune* accompanied the group and filed a story representing Wilde as a conscious performer in the theatre that night, although not on stage. Wilde was gorgeously dressed, the reporter noted – wearing a fur-trimmed ulster over a "faultless shirt front ... relieved by one enormous stud, of some colored stone, in the center, and a red silk handkerchief protruded from his waistcoat." Entering late, Wilde and his party occupied two boxes that connected with the stage, with Wilde at first sitting in the rear box out of sight. In a short while, however, he moved conspicuously to the forward box where the audience could get "a pretty good view of him" – almost as good as their view of the actors on stage. Consequently, according to the *Tribune*, "There were numberless opera glasses turned toward the poet" instead of toward the stage where *Patience* was being performed. Wilde all the while was watching the play attentively until J.L. Ryley, the actor playing Reginald Bunthorne, finally came on stage. Ryley was made up as Wilde, in contrast to the London production in which the connection of Bunthorne with Wilde was generally understood but less direct. In a remarkable juxtaposition, the audience suddenly had both Wilde and his double, Bunthorne, performing before them, and the *Tribune* writer noted the moment with care: "When *Reginald Bunthorne* (J.H. Ryley) came on the stage, the whole audience turned and looked at Mr. Wilde. He leaned toward one of the ladies and said with a smile, looking at *Bunthorne*, 'This is one of the compliments that mediocrity pays to those who are not mediocre.'"[16]

Or was it the other way round? After all, it was Wilde who had come to see Bunthorne, just as he had on opening night in London some months ago; and it was Wilde, made up as Bunthorne, who would be bringing his own act to Chickering Hall in just a few days. Moreover, the *Tribune* reported that during an intermission Wilde and his party went behind the scenes to be introduced to the actors – all but Ryley, the actor playing Bunthorne, who snubbed Wilde by closing the door of his dressing-room and talking to no one. Yet, gazing coolly on his double from a stage-side box, Wilde claimed ownership of the very role that J.H. Ryley was performing before his eyes at the Standard Theatre, an ownership based, in Wilde's mind, on the debt that mediocrity owes genius. Neither his American tour – a "side-show" to *Patience*, as one journalist put it – nor events that followed would vindicate Wilde's claim of ownership over his self-enactments. Nor would they entirely discredit it, for if there had been no Wilde, could there have been a Bunthorne to begin with?

## POSING FOR THE CAMERA

The question that cried out for an answer when Wilde met – or almost met – Bunthorne in a New York theatre was not only "who was who" in this almost farcical proliferation of Wildes and Bunthornes, but who, or what, owned and controlled the pose called "Oscar Wilde"? That question found an intriguing context, if not exactly a clear answer, when Richard D'Oyly Carte, the Savoy opera producer who had signed up Wilde for this "side-show" in the first place, arranged a publicity photo-shoot for him on January 10, the day after his first lecture. Wearing the self-parodying costume inspired by Bunthorne, Wilde posed – or rather, *was* posed – for twenty-seven separate photographs in the Union Square studio of the pre-eminent celebrity photographer, Napoleon Sarony.

Photographing celebrities was a profitable business for Sarony, and one that also paid well for his famous subjects, most of whom were actors or performers of some type. The sitting fees paid by Sarony were the subject of much haggling and varied widely – $300 for actress Fanny Kemble, $1,500 for Sarah Bernhardt, $5,000 for Lily Langtry – and his sessions with performers such as these generated multiple poses captured in "cabinet photos" (3.75 by 5.5 inches) and occasionally larger "panel" photos. Mounted on cards with rounded corners and beveled edges, trimmed in maroon or gold, these photos were displayed in Sarony's showcase windows and widely distributed for sale by theatres, hotels, shops, and mail order. Celebrity images had market value, then as now, but Sarony's portraits were also distinguished by a lifelike spontaneity unusual for the time – a variety of poses, gestures, and expressions that made his work stand out from the dull sameness of most photography. Notwithstanding the long exposure times of up to a full minute, Sarony was able to avoid the stiff, wooden poses that make the photographs of most of his contemporaries seem so unlifelike. Concealed headrests, as well as "eye rests" to give sitters something to fix their gaze on, helped to minimize eye and body movement during the long exposures.[17]

Yet in his session with Wilde, as with all of his subjects, Sarony took no pictures himself, and was uninvolved in the processing and printing of film; he set up the large studio camera, but his main assistant actually shot the pictures. Posing the sitter was Sarony's primary function in these photo sessions, and by all accounts he was meticulous, demanding, and even tyrannical in doing so. Sarony was known for his harsh treatment of clients who would not or could not comply with his instructions about how to "pose," often stalking out of the studio and leaving them to deal with his assistants. According to the newspaper cartoonist Thomas Nast, writing about Sarony in the *Photographic Journal of America* in 1895: "With that class of persons who wished to be allowed to pose themselves he would have nothing to do. He knew his own profession, and insisted upon having absolute liberty to do his work as he thought best. More than one well-known actress has been reduced to tears because Sarony would not 'take her' any more."[18]

Like the portraitist Basil Hallward in Wilde's as yet unwritten novel *The Picture of Dorian Gray*, Sarony seemed actually to project himself into the poses of his subjects, infusing his identity into theirs. "What distinguished a Sarony portrait was his ability to make everyone he photographed look like Sarony ... the same feeling in every picture. Partly from imitation and partly from carrying out his directions, all his sitters seemed to catch the Sarony tricks of expression and pose. If they did not he would not take them at all."[19] The most significant and best-known of Sarony's portraits of Wilde – No. 18 in the series of twenty-seven poses – displays Wilde in his comic-opera costume, holding a book in his right hand, at an angle that draws attention to his knee breeches, silk stockings, and brightly shining pumps. His head supported by his left hand, Wilde stares at the camera with a faraway gaze that makes him appear curiously detached from himself. One commentator has suggested insightfully that it is an elaborately posed photograph with "a bizarre composition in which Wilde resembles a marionette, with Sarony having snipped the strings."[20] As in Wilde's lecture tour and society appearances as a Bunthorne look-alike and side-show to *Patience*, the subject in "Oscar Wilde, No. 18" performs himself in a pose over which he had only limited control. Appropriately, and as usual with Sarony's portraits, the elaborate signature of the photographer dwarfed the small type of the sitter's name in the caption ("Oscar Wilde").

In Sarony's photographic studio, as with Wilde's appearances in society and lecture halls as a character out of Gilbert and Sullivan, the issue would be who controlled the self that Wilde was performing. Was he the autonomous, revolutionary advocate of beauty over commerce, "the majesty of the sea" in comparison to the "bubble" on the wave that was Bunthorne? Or was he performing, as the *New York Herald* put it, with a "managerial collar around his neck," not the enemy of commercialism but its agent – "the acme of advertising" and a walking, talking "side-show" to *Patience*?[21] The Sarony photograph entitled "Oscar Wilde, No. 18," like Wilde's appearances in America as a Gilbert and Sullivan parody of himself, shows how pervasively his self-performance was infiltrated by the very forces he wanted to oppose. In the case of the photograph, the external factors that exerted pressure upon Wilde's pose and the "meaning" of his image on film went beyond the dictatorial ordering of the pose by Sarony himself. This image of a satin-and-silk Wilde was soon to be the centerpiece of litigation that would become a landmark precedent in the law of copyright and intellectual property, revolving around the issue of who originated and "owned" the pose that Wilde, under Sarony's direction, adopted in the photo. It is significant, however, that Wilde himself had no role in these proceedings, which were as remote from him personally as his detached gaze in the photograph might suggest.

Soon after Sarony's "Oscar Wilde, No. 18" was offered for sale, 85,000 unauthorized copies of the photograph were printed by a New York department store, Ehrich Bros., in an advertisement for hats. Sarony sued the printer for infringement of copyright and won his case in New York district court, but the Burrow-Giles Lithographic Company appealed the decision to the United States Supreme Court in December 1883 – a year after Wilde had returned to England. The basis of the appeal to the Supreme Court in *Burrow-Giles* v. *Sarony* was that the photograph of Wilde was merely the visual record of something, or rather *someone*, already in existence, and therefore not copyrightable; in other words, Sarony could not claim copyright over Oscar Wilde, since he did not "create" or "author" him. David Graham, counsel for the Burrow-Giles printing firm, explained this interpretation of the photo in a little-noted "Brief and Points for Plaintiff-in-Error" in the Supreme Court records of the case: "In photography, the true object sought after is a truthful representation of the subject, and putting Oscar Wilde into a new attitude ... does not change Oscar Wilde into another person ... the camera 'represents the scene *as it is*; *nothing is added, nothing omitted*.'"[22]

Figure 2. Napoleon Sarony's portraits of Wilde were appropriated
by commercial firms to advertise their products. "Oscar Wilde,
No. 18" was transformed into an ad for hats by a New York
department store, generating a lawsuit by Sarony alleging
violation of his propriety rights in the posed image of Wilde.
(Library of Congress)

The issue, then, was whether the gorgeously clad, dreamy-eyed figure
in Sarony's "Oscar Wilde, No. 18" was Wilde himself – "nothing added,
nothing omitted" – or a pose that the photographer had created in the
process of reinventing "Oscar Wilde" from the outside.

Under this striking headline – "DID SARONY INVENT OSCAR WILDE?" – the *New York Times* summarized the argument in the Supreme Court against Sarony's claim of copyright on the photograph: "Mr. Sarony had not produced or invented Oscar Wilde, but had merely arranged him, that is, had newly arranged something already extant ... Mr. Sarony was not the creator of Oscar Wilde, and a photograph was not such an original as could be copyrighted."[23] The contrary point of view, Sarony's own, insisted that the photographer had created, if not Wilde himself, the pose in which Wilde was photographed and would be marketed for sale across the country.

On March 17, 1884, the Supreme Court finally upheld the lower court ruling that Sarony was indeed the "author" of Oscar Wilde as he appeared in the contested photograph:

[Sarony] was the author, inventor, designer, and proprietor of the photograph in suit, the title of which is "Oscar Wilde, No. 18" ... the same is a useful, new, harmonious, characteristic, and graceful picture, and ... said plaintiff made the same at his place of business in said city of New York, and within the United States, entirely from his own original mental conception, to which he gave visible form by posing the said Oscar Wilde in front of the camera, selecting and arranging the costume, draperies, and other various accessories in said photograph, arranging the subject so as to present graceful outlines, arranging and disposing the light and shade, suggesting and evoking the desired expression, and from such disposition, arrangement, or representation, made entirely by the plaintiff, he produced the picture in suit, Exhibit A.[24]

Having "authored" Oscar Wilde as posed in photograph No. 18, Sarony then legally demonstrated his exclusive ownership of the pose, in the opinion of the U.S. Supreme Court, by signing the photo with his name and writing the word "copyright" on it. To gain copyright, Sarony also had to deposit two copies of the photo with the Librarian of Congress, inscribed with the name of the "author," and pay a fee of fifty cents. These requirements having been met to the satisfaction of the highest court in the land, "Oscar Wilde, No. 18" was duly absorbed as a piece of property (not Wilde's, but Sarony's) in the commercial and legal ethos that the artistically dressed man in the photograph would spend his short life trying to undermine. Oscar Wilde's pose in this instance, as would always be the case in his consciously theatrical life, was both limited and governed by external forces over which he had only the most limited control, when he had any at all.

In *Burrow-Giles* v. *Sarony* there was never any consideration given to the possibility that Wilde was the "owner" of the pose in the photograph – only

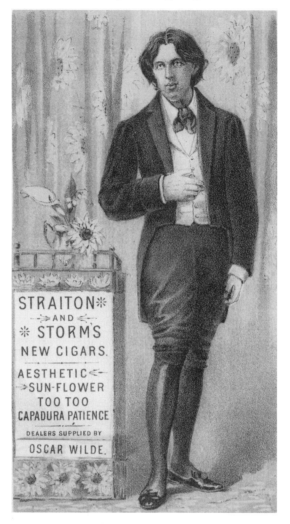

Figure 3. One of Sarony's photographs of Wilde was
turned into an advertisement for Straiton and Storm's New
Cigars. (Library of Congress)

the competing claims that anyone at all (such as the Erich Bros. department store) could appropriate it, or conversely that Sarony held exclusive
rights to it. Wilde did not appear in the case, remaining weirdly detached
from this contest over his own posed image, and seems to have left no
recorded comment or opinion that has survived. The case, however, would

become an important legal landmark; it is still routinely cited by courts in the United States in determining issues of intellectual property and copyright pertaining to everything from works of art to pirated telephone directories. Although little-noted in literary studies and almost always ignored by Wilde scholars, *Burrow-Giles* v. *Sarony* is discussed at length in law textbooks and featured in law school syllabuses dealing with copyright, "art law," and intellectual property.[25] However, some recent legal scholarship, while conceding the importance of *Burrow-Giles* v. *Sarony*, argues that the case of Wilde's photograph left the law in a "murky" condition by reserving copyright for "authors" or "originators" without clearly restricting the meaning of such terms. What the Sarony case ultimately meant, therefore, was that "the Supreme Court seemed ready to accept almost any authorial contribution as sufficient" to vindicate a claim of copyright.[26]

Although Wilde's posed image was his own, and Wilde himself not the invention of Sarony, the photographer argued successfully that "arranging" and "disposing" the subject were enough to entitle him to exclusive rights as author and proprietor of this photographic version of Oscar Wilde. Wilde's posing for Sarony, and what came of it later in the Supreme Court, was a subtle yet powerful demonstration that one's self-enactment, no matter how audacious, would always be conducted within the oversight of social regimes of regulation and power. That was the moral of "Oscar Wilde, No. 18," just as it was the implied lesson of Wilde's visit to America, from east to west and back again. Although a conscious performer, one who desired above all to perform autonomously, Wilde's American experience was significantly "authored" by others – by Ricard D'Oyly Carte in setting up this "side show" in the first place, by Napoleon Sarony in his photographic studio, and by Gilbert and Sullivan in a Savoy opera called *Patience*.

In rendering its decision in *Burrow-Giles* v. *Sarony*, the Supreme Court attempted to lay out what it believed to be the central issue in any case involving the copyright of a photograph: "Whether a photograph is a mere mechanical reproduction or an original work of art is a question to be determined by proof of the facts of originality, of intellectual production, and of thought and conception on the part of the author; and when the copyright is disputed, it is important to establish these facts."[27] The phrasing of the Supreme Court ruling, although not the thought behind it, anticipates *The Work of Art in the Age of Mechanical Reproduction* (1936), in which Walter Benjamin would argue that this Victorian concern with whether photography was "art" was a distraction from the main point about this new technology of representation – namely, that photography, arising at the same time as socialism, changed the nature of art by politicizing it. Photography transformed art into a collective experience, removing it from the domain of "cult value" in which the "aura" belonging to a unique art object was accessible to very few people – the privileged few who had access to its location in time and space, which was not duplicable.[28]

Wilde's self-conceived purpose in visiting America was in this way consonant with Benjamin's idea of photography, for "I am here to diffuse beauty," he told reporters, so that even those who dwelt amid Hoboken smokestacks would know how to conduct "the search after the secret of life." But while "exhibition value" began to prevail with the advent of photography, making it possible for millions to have access to a work of art through mechanical reproduction, Benjamin points out that "cult value does not give way without resistance." One form of that resistance can be seen in the development of copyright and art law, for the effect of the court case revolving around "Oscar Wilde, No. 18" was precisely to limit circulation and accessibility of the photograph in order to serve the exclusive property rights of its "author," Napoleon Sarony. Wilde, on the other hand, had come to America cultivating an outrageous pose that – despite his self-advertised aestheticism – was calculated to *politicize* art by diffusing it everywhere. This revelation of art to everyone, rich and poor, was the essence of the aesthetic yet egalitarian ideology that underlay Wilde's approximately 150 lecture appearances across America.

### AFTER AMERICA: MORE PORTRAITS OF OSCAR WILDE

In subsequent years, following his return from America, Wilde continued to probe the delicate balance between posing and being dis-posed, figuring it as a continuum of the possibilities and problematics of self-fashioning. In this process the paradoxical relationship of artist and model was highly suggestive, and Wilde returned to it again and again, as if haunted by his own ambivalent experience of modeling in Napoleon Sarony's studio for the stage-managed photographs that would help bring into being the celebrity persona "Oscar Wilde." In "The Relation of Dress to Art," written for the *Pall Mall Gazette* in 1885, Wilde discusses the artist's model as an empty being who, in a kaleidoscope of costumes, is guilty of "ruining" modern painting, "reducing it to a condition of mere pose and pastiche." He is almost tempted at this moment to agree with James McNeill Whistler that a painter should represent only the dress of modern times, and the actual environment, in order to move art toward authenticity and mediate the harmful effects of that "impostor," the model. Although

Wilde is only half-serious, playing with the idea, he is concerned enough to ask: "Do we not all recognize him, when … he reappears on the walls of our summer exhibitions, as everything that he is not, and as nothing that he is, glaring at us here as a patriarch of Canaan, here beaming as a brigand from the Abruzzi."

The model, from this perspective, is not only an empty suit of dress-up clothes, but a harbinger of the decline of civilization itself – "this poor peripatetic professor of posing" who is "the sign of the decadence, the symbol of decay."[29] If the great artist reinvents his subject matter in this way, then the rough edges of real life and the vacuity of the model have something important in common: they provide the artist with the raw material which he touches and transforms with magical powers, and in this sense the model is no less "empty" than the uninspiring surface of Nature which presents us with nothing beautiful or quite "real."

This defensive embrace of authenticity and even realism in "The Relation of Dress to Art" may be uncharacteristic of Wilde in the long run, but it allows us a glimpse of some undercurrents of anxiety about living life as a masquerade, or at least about one way of doing so – that of the model, bankrupt of self-determined identity. But the model, after all, is only one of the elements in the composition of a great picture, and all of them must become "what they are not" in order for the picture to rank as great art. In "Mr. Whistler's Ten O'Clock" (1885), Wilde cites with admiration the painter's antagonism to Nature by virtue of his preference for "dim dawns and dusks, when the mean facts of life are lost in exquisite and evanescent effects, when common things are touched with mystery and transfigured with beauty; when the warehouses become as palaces, and the tall chimneys of the factory seem like campaniles in the silver air."[30] Seen from this angle, the artist "poses" not only the model, but Nature itself, creating something beautifully real on the barren surfaces of what was there before. As Wilde would say in a later essay, "The Decay of Lying" (1888), modern fogs were invented by Impressionist painters, and sunsets by Turner.

In "The Model Millionaire," a story from 1887, Wilde considers the possibility of conferring greater agency upon the model – in this case a millionaire who acts out his fantasy of being painted as a penniless beggar in a life-size portrait, "a living Velasques!" The painter, Allen Trevor, faithfully executes this fantasy in oils and brings it to life by lying to his friend Hughie Erskine that the millionaire baron posing as a beggar on the platform in his studio is just that – a beggar. The pose fades to real life when Hughie is convinced of the truth of the masquerade and quietly gives the "beggar-man" a sovereign; then, next morning, the posing millionaire sends Hughie a check for £10,000, a sum that will make it possible for the (really) penniless Hughie to marry his sweetheart. "The Model Millionaire" makes a case for the power of the pose to shape and organize reality, and in this story it is the model who leads the artist toward the materializing of imagination on canvas and in actual fact, putting flesh on a fantasy of social equality in which poverty and wealth trade places and mutual happiness is the result.

But "The Model Millionaire" communicates the aura of a daydream, and its easy resolution of conflict – between pose and reality, artist and model, wealth and poverty – is really no resolution at all. In 1889, however, Wilde offered a different and somewhat more nuanced perspective of the model in his essay "London Models" for the *English Illustrated Magazine.* Here, the model is neither a sign of the decay of civilization, as in "The Relation of Dress to Art," nor the fairy-tale reconciler of opposites and happy endings, as in "The Model Millionaire." He, or she, is also not quite the empty suit of clothes that constituted the model in "The Relation of Dress to Art." There is something inside, although (and fortunately) models do not usually present it to the artist. Instead, "They career gaily through all centuries and through all costumes, and, like actors, are only interesting when they are not themselves." If they are actors, there is surely someone behind the mask, but probably not anyone we would care about or enjoy knowing. Female models talk a great deal, for example, but say nothing; and if "physically they are perfect," intellectually they are dull as a class. Even models who pose in the nude are scrupulously respectable, well-behaved, and aspire to marry well. These commonplace, philistine character traits of models are interesting only by way of contrast to their dramatic achievements as "actors" – the poses they strike and the parts they play, erasing their banal personalities to give expression to the artist's, who *he* is, or wants to be. Rather than the symptom of a burnt-out civilization, the professional model is primarily conceptualized in "London Models" as a dramatic medium for the self-expression of the artist and the realization of his art. The powerlessness of the model/actor in this dynamic is worth noting, however: "'What do you sit for?', a young artist asked a model who had sent him her card ... 'Oh, for anything you like sir,' said the girl; 'landscape if necessary!'"[31]

For Wilde, then, every great picture is a kind of forgery – the painter's representation of what his model or landscape is *not* – but in a story first published in 1889 and later revised and expanded, "The Portrait of Mr. W.H.," the eponymous portrait really is a forgery in the dictionary sense of the word. Understanding the portrait of "W.H." in this way – as a pose with no real person behind it, although one is falsely claimed to be – can help us toward an understanding of the nuances in Wilde's developing thought about posing, dis-posing, and theatricality. At issue in the story is an allegedly Elizabethan painting of a young man "of quite extraordinary personal beauty," with the dreamy eyes and delicate red lips of a girl, his hand resting on an open book. The description is weirdly evocative of Sarony's famous portrait of Wilde himself, "Oscar Wilde, No. 18," in which a youthful and effeminate Wilde gazes wistfully at the camera, his hair impeccably coifed and his hand on an open book. Sarony's portrait was part of an effort to reinvent Oscar Wilde as a celebrity personality; and in writing "Mr. W.H.," Wilde was from one point of view composing a portrait of himself – but with results no less equivocal than the portrait that Sarony had captured on film a few years before in his Manhattan studio.

In defense of literary and artistic forgeries, the narrator's friend Erskine conjectures that all art is "to a certain degree a mode of acting, an attempt to realize one's own personality out of reach of the trammeling accidents and limitations of real life." If the premise of the story is that all art is theatrical self-portraiture, then one is compelled to entertain the possibility that the portrait of W.H. is in fact a portrait of the artist himself. The portrait was allegedly found by chance in an old trunk by Erskine's friend Cyril Graham, who offered it as evidence for his theory that Shakespeare's sonnets were dedicated to the beautiful youth in the picture, identified in gold letters in the corner of the portrait as "Willie Hughes." From textual evidence within the sonnets, Cyril had already identified Hughes not only as the W.H. to whom Shakespeare dedicated his love poetry, but also as the boy-actor for whom he wrote the great roles in his plays – Juliet, Desdemona, Cleopatra, and the rest. "To have discovered the true name of Mr. W.H. was comparatively nothing," the narrator states after he has become a believer himself in Cyril Graham's theory, "but to have discovered his profession was a revolution in criticism." W.H. was an actor, "and the love that Shakespeare bore him was as the love of a musician for some delicate instrument on which he delights to play"; W.H. excited homoerotic passion in the poet and yet enabled "a kind of mystic transference of the expressions of the physical sphere to a sphere that was spiritual, that was removed from gross bodily appetite." For Shakespeare, the narrator proposes, W.H. the actor was "the interpreter of his vision, as he was the incarnation of his dreams." Willie Hughes, in this profound sense, *was* Shakespeare.[32]

At the same time, of course, Wilde himself forms the third corner of a homoerotic triangle by virtue of calling into being through his own artistry a gay Shakespeare and the cross-dressing actor who not only inspired the playwright, but embodied Shakespeare's enactment of himself. For all art is "a mode of acting," as Erskine announced at the beginning of the story, "an attempt to realise one's own personality on some imaginative plane beyond the reach of the trammeling accidents and limitations of real life."[33] By these terms, the portrait of Mr. W.H. is the portrait of yet another effeminate "actor," Oscar Wilde – and as such, an attempt at both artistic and sexual self-realization. Within the frame of the story, the portrait is also the self-projection of Cyril Graham, whose cross-dressed performance as Rosalind at the then all-male A.D.C. at Cambridge was the best that Erskine had ever seen. In turn, as Erskine reflects with sensuously half-closed eyes, the narrator of the story reminds him of Cyril. At the center of these concentric circles of identity is Wilde himself, the author and therefore ultimate actor of the fiction, writing himself into "The Portrait of Mr. W.H." – an artistry of the self that encompasses and integrates Wilde's unconventional aesthetics and, at the time, unspeakable sexuality.

But what does it signify that the portrait is a forgery, and that Cyril Graham, its "discoverer," commits suicide when his lies are exposed and his theory of the sonnets discredited? And why, at the end of the story, does the portrait inspire the narrator when he looks at it on the wall of his private library to think, in spite of everything, "there is really a great deal to be said for the Willie Hughes theory of Shakespeare's Sonnets"?[34] We must consider, first of all, that the portrait of W.H. has become the private possession of the narrator by the end of the story, that it hangs in the library of his own exclusive home, and that he never discloses the story behind it when guests inquire. All of that is kept secret, as is the painting itself except for an elite circle of observers. These extreme limits placed on the circulation of the picture, making impossible any open access to what it is and "means," may remind us of the effects produced by Sarony's successful claim of copyright over the posed photograph of Wilde, "Oscar Wilde, No. 18," which limited access to the work by giving the photographer sole proprietary rights in it – on the basis that he had "created," "arranged," and "disposed" the image in the picture in a way that made it his own. Such limits on the accessibility of the work of art are irreconcilably opposed to Wilde's own expressed belief – the great theme of his lectures in America – that art had to be democratized and brought to the people. When a picture is not reproduced and circulated, whatever it expresses belongs to the private sphere, an individual or an elite group, and its effects and meanings are rendered mute, or nearly so, even if the aura of a unique original is intensely experienced by one or a few. In the case of "The Portrait of Mr. W.H.," what is denied full expression is Wilde's own enactment of himself, of his aesthetics and sexuality, as embodied in the portrait. There may be, as the narrator says at the end of the story, "a great deal to be said for the Willie Hughes theory of Shakespeare's Sonnets," but he simply refuses to say it – and this choice of closeted silence provides an equivocal ending for "The Portrait of Mr. W.H." The portrait is and will continue to be confined to the four walls of the narrator's private library, and its profound meanings are to remain a secret locked in his heart.

Unseen, unreproduced, and unknown except to a few, the portrait of Mr. W.H. possesses in rich measure what Walter Benjamin called "aura," the authenticity of a unique work of art that has not undergone "mechanical reproduction" and been communicated to masses of people. Benjamin's concept of aura helps us to detect the pulsating tensions between truth and lies in "The Portrait of Mr. W.H.," in which Wilde seeks to communicate deeply held convictions about art, gender, and sexuality in a narrative framework pervaded by an anxiety, etched in the imagery of despair and suicide, that what the author wants to communicate is an "act" – a pose. This interleaving of the true and the theatrical in an anxious project of self-identification is further complicated by the narrator's refusal at the end of the story to say anything to the world about the picture and what it really means, even though "there is a great deal to be said." Part of what is left unsaid is a point Benjamin makes about portraits as an artistic genre in the modern world: they are the last refuge for the "cult value of the picture" in an age of mechanical reproduction, meant to be the faithful record of some actual person, the last bastion of truth.[35] The portrait of W.H., however, goes against the grain of this genre of authenticity by posing as something it is not, for the "Willie Hughes" depicted there never existed in the first place. At the same time, the portrait of the imaginary W.H. was dis-posed by Oscar Wilde as a histrionic "act" to realize himself artistically and sexually, for art is "a mode of acting," an attempt by the artist to perform and develop his own personality.

Wilde's desire to speak the "truth" of this vision of a performative art and characterological homosexuality is undermined, however, by a compromised ending in which nothing to the point is *said* by the narrator of the story, who finally declines to narrate at all, and the portrait that speaks both truth and lies is silent too – emitting a Benjaminian aura in a private space where few can ever see it and none will know of the combustible mixture of truth and falsehood that lies beneath its painted surface. Consequently the vexed truth that it was meant to speak will remain uncirculated in the social world, namely, as Wilde imagined it, a homosexual aesthetic whose creative power would transcend both mimesis and the physical expressions of same-sex desire. This shrinking away from the democratization and politicization of art represents a serious compromise of Wilde's own stated principles, leaving his portrait of W.H. in the barren realm of art for art's sake, to be enjoyed on a purely aesthetic plane by an elite group with no attention to its social or artistic meanings and purposes.

To read "The Portrait of Mr. W.H." in this way – as the story's betrayal of its own deepest motives – is to see it in a different light from much recent and intriguing criticism. For example, Alan Sinfield makes the point that there could be no convincing or authentic portrait of Mr. W.H. in Wilde's story because, as yet, modern homosexuality had not been invented, and so there was nothing "real" to paint, and therefore by implication nothing for the portrait to say to the world. In other words, nothing yet existed, and would not until the time of Wilde's trials, that could provide a "reality" to serve as a model for W.H.'s portrait.[36] Although Sinfield is a brilliant and fascinating critic of Wilde, it is worth balancing his argument with what Wilde himself has to say in "The Decay of Lying": "Life imitates art," not the other way round, and it is only inferior work that models itself on actual life. Not unlike Sinfield in this way, William A. Cohen argues in his engaging analysis of "The Portrait of Mr. W.H." that the riddle of the story is not answered by any pre-existent sexual category, the lack of which accounts for the effect of indeterminacy that the story produces.[37] Moe Meyer argues that the story breaks down because Wilde, in order to establish a homosexual identity, erases the identity of the model in W.H.'s portrait and claims it for himself – noting that the boy in the picture could be the signifier of his own identity, or Wilde's perhaps, but not both.[38] All of these critiques are founded on the assumption that Wilde and his world were unable to conceive "who" was pictured in the portrait of W.H. because they lacked the interpretive apparatus to do so. This assumption was founded on another, that there was no social category of homosexuality, in England at any rate, until one was produced a few years later by Wilde's trials for gross indecency – a point of view that has been convincingly discredited by recent historians of gender and sexuality, as this book will discuss in more detail in its chapters on the trials.

Perhaps the best commentary on "The Portrait of Mr. W.H." – and on *The Picture of Dorian Gray*, Wilde's more elaborate fiction on acting and posing – is to be found in the author's own work when he was writing about something else. In *The Critic as Artist: A Dialogue*, written in 1890 and revised for book publication in *Intentions* (1891), Wilde formulates the idea that "language is the parent, not the child, of thought," adding, "the one duty we owe to history is to re-write it."[39] This assertion of the power of language to create rather than merely imitate conditions of being is what lies at the foundation of "The Portrait of Mr. W.H.," for the story is an audacious rewriting of Shakespeare with the aim of creating, through Wildean speech acts, new modes of both art and life. Wilde seeks to realize the sexual potential of his own personality through literature, and its literary potential through sexuality. In this development of self, as in all progress, what the world calls "sin" is an indispensable element, as Wilde writes in *The Critic as Artist*, because it produces an "intensified assertion of individualism" and leads us toward a "higher ethics" through rejection of normative morality.[40] For Wilde, the task of the poet is to create from the chaos of actual life "a new world that will be more marvelous, more enduring, and more true than common eyes look upon."[41]

Criticism, however, is even more artistic than literature in Wilde's aesthetic because it concerns itself only with one's personal impressions, turning upside-down Matthew Arnold's famous dictum that criticism should "see the object as in itself it really is." Criticism refers even less than literature to anything external to itself, for the critic actually re-creates the work of art he addresses – whatever it might be, Shakespeare's love poetry or the portrait of W.H., for example – and does so absolutely on his or her own terms. In this sense criticism is the noblest form of autobiography, the record of the ideas and "imaginative passions" of the critic's own mind, untied from all mundane conditions of accuracy. Thus the critic of painting, for example, need not be concerned with what is really "in" the painting, any more than an actor playing the part of Hamlet should concern himself with what Shakespeare "meant" by creating such a character. For Wilde, anticipating postmodern critical theory, truth is simply a matter of style: "The meaning of any beautiful created thing is, at least, as much in the soul of him who looks at it as it was in his soul who wrought it," and "Beauty has as many meanings as a man has moods."[42] From this point of view, Wilde notes, it is irrelevant that Walter Pater's famous misreading of Leonardo's "Mona Lisa" – "she is older than the rocks among which she sits, like the vampire, she has been dead many times, and learned the secrets of the grave," etc. – has nothing whatever to do with what the painter himself intended. By the same token, meanings may be legitimately read into the portrait of Mr. W.H. – by Cyril, Erskine, the narrator, Wilde himself, and of course the reader – that have nothing to do with the actual facts of the matter. "And so the picture becomes to us more wonderful than it really is," Wilde writes, "and reveals to us a secret of which, in truth, it knows nothing."[43] These lines from "The Artist as Critic" refer to Pater's fanciful yet profound criticism of the "Mona Lisa," but can be applied with equal force to the forged and misrepresented portrait of Mr. W.H. in Wilde's story.

Wilde functions as a critic in "The Portrait of Mr. W.H." – of painting, of poetry, of life – but also as the artist who created the piece. As such, as Erskine suggests, the author is performing himself into the story, acting a part. As Wilde makes clear in *The Critic as Artist*, this self-enactment of the artist in the process of creation takes place in all authentic art, whatever form it may take. In painting, for example, "the very landscape that Corot looked at was, as he said himself, but a mood of his own mind." All art is drama, then, and as for the theatre itself,

those great figures of Greek or English drama that seem to us to possess an actual existence of their own, apart from the poets who shaped and fashioned them, are, in their ultimate analysis, simply the poets themselves, not as they thought they were, but as they thought they were not; and by such thinking came in strange manner, though but for a moment, really so to be.[44]

Shakespeare and all great artists reveal themselves most completely when posing and speaking behind a mask in their art. Their characters are themselves; their portraits are self-portraits. In Wilde's own terms, therefore, the portrait of Mr. W.H. is above all a portrait of himself – of Oscar Wilde posing – and so is the portrait of Dorian Gray.

### THE POSE THAT CAME TO LIFE

Posing had become supremely important in Wilde's evolving thought; and although particular poses would be artistic and self-developing to varying degrees, "still to have a pose at all is something ... a formal recognition of the importance of treating life from a definite and reasoned standpoint."[45] The central aim of posing was what Wilde called self-culture, the development of the individual's full potential in both art and life, but this noble aim was always, for Wilde, complicated and darkened by the shadow of its opposite – what I have called "dis-posing." Whether the topic is an artist projecting a pose or attitude into his work, or a model striking a pose in a studio, Wilde's discussions of posing as self-performance are always vexed by the issue of who, or what, directs and controls – dis-poses – the pose. This was the central issue of the landmark copyright case involving his own portrait, "Oscar Wilde, No. 18," a photographic pose that the Supreme

Court determined to be the creation and property of someone else. It was the issue, too, in much of Wilde's writing on painting, such as "London Models" and "The Relation of Dress to Art," in which the model's identity is more or less evacuated in order to provide the means for embodiment of the artist's own self-imaginings. This imperializing appropriation of the model's identity occurs again in "The Portrait of Mr. W.H.," in which the model, whoever he was, has been transformed into the sign of a homoerotic aesthetic that seeks to realize Wilde's own aspirations for a performative artistic and sexual identity. But, as we have seen, this pose is embedded in a narrative of suicide and despair, and the pose that started it all – the pose as recorded in the actual portrait of W.H. – is rendered inaccessible to the social world that it was meant to transform. In the end it is merely an owned artifact in someone's upscale dining room, a performance without an audience.

Wilde would return in his next major fiction to these same issues of agency and control in relation to the pose. In *The Picture of Dorian Gray*, written and rewritten from 1889–91, the title character seizes control of the portrait he sat for, rigidly enforcing its "cult value" and "aura" by reserving it as *his* own unique possession, hiding it away in an attic room and allowing no one else to see it at all. While Sarony's portrait of Wilde and the ensuing litigation exemplified the individual's lack of autonomous control over his own "posing," Dorian Gray in Wilde's novel not only claims exclusive proprietary rights in the portrait of himself, he makes it a stage upon which he can reinvent himself in performance. "It is not my property," the painter Basil Hallward declares when Lord Henry Wotton makes a name-your-price offer to buy the picture of Dorian Gray: "I will give you anything you like to ask for it. I must have it."[46] The portrait thus belongs to the model alone, as Wilde sets up his narrative at the beginning. Withdrawing his portrait from the circuits of distribution and commerce, Dorian somehow wills and speaks himself into co-identity with the picture – an aesthetic re-rendering of himself that seems to be, until the end of the novel, beyond the reach of courts of law and other forms of regulation, including any control of the painter over his own creation. Indeed, when Basil Hallward attempts, belatedly, to exert his claim and put the painting on exhibition, Dorian takes the artist upstairs to the room where the portrait is hidden and stabs him to death in front of it.

This fatal confrontation between artist and model is set in motion early in the story when Basil Hallward shows Dorian Gray the finished portrait, signing it with long, sloping letters in the corner of the picture, similar to the distinctive signature with which Sarony signed his famous photographs, including "Oscar Wilde, No. 18." Dorian and his new friend Lord Henry Wotton look on the portrait with breathless admiration, and Dorian reflects sadly on the differences that divide his painted and bodily self:

"How sad it is!" murmured Dorian Gray, with his eyes still fixed upon his own portrait. "How sad it is! I shall grow old, and horrible, and dreadful, but this picture will remain always young. It will never be older than this particular day of June ... If it were only the other way! If it were I who was to be always young, and the picture that was to grow old! For that – for that – I would give everything! Yes, there is nothing in the whole world I would not give! I would give my soul for that!⁴⁷

Although Dorian does not know it yet, his spoken wish to trade places with his own portrait, taking on its ageless beauty as his own, is to be gratified. This metamorphosis is the result of a statement-event that seems actually to make the wish come true – "If only it were the other way!" – thereby reconstituting Dorian as his own portrait, "the finest portrait of modern times ... one of the greatest things in modern art," while the painting itself is left to absorb the shocks of time-bound reality in place of the "real" Dorian.⁴⁸ The scene prefigures the concept of "performative" speech that would be theorized many decades later by J.L. Austin, who noted the existence of a type of discourse that could "perform" a new reality, in contrast to so-called "constantive" speech that referenced something already extant. For example, a man and woman, in one of Austin's famous examples, fashion a new reality when they *speak* the vows of matrimony under proper circumstances, performing themselves into a different condition of existence through an autonomously creative use of language.⁴⁹

   Although Dorian Gray certainly transforms himself in Basil Hallward's studio – trading places with his own portrait when he *speaks* his desire to do so – he nevertheless falls short of J.L. Austin's ideal of "performative language" and calls into question the principle behind it. Unlike Austin's imagined speaker of pure agency who makes things happen through words and controls outcomes, Dorian Gray is no more in charge of his posed portrait, or of himself, than Wilde was in control of the portrait that he posed for in Napoleon Sarony's studio. Dorian's performative transformation fails after all, for his other self, ravaged by time and sin, is displaced onto the canvas where it continues for the duration of the novel to admonish, fascinate, and torment him, the man the world recognizes as Dorian Gray. Defying morality and custom as well as the processes of time, Dorian launches a hedonistic and implicitly homoerotic quest for new sensations that will release him from the confines of fixed identity and open the door to what the novel terms a "multiplication of personalities." Meanwhile, however, his hidden portrait receives the imprint of each crime and sin, the beautiful face becoming hideously unlike its original although still recognizably Dorian's own.

Near the end of the novel, gazing on this decaying image of himself behind closed doors, Dorian perceives the painting as the intolerable voice of conscience and a "monstrous soul-life" that he must kill. At this decisive moment the speech act by which Dorian remade himself as his own portrait unravels completely – for when he stabs his portrait, it is he who is destroyed and not the painted image of himself. Knife in hand, he approaches the picture:

There was a cry heard, and a crash. The cry was so horrible in its agony that the frightened servants woke, and crept out of their rooms … When they entered, they found hanging upon the wall a splendid portrait of their master as they had last seen him, in all the wonder of his exquisite youth and beauty. Lying on the floor was a dead man, in evening dress, with a knife in his heart. He was withered, wrinkled, and loathsome of visage. It was not till they had examined the rings that they recognized who it was.[50]

As Wilde became a quotation of his own image in a Gilbert and Sullivan play, Dorian Gray becomes a quotation of his own portrait, his body reiterating the picture's ghastly alterations in form and coloring that were conscience to him. He has changed back into "himself" – himself, that is, as marked and defined by the moral and social codes of the world in which he lives. As Matt Cook has written in a somewhat different context about the ending of the novel, "When Dorian plunges the knife into the painting … a personal transgressive odyssey is brought to an end: the formal divisions between inside and out, the public and the private are re-established and the policeman makes his entrance."[51]

Like Wilde's own posing for Napoleon Sarony, the posing of Dorian Gray in Basil Hallward's studio demonstrates that self-performance can never be entirely autonomous. Contrary to the intentions of their models, the posed portraits of both Wilde and Dorian would become saturated in due course by the regulatory power of the social world in which they lived – systems of law, commerce, and morality. Wilde's aesthetic pose in America was intended to challenge "the commercial spirit" with the transformative power of art, but in the end it was the law, mediating the opposing claims of who "owned" Wilde's pose, that had the last word on "Oscar Wilde, No. 18" and incorporated it into the social machinery that Wilde wanted to oppose. By the same token, Dorian Gray's posed portrait, and the speech act by which he merges himself with it, represents an attempt to live beyond the reach of the moral law. But in the end, Dorian's remorseful, knife-wielding attack on his own portrait becomes an attack on himself – that is, his aestheticized self, Dorian Gray as reconstituted by his own portrait. Lying dead on the floor with a knife in his heart, Dorian is an exemplum of the moral law he had aimed to transcend: "The wages of sin is death."

# *Pure Wilde*

## Feminism and masculinity in *Lady Windermere's Fan*, *Salomé*, and *A Woman of No Importance*

Wilde's great plays of the 1890s are the acting out of the author's conflict and to a high degree his compromise with an increasingly powerful variety of late-Victorian feminism – rigid in its insistence that the "law of purity" be applied to men and women alike. An examination of the numerous manuscript drafts of the plays reveals that they began as expressions of Wilde's adamant hostility to the gender ethics of "purity" feminism, and what it required of men, a hostility that was also the source of a great deal of melodramatic excess marking these plays throughout their textual history. The sole exception is *Salomé*, whose surviving manuscript, written in French, is uncharacteristically (for Wilde) clean and almost unmarked by revision.[1] Interestingly, *Salomé* is also the only play by Wilde that stands in virtually unmediated conflict with the purity feminism of the *fin de siècle*.

With the sole exception of *Salomé*, banned from performance in England in his lifetime, Wilde toned down the intensity of his conflict with an increasingly powerful women's movement in the process of revising his plays. In Wilde's earlier society comedies in particular – *Lady Windermere's Fan* (1892) and *A Woman of No Importance* (1893) – the act of manuscript revision is also an act of political accommodation and compromise with the forces of feminism and social purity. It is important to remember that Wilde was writing and revising these manuscripts in the shadow of the most spectacular victories ever recorded by Victorian feminists, who only a few years before worked hand in hand with "social purity" activists to compel Parliament to end the notorious Contagious Diseases Acts and legislate the Criminal Law Amendment Bill under which Wilde himself would later be tried and imprisoned for the new crime of gross indecency. On one hand, then, Wilde was personally endangered by the puritanical feminism of his historical moment, while on the other hand the solidarity of feminist and social-purity reformers placed a major obstacle in his path toward realizing a performative masculinity that would be unshackled

from restrictive moral codes and re-map the boundaries of gender as the
Victorians understood it.

This vision of a freely performed gender identity was the motivating
force behind Wilde's tour of America and much of the fiction and criticism that he wrote just before his success as a playwright in the 1890s –
especially "The Portrait of Mr. W.H.," *The Artist as Critic*, and *The Picture
of Dorian Gray*, as we have seen. These works imagine a perfection of
self-development through a form of acting, or "posing," in which an individual really makes himself anew through the resources of an intense, aesthetic individualism that traverses the borderlands of morality, sexuality,
and gender. At the same time, from Wilde's point of view, the stern morality of feminists and social-purity reformers was itself a pose – a "moral
pose," as he called it in "The Critic as Artist," adding that "of all poses, a
moral pose is the most offensive."[2] From this theatrical standpoint, indeed,
*every* thought-out attitude toward life, every self-conscious work of art,
and every strategy of self-representation is finally an "act," a performance.
That is why it is important to have a pose of some kind, even if it is an
"offensive" one like the pose of morality – for without a conscious pose,
without an "act," one is also without individuality and can have no reasoned criticism of life.

The process of revising his plays became a give-and-take in which Wilde
listened to and absorbed the arguments put forward by radical feminists
and their allies in the social-purity movement. His morally vigilant women
characters invariably became less single-mindedly "moral," less hypocritical, and simply more likable the more Wilde revised his comedies, but
not without cost to the characters who were most like Wilde himself.
Aesthetic, effeminate, and dandified characters had to yield ground on a
number of fronts in order to make room for the enlarged sympathy that
Wilde's multiply layered revisions tended to claim for his upright women
characters. His radical feminists had to change too, not only through
authorial revision of their character traits, but also by learning to adjust
their demands for purity, especially male purity, to a more tolerant and
humane outlook than they started with. This conciliatory rewriting of
strident and heavy-handedly melodramatic passages resulted in plays with
more believable characters and more credible narratives than they began
with. At the same time, however, Wilde often had to second-guess and
rein in his own views and inclinations as embodied in the dandified and
amoral men (and a few women) who represent them in these plays. On
occasion, indeed, spectators felt they were witnessing a sermon on stage,

rather than a self-expressive authorial performance through his created characters such as Wilde had theorized in *The Critic as Artist*.

In the earliest manuscript drafts of *Lady Windermere's Fan*, for example, the as yet unnamed heroine insists upon strict application of "the same laws for men as there are for women." But in this original version the character who would eventually be called Lady Windermere is a cynical hypocrite, and the mission of the play is to expose the sensual and self-indulgent nature that her devotion to "purity" conceals. In later versions, however, and most notably in the final one, Lady Windermere has matured into a rounded character whose feminism is flexible, yet sincere. Her personal purity, although called into question in earlier drafts, is authenticated and approved by the final curtain of the performed version of the play, and the Wildean dandies who mock and deride the moral ideal of purity in *Lady Windermere's Fan* have mostly disappeared by the fourth act and in some cases become "good" themselves. If we were to imagine a "preface" that Wilde never wrote for *Lady Windermere's Fan*, *Salomé*, and *A Woman of No Importance*, we could do no better than recall the vision of a performative gender identity as expressed in his earlier fiction and criticism on one hand, and on the other hand the writings of his adversaries – the purity feminists who significantly determined the plot and characterization of these plays and helped lay the groundwork for the ultimate catastrophe of his life.

## "THAT BEAUTIFUL WORD OF 'PURITY'": A PREFACE TO WILDE'S PLAYS

Although the puritanical gender code of late-Victorian feminism powerfully affected Wilde's career and created the social conditions that made possible his courtroom trials on charges of gross indecency, the movement is not now widely understood or adequately historicized. As historian Barabara Caine has pointed out, purity feminism requires far more scholarly attention than it has received.[3] In particular, the importance of the movement needs to be better understood, as well as *why* it was important. Running beneath the fascinating narrative of its social and political campaigns – but buried for the most part in little-known or long-forgotten speeches, pamphlets, and polemical books – is a new if fitful recognition that traditional conceptions of gender are regulatory fictions, not the expression of a universally "true" manhood or womanhood or core personal identity. In this regard Wilde and certain late-Victorian feminists are on the same important page as Victorians who anticipate Joan Rivière and Judith Butler in realizing that gender is not a manifestation of biological sex, but a ritualized drama, or "masquerade" in Rivière's phrase, through which the body takes on cultural meaning and typically serves the purposes of entrenched social power.[4]

In this environment in which gender codes and identities were under attack and increasingly destabilized, Wilde and purity feminists in particular agreed on the need for a radical critique of normative masculinity. They clashed, however, in their prescriptions of what should replace it. Wilde's career as a popular playwright was in important respects the direct result of his conflicts and compromises with these late-Victorian reformers over the re-scripting of masculinity, and his most famous plays, from *Lady Windermere's Fan* to *The Importance of Being Earnest*, were organized by it through an arduous process of revision. To see Wilde's drama in context – the drama of his life as well as the plays he wrote – requires that it be situated in relation to the coordinated efforts of late-Victorian feminists and social-purity reformers, the twinned forces that energized his work as a playwright and in the end brought him to ruin.

This historically important convergence of Oscar Wilde and purity feminism becomes evident in retrospect with the enactment of the Criminal Law Amendment Bill of 1885, the legislation that created the crime for which Oscar Wilde would be imprisoned a decade later. Yet the focus of the Criminal Law Amendment Act as a whole was not gross indecency between men, but rather a number of heterosexual behaviors that until the 1885 Act had been legal. For example, "the defilement of any girl under the age of thirteen" became a felony in that year, or a misdemeanor if the girl were between the ages of twelve and sixteen. Girls under sixteen could no longer be "detained" in brothels under terms of the new legislation. A law to protect young girls from seduction and prostitution had become a primary objective of feminist and allied social-purity groups, one closely connected to their campaign against state regulation of prostitution through the Contagious Diseases Acts and other forms of police control. Yet the overall effect of the Criminal Law Amendment Act was to criminalize a range of sexual conduct by men, from prostituting and having sex with children to being "grossly indecent" with each other.[5] The Act and its supporters thereby contested the traditional view that the core "nature" of men (as it was thought to be) was marred by lusts that it was impossible to tame and futile to complain against. In addition to the common perception that men were by nature irredeemably carnal, reformers had to overcome unwillingness on the part of many people to discuss or even acknowledge the existence of what the new law dealt with – the sexual trafficking of working-class children for the profit and pleasure of affluent men.

By 1885, frustrated by previous failures of Parliament to enact the Criminal Law Amendment Bill, allied feminist and social-purity leaders joined with W.T. Stead, editor of the *Pall Mall Gazette*, to produce a journalistic exposé of child prostitution. In collaboration with Josephine Butler of the Ladies' National Association and Florence Booth of the Salvation Army, Stead arranged to buy a thirteen-year-old working-class girl from her own mother in a Marylebone slum as the basis of a sensational series of articles in the *Pall Mall Gazette*, beginning in July 1885 and creating an election-year furor. The aim of this coalition of feminism, social purity, and journalism – "to drag this great evil to light," as Stead wrote at the beginning of his series of articles – was spectacularly successful, even though Stead went to prison for his efforts and more than a hundred newsboys were arrested for selling a publication with "indecent" content. The conspiracy of silence that had long protected men who trafficked in the children of the poor was effectively broken.

Although the Criminal Law Amendment Bill had been stalled in Parliament for two years, M.P.s were suddenly swamped with letters from their constituents, and monster rallies were held in support of the legislation. Salvation Army soldiers and cadets marched to Parliament with a petition signed by 393,000 people. Amid this uproar, a committee of M.P.s and bishops of the church certified what had become obvious: Stead's allegations about child prostitution and sexual abuse were "substantially true."[6] The bill was passed in August, hard on the heels of Stead's triumph of investigative journalism in the *Pall Mall Gazette* and the excitement it had created. Stead went to prison, not for what he wrote but for posing as a man who procured a girl "just over 13" for prostitution, executing all the details of the transaction "short of actually consummating the crime he [was] pretending to wish to commit."[7] He had presented himself in the guise of an elderly man to Eliza Armstrong, the thirteen-year-old girl he had bought and paid for; she screamed when she saw him approaching her bed, but Stead never touched her. He went on to write a jailhouse biography of Josephine Butler, celebrating her relentless efforts on behalf of purity feminism to enact the Criminal Law Amendment Act that would bring Wilde himself to prison ten years later.[8]

When it was pushed through Parliament in 1885, there still remained one great but unfinished crusade of the purity reformers – total repeal of the Contagious Diseases Acts. The CD Acts, as they came to be known,

were introduced in 1862 to empower police and magistrates to con-
fine suspected prostitutes in lock hospitals for forced treatment in order
to control the spread of syphilis and other sexually transmitted diseases
among military men, although the men themselves were not subject to
any such surveillance. Feminists, led by Josephine Butler and her Ladies'
National Association, pointed out that these Acts "so far as women are
concerned ... remove every guarantee of personal security which the law
has established and held sacred, and put their reputation, their freedom,
and their persons absolutely in the power of the police." The Contagious
Diseases Acts targeted only women, leaving unpunished, in the words of
an LNA manifesto, "the sex who are the main cause, both of the vice and
its dreaded consequences; and we consider that liability to arrest, forced
medical treatment, and (where this is resisted) imprisonment with hard
labour, to which these Acts subject women, are punishments of the most
degrading kind."[9] In her memoir Butler argues that the CD Acts aimed
at "the enslavement of women," but in particular a class of women – "the
daughters of the people."[10] It was working poor women who could not survive otherwise who swelled the ranks of prostitutes in the Victorian era,
as Butler knew and as has been documented more recently by historian
Judith Walkowitz.[11] Prostitutes were thus vulnerable to oppression on the
grounds of class as well as of gender.

From the perspective of purity feminists, then, it made sense to regard
prostitutes compassionately as their sisters, degraded, policed, and sexually victimized by men. Josephine Butler received prostitutes into her
own home "in the hour of trouble, sickness, and death," sometimes asking house guests to go to a hotel so that she could receive these outcast
women "as if they had been my own sisters."[12] Ellice Hopkins, founder
of the militant White Cross Army, established homes for prostituted
and sexually abused children – "poor, degraded mites of nine, eight, and
seven, coming into my hands," as she wrote in a tract informing working-
class fathers of new protections afforded their daughters under the newly
enacted Criminal Law Amendment Bill.[13] Like Butler, Ellice Hopkins
expressed compassion for prostitutes, blaming instead of these women "a
fearfully debased manhood that is in our midst that respects nothing."[14]
Elsewhere, in the 1883 manifesto of the White Cross Army, Hopkins again
protests the injustice of making women accountable for vice and conta-
gion, and reflects hopefully that a new attitude may be taking hold. "This
weary hammering away at degraded women, while leaving all the causes
that make them degraded untouched, is beginning to be recognized as
not a very fruitful method," she writes. Campaigning for abolition of the

Contagious Diseases Acts and passage of the Criminal Law Amendment
Bill, Josephine Butler, Ellice Hopkins, and their many followers in the
mid-1880s sought to restore liberty and dignity to the girls and women
who had become, as Butler put it, "police-made slaves," and to fix blame
for this state of affairs on the men who regulated and paid for sex, not on
the women who sold it. "It is this stronghold," wrote Butler, "which must
be attacked."[15]

Victorian feminism was far from monolithic, however, and the opposition to the Contagious Diseases Acts, led by Josephine Butler and her
allies in the Ladies' National Association, was not shared by all leaders of
the Victorian women's movement. Emily Davies and Frances Cobbe, for
example, represented a feminism devoted single-mindedly to emancipa-
tion (which Butler also advocated), critiquing women's oppression from
the perspective of a political and economic liberalism deeply influenced by
John Stuart Mill. More cautious than Josephine Butler, and more decor-
ous, they remained silent on issues of state-regulated prostitution and the
social control of women's bodies. Among the most prominent of Victorian
feminists was Millicent Fawcett, a moderate and pragmatist who at first
kept silent about the Contagious Diseases Acts, opposing them but choos-
ing to focus her efforts on the campaign for women's suffrage. By the
mid-1880s, however, Fawcett was increasingly concerned with the sexual
oppression of women by men and had become a founding member of the
National Vigilance Association. Like Butler and Ellice Hopkins, founder of the militant White Cross Army, she now combined advocacy for
women's suffrage with the NVA's campaign for social purity. "The more I
dwell upon the details of Josephine Butler's life and work," Fawcett would
write in this later phase of her own career, "the more I become convinced
that she should take the rank of the most distinguished Englishwoman of
the nineteenth century."[16]

It is unclear how many feminists were involved in these purity campaigns, but the number was surely enormous, involving not only members of the National Vigilance Association, but the Social Purity Alliance
which preceded it, the White Cross Army, the Ladies' National Association
which had been formed to fight the CD Acts almost from the beginning,
and the newly emergent Women's Liberal Association, an offshoot of the
Liberal Party. The new moral fervor transcended any single organization,
although the National Vigilance Association became perhaps its most
radical exponent by harassing prostitutes as well as their clients and by
fiercely opposing birth control and "impure" literature. Eventually Butler
herself would resign from that organization, so great was its clash with her

own liberal principles, but her devotion to the cause of social purity would be undiminished. Across this wide range of organizations and activities, Butler identified as "the central principle" a common insistence upon the purity of all members of society, men as well as women, as the only way to end the double standard of morality and the sexual control of women by men.[17] But underlying this conscious goal was a revolutionary, although unsystematic rethinking of gender itself which must begin to be taken into account in order to measure at all accurately the significance of *fin-de-siècle* feminism.

In their campaigns for gender equality, Butler and her allies were single-mindedly focused on attacking the entrenched belief that men were naturally unchaste and that regulated prostitution was necessary in order to appease the brutish appetites of men and protect the virtue of "good" women. The agitation against the CD Acts and on behalf of the Criminal Law Amendment Act was founded, therefore, upon the assumption that this view of masculinity as a naturalized category of gender was fraudulent. It was exposed as a self-serving fiction rather than an expression of biological or any other kind of fact. In attempting to demolish this construction of masculinity and replace it with another, Victorian feminists on the side of social purity were implicitly, and sometimes explicitly, recognizing the performativity of gender in their "great crusade" against the sexual control of women by men. It was a move that held tremendous potential for change in the way gender was understood. In Butler's view, for example, the Contagious Diseases Acts had brought into existence a "diabolical triple power" of doctors, magistrates, and police whose purpose was to place certain women under surveillance and enforce their degradation as embodiments of the Victorian nightmare of feminine evil and uncontained sexuality.[18] These women, Butler recognized, were "maddened, hardened and stamped underfoot by men," actually defined into being by medical and legal authority. The "tortured and fiendish" womanhood of Victorian prostitutes was, for Butler, nothing more nor less than the creation of men "bowing down before the unrestrained dictates of their own lusts" – lusts which they falsely imagined to be natural and unchangeable, determined by their masculine gender.[19] The essence of Butler's view, then, was that at least some authorized paradigms of both masculinity and femininity were performed, not "real."

Even before the full repeal of the CD Acts in 1886, the rhetoric of the movement was deeply colored by its adherence to a single standard of purity for both men and women and, crucially, by a recognition that dominant readings of gender in no way expressed a "true" masculinity or femininity.

Josephine Butler, in a little-known polemic of 1882 entitled *The Hour before the Dawn: An Appeal to Men*, advocates what she describes as "two radical principles – namely, the sacredness of the home, and the duty of men to live and to suffer women to live in purity." Butler excoriates the Contagious Diseases Acts in the context of the "unequal standard of morality for the sexes," which is in her view the ultimate cause of prostitution and contrary to every principle of justice. "The law of personal purity obliges men and women equally to rule their lives by their highest spiritual ideal," Butler proclaims, quoting the manifesto of the Social Purity Alliance. The idea that "unchastity is a 'necessity' for man" is false to the core – nothing more than "man's invention, for his own base convenience."[20] Similarly, in *Sursam Corda*, her address to the Ladies' National Association in 1891, Butler attacks the eminent historian and social critic W.E.H. Lecky for his romanticized description of the prostitute as the "priestess of humanity," charged with the mournful office of bearing the sins of men. "What beautiful language, what subtle arguments," exclaims Butler, "have men brought, in all ages, to the support of the recognised indulgence of their own selfish interests and degraded passions!"[21]

Embedded in such pronouncements is the same insight that would produce theories of performative gender a century later. In understanding the Victorian idea of masculinity as something manufactured and sustained to further the interests of men, Josephine Butler anticipates Judith Butler's assertions more than a century later that gendered identity is brought into being by gestures and enactments that create the illusion of an organizing gender core, an illusion "discursively maintained for the purposes of the regulation of sexuality."[22] Although Josephine Butler's much earlier observations are not presented as a fully developed theory of gender, she nevertheless argues for a reconsideration that would reveal the performativity of gender and destabilize masculinity as a naturalized category of identity. It has not yet been fully noted what a crucial turning point this was in constructing what it meant, or might mean, to be a "woman" or a "man."

In the early years of the CD Acts Butler visited the garrison towns where they were in effect and personally met many "Queen's women," as the prostitutes called themselves, as well as soldiers who were quartered in those places. One of the men, recalls Butler in a little-known pamphlet, *Truth Before Everything*, explained the behavior of himself and his fellow soldiers as the result, not of their own nature, but of the expectations of those above them. "*They expect us to be bad, and we are bad*," a young soldier told Butler, who italicized his comment, and then drove home the point herself: "'They – the authorities – expect us to be bad.' That boy expressed the whole truth concerning the effect of this degrading State institution, in those few simple words. Why should not the authorities give a trial to the plan of *expecting* these soldiers to be *good?*"²³

With these words Butler rejected the idea that the Contagious Diseases Acts could be justified by appealing to the gendered "nature" of men as inevitably corrupt, thus requiring the sacrifice of a whole class of women. As suggested by the comments of the young soldier, Butler argues that the sordid behavior of some men is nothing more than the acting out of a script that has been written by "the authorities" to enforce their view of what men are or should be. By this view, being a "man" is a performative event rather than the outward manifestation of "real" or natural masculinity that would justify the policing and "enslavement of women" brought about by the Contagious Diseases Acts.

By the same token, and crucially, the *new* masculinity that Butler advocated was implicitly performative in nature, rather than expressive of a natural gendered identity. In asking the question "Why should not the authorities give a trial to the plan of *expecting* these soldiers to be *good?*," Butler concedes, unselfconsciously, that her purified masculinity is itself a script to be performed – an acting out of the projected expectations of external authority rather than the manifestation of an essential masculine nature or even the result of a humanist individual choice by which a particular man would determine for himself what it meant to be male.

Rhetorically as well as ideologically, these developments marked a significant historical moment. The term "masculinity" was becoming a signifier whose content was in doubt, contested by opposing parties with regard to what the concept, and gender itself, could be said to mean, if anything, in and of itself. The terms "purity," "puritan," and "puritanism" had also become battlegrounds. On one side Josephine Butler asserted, "It is a beautiful word that of Purity," yet she worried that because of its political cachet many societies had begun to use that name without fully endorsing the program of feminist social purity. For example, she writes in *Truth before Everything*, some groups oppose "impure" literature and yet support the state regulation of vice. While on one hand even her foes appropriated the term "purity" to work at cross-purposes with feminists like herself, on the other hand there were enemies passionately eager "to get rid of this 'damnable Puritanism' which is so irksome to them." For this latter group the hated term "purity" was beginning to stand for the reforms of gender that radical feminism was promoting. "Nothing, they know," writes Butler, "would so rapidly and forcibly conduce towards their liberation from this oppressive yoke [of "purity"] than that the State should itself proclaim … that free fleshly indulgence is necessary for man, and therefore not to be blamed, but rather to be facilitated."[24] Around the word "purity" the cultural battle-lines were drawn on the issue of gender; and in the dramas of Oscar Wilde, as well as in his courtroom trials and imprisonment, clashing ideologies of masculinity and femininity would be acted out.

In literature the new gender ideology of purity was circulated by the most widely read feminist novel of the *fin de siècle*, *The Heavenly Twins* (1893) by Sarah Grand. In one strand of the book's complicated narrative, a bride discovers that her husband has had sexual relationships before their marriage, making him a "moral leper" with whom she will tolerate no intimacy, physical or emotional. Their marriage is never consummated. *The Heavenly Twins* was an instant and huge success, and more than any other text it created an awareness of what seemed to some men the most problematic demand of the developing women's movement. Sarah Grand expressed that demand in her own voice in a magazine article that appeared shortly after the publication of *The Heavenly Twins*. "Man morally is in his infancy," she wrote in 1894. "There have been times when there was a doubt as to whether he was to be raised or woman was to be lowered, but we have turned that corner at last; and now woman holds out a strong hand to the child-man and insists … upon helping him up."[25]

Some men, who had little sympathy with feminism in the first place, turned the feminist demand for male purity into ridicule. For example, in Sydney Grundy's hit play *The New Woman* (1894), a young woman named Enid Bethune, sounding like a member of the Ladies' National Association or White Cross Army, proposes that "a man, reeking with infamy, ought not to be allowed to marry a pure young girl." "Certainly not!" responds Victoria Vivash, a feminist of a very different order – "she ought to reek with infamy as well."[26] But *The Woman Who Did*, as Grant Allen characterized her in the title of his notorious novel of 1895, was comparatively rare among late-Victorian feminists. It was *The Woman Who Didn't*, as Victoria Cross entitled her fictional rejoinder to *The Woman Who Did*, that registered more accurately the dominant tone of late-Victorian feminism.[27] There were exceptions like George Egerton, who celebrated female sexuality in her fiction of the 1890s, and Mona Caird, whose novels and journalistic writing advocated free love. But for most of those in the organized women's movement – members of the Ladies' National Association, Women's Liberal Association, and other groups – gender equity had little to do with loosening the sexual restraints placed upon women, but much to do with raising the standard of conduct for men. On the agenda of feminist leaders such as Millicent Fawcett and Josephine Butler, the reconstitution of masculinity along lines of purity went hand in hand with other defining issues of the movement – votes for women, access to higher education and professional careers, and resistance to the police surveillance of women carried out under the Contagious Diseases Acts.

## WILDE'S FEMINIST PHASE

Wilde was in close contact with prominent figures in the women's movement as editor of *The Woman's World* from 1888 to 1890, a magazine formerly known as *The Lady's World* but reconceived under Wilde's editorship to focus on women's suffrage, education and employment, and a range of social issues from women's perspectives. Wilde commissioned Emily Faithfull to write on women's employment, Millicent Fawcett on women's suffrage, Clementina Black on the abysmal working conditions of barmaids, Mrs. Oscar Wilde herself on "rational dress" for women, and Lady Sandhurst – Constance Wilde's close friend and a leader of the Women's Liberal Association – on women in politics. Articles and interviews featured in *The Woman's World*, various and wide-ranging, sometimes revolved around the feminist agenda of morality that was circulating widely in contemporaneous literature and would later become central to Wilde's own plays. In 1889, for example, Millicent Fawcett's essay "Women's Suffrage" emphasized not only votes for women but society's need for women who could transform the public sphere, once they were part of it, with an infusion of domestic virtue. "We want women," she wrote in Wilde's magazine, "to bring their true woman's influence on behalf of whatsoever things are true, honest, just, pure, lovely, and of good report, to bear upon the conduct of public affairs."[28] In a lengthy interview in 1890, Lady Sandhurst mixes advocacy of women's suffrage with "moral earnestness" in both personal life and politics.[29] Lady Sandhurst had by this time greatly influenced her friend Constance Wilde, bringing her into the Chelsea branch of the Women's Liberal Association and encouraging her efforts in the Rational Dress Society, whose official publication, the *Rational Dress Society Gazette*, she edited during the same period that her husband was editor of *The Woman's World*.

Although it seems improbable from the perspective of Wilde's playwriting in the 1890s, his years as editor of a woman's magazine were marked not only by sympathy for women's aspirations in general, but for the rigidly moral framework in which they were so often expressed. In a review that Wilde himself contributed to his magazine in 1889, he expresses the view that society should empower women politically because to do so would bring about the "moralization" of the corrupt, male-dominated world of politics. "The family ideal of the State may be difficult of attainment," Wilde writes in language unimaginable for him only a year or two later, "but as an ideal it is better than the policeman theory. It would mean the moralisation of politics. The cultivation of separate sorts of virtues and separate ideals of duty in men and women has led to the whole social fabric being weaker and unhealthier than it need be."[30] It was the same point that Josephine Butler had made the year before in a speech entitled "Women and Politics," given before the Women's Liberal Association at Portsmouth, in which she declared that "women must work for the Parliamentary vote." In the words of one report summarizing the speech, "Mrs. Butler said she felt very strongly the necessity that women should be politicians ... Until they did so we should not have our Legislature such as it ought to be, or public opinion purified as it should be ... It would have a perceptible effect on Parliament."[31]

But the enthusiastic endorsement of women's moral influence in the public sphere soon disappeared from Wilde's writing; in fact, his plays of the 1890s were built on reversals and modifications of this feminist politics of purity – to a greater or lesser degree, depending upon the play and the several stages of revision that they went through.

REWRITING *LADY WINDERMERE'S FAN*

It would be interesting to speculate how much of Wilde's advocacy of feminist causes during his time as editor of *The Woman's World* was itself a pose, only one of a spectrum of attitudes in a histrionic life whose aim was the multiplication of personality. However that may be, it is certain that as editor of *The Woman's World* he was pitching the magazine's editorial content to make it consumable by a *fin-de-siècle* feminist clientele whose agenda included jobs for women, votes for women, and an emphasis upon moral earnestness for men and women alike. Once Wilde was no longer selling journalism to the commercial niche that the readership of his magazine represented – once, that is, he had become a novelist and, soon after, a popular dramatist – the tone of his writing with respect to women and feminism underwent a fundamental change. Instead of advocating a feminist agenda, as he had done as a journalist, Wilde began producing texts in which women, especially feminist women, were a disruptive presence. The society dramas written between 1891 and 1894 began as sometimes crudely exaggerated attacks on the contemporary feminism that Wilde had catered to as editor of *The Woman's World*. His laborious revisions of these same plays tend to reduce their melodramatic hostility to purity feminism, often resulting in greater aesthetic coherence while diminishing some important characters who share Wilde's own distaste for a regulatory and strict morality.

Against this background of Wilde's changing representation of women, the first of his popular society dramas, *Lady Windermere's Fan*, was being drafted and re-drafted to modulate and refine its adversarial focus on feminist demands for a reconfiguration of gender. In the earliest known version of the play – a holograph manuscript in Wilde's hand, generically entitled *Play* – the plot organizes itself quickly around ideas associated with purity feminism after a wobbly opening scene in which Wilde is clearly trying to find his way. This first manuscript draft of *Lady Windermere's Fan*, housed in the British Library and rarely cited in criticism of the play, opens with a slanging and crudely flirtatious Lord Darlington in conversation with Lady Windermere, whose outwardly rigorous virtue, Wilde implies, is only skin-deep. Using language markedly more self-righteous than she employs in later versions of the play, Lady Windermere says to Lord Darlington, on the subject of women's purity: "I think a woman who has done anything wrong brings a taint wherever she goes. And if she really repents she will never want to go into society again."

But the rest of the conversation in the first draft, although unattached to the names of speakers, closely resembles what is spoken at the same juncture in the final version of *Lady Windermere's Fan* – with one exception. All but the last line of the following exchange remained intact in the play's final draft:

LORD DARLINGTON: And men? Do you think that there should be the same laws
    for men as there are for women?
LADY WINDERMERE: Certainly.
LORD DARLINGTON: … You make no exceptions?
LADY WINDERMERE: None.
LORD DARLINGTON: What a fascinating Puritan you are, Lady Windermere.
LADY WINDERMERE: …The adjective is *de trop*.

Everything about this dialogue, as far as Lady *Windermere's* lines are concerned, matches the tone of Josephine Butler and purity feminism except for the last line: "the adjective is *de trop*," an abrupt slip into French that is suggestive, in this Victorian context, of a worldly and less-than-earnest woman. Scenes in the manuscript that were to be staged in Lady Windermere's "*boudoir*" strike the same note, as do some remarks

of Lady Windermere when she believes she has discovered her husband
has been having an affair with a woman named variously in the manuscript "Mrs Alwynne," "Mrs. Evlynne," and "Mrs. Erlynne." Breaking into
her husband's checkbook and discovering that he has paid large sums of
money to this woman, Lady Windermere snaps at him with another brief
lapse into French: "You go for your *amours* into an expensive market."[32]
Such expressions as these, implying that beneath the mask of the "Puritan"
is a cosmopolitan and sexually knowing woman, were without exception
deleted by Wilde as he revised *Lady Windermere's Fan.* The result is a very
different portrait of this "Puritan" woman than the one Wilde had begun
to draw, a character who, in revision, became less susceptible to inferences
of cynicism and hypocrisy, and on balance was represented more sympa-
thetically despite her remaining flaws.

This softening of a "Puritan" woman through the processes of revision
would become the paradigm of Wilde's society comedies, as if the author
were negotiating the concepts of gender she espoused and interrogating
his own deep hostility toward them. By modulating his attitude toward
women who insisted that the law of purity be applied equally to men and
women, Wilde rescued his heroines from caricature, humanizing them
and making possible some rapprochement with the men in their lives.
Further examination of the first draft of *Lady Windermere's Fan* in relation to later versions shows how Wilde's second-guessing of his initial
conception of Lady Windermere influenced the sweep of the play as a
whole as well as the shape of plays yet to be written. The original Lady
Windermere's puritanical rhetoric is almost comically melodramatic
when describing "Mrs. Erlynne," the name Wilde finally settles on for
the woman who, unknown to Lady Windermere, is her own mother and
also the woman she suspects of having an affair with her husband. Lady
Windermere vilifies Mrs. Erlynne as "that vile painted woman whose
very sight is a degradation, whose touch an infamy," language that disappears in later drafts of the play. Lady Windermere's overheated rhetoric
in the first draft is applied to men too, especially her own husband, to
express dismay that he has not lived up to the standard of purity that,
so far at least, she has fully satisfied in her own behavior. But when Lord
Darlington suddenly declares to Lady Windermere that he loves her and
asks her to "come away with me," she immediately decides to do so in
anger over her supposed betrayal by her husband. "As there is no honour
amongst men – let there be no purity among women," she exclaims in the
first draft. "Evil for evil, pain for pain, sin for sin! Yes, I shall leave him –
and let him know for whom."[33]

Lady Windermere's sudden, blunt, and vengeful renunciation of her deeply held belief in the ideas of purity feminism ("as there is no honour amongst men – let there be no purity among women") disappear in the finished play. In the final version she never abandons her beliefs so cynically and self-consciously; instead, shaken by her husband's supposed unfaithfulness, she becomes vulnerable to Lord Darlington's appeals that she run away with him: "Let me think! Let me wait! My husband may return to me ... Ah, give me time to think. I cannot answer now. (*Passes her hand nervously over her brow*) ... How alone I am in life! How terribly alone."[34]

Then, in this final revision, Lady Windermere sits distracted through a conversation with a group of women before excusing herself from the room with scarcely a word, let alone the words that Wilde originally gave her: "let there be no purity among women." Roiled with shock and hurt, she writes a letter to her husband to say that she is leaving him; but gone is the first draft's violent rhetoric against men and against Lady Windermere's supposed rival, Mrs. Erlynne. Gone, too, is Lady Windermere's bitter speech renouncing the whole concept of purity for men and women alike, along with her abrupt transformation from a disciple of the social-purity movement to a character on the edge of becoming a "fallen woman" herself. In the first draft, Lady Windermere's purity feminism is a sham that quickly collapses when tested by life, and in the original version of the play she just as quickly discards her supposed ideals without reflection. The final version, by contrast, revises this hypocritical and vengeful woman into a new Lady Windermere who is mistaken but sincere, rattled, clueless – and although about to leave her husband, her conduct would be unimaginable except in the state of crisis and delusion that has engulfed her. Even so, the drama reviewer for the *Pall Mall Budget*, viewing the heavily revised play in its first production, complained that Wilde had presented a heroine "Puritanic in feeling, and bitterly virtuous in ideas – and assumes that in a few minutes ... she is induced [by Darlington] to commit cold-blooded adultery."[35] Although some basis remains for these objections even after Wilde's thorough revision of Lady Windermere's character, it is important to note that the heroine, as she appeared on opening night in 1892, was immensely less "cold-blooded" and cynical than Wilde had made her out to be in earlier drafts.

Wilde's drastic revision of the character of Lady Windermere enables him to stay on speaking terms in this play with the feminist and social-purity views of gender identity represented by her in the first two acts. In revised form, Lady Windermere is characterized as being reasonable and honest enough to be won over from her radical position and embrace an ideology of gender that has no stake in a rigid ideal of purity, whether for men or women, and that calls into question the usual categories of "good" and "bad" without betraying the *donné* of her character. The key to this transformation, in the original manuscript as well as in all succeeding drafts of the play, occurs after Lady Windermere writes a letter to her husband announcing her decision to leave him and then goes to Lord Darlington's rooms, intending to elope. But Darlington is entertaining friends, and Lady Windermere must conceal herself while he confesses that he is in love with a "a good woman" – Lady Windermere, of course – expressing himself in the first draft much as he does in the final version of the play:

DARLINGTON: She has purity and innocence. She has everything that we men have lost.
"C.G." [CECIL GRAHAM]: What should we men do ... with purity and innocence? Not a single pretty woman would speak to us.
DARLINGTON: How corrupt you are, Cecil.[36]

This conversion of the dandified and amoral Darlington into a sympathizer with purity feminism is more improbable in the first draft than in the finished play, and the same can be said for Lady Windermere's alteration from a purity ideologue into a woman who demands perfection from no one and calls into question the settled definitions of "good" and "bad." By making Darlington less coarse at the outset, and Lady Windermere less strident and hypocritical, Wilde prepares the way for a more convincing accommodation in the finished play between the sexual politics of purity and a larger, more tolerant view. Mrs. Erlynne, the supposedly "bad" woman of the play, pursues Lady Windermere to Darlington's rooms and persuades her to return to her husband, sacrificing herself to enable the daughter who does not know her to escape undetected. In all versions of the play, consequently, Lady Windermere – no longer advocating purity as a law for women *or* men – pronounces Mrs. Erlynne a "good woman" and understands at last the difficulty of dividing people into "the good and the bad."

But Lady Windermere ends the play, in all versions, as much married to her husband as she was at the beginning, as devoted and faithful to him as before, and as "pure," as she would have said in the first half of the play, as ever. She has modified her application of the categories of good and bad, but the categories themselves remain intact; and she has renounced her insistence upon purity without becoming "impure" herself. Nevertheless, Lady Windermere has traveled an immense distance from her starting point as a rigid puritan in matters of gender, a distance that would have been implausibly immense for the hypocritical and overwrought woman imagined by Wilde in the first draft of the play. By smoothing these hard edges of Lady Windermere in revision, Wilde makes her ultimate conversion into a tolerant yet still highly moral woman more credible than it was in his original conception. His revisions of the final act, too, add force and coherence to the play's guiding thesis that people cannot be divided into the good and bad by an inflexible rule of so-called purity. Notably, the fact that the "good" daughter and the "bad" mother share the same name – Margaret – in the final version of the play (whereas they are called "Violet" and "Angela" in the first draft) drives home the point of our common humanity and fallibility.

Such revisions as these do not alter the fact that *Lady Windermere's Fan* is framed as an assault upon the gender ideology of late-Victorian feminism and the social-purity movement, but they dilute the stridency and melodrama of Wilde's opposition and enable a reasonably harmonious accommodation with those on the other side of the issue. This approach would not solve the crisis that feminist puritanism of the *fin de siècle* would eventually pose for Wilde, as his later arrest and conviction on charges of gross indecency make abundantly clear. In a few years, he was to be the pawn and victim of the puritanism with which *Lady Windermere's Fan* was finally able to make peace. But Wilde's approach in composing the play was at the very least tolerant and large-minded, worked out in revision through the second-guessing of his own biases on gender and sexuality, and it would set the tone and become the pattern for his stage comedies to follow. Not coincidentally, this pattern of revision also made for much better plays than the ones he conceived in first draft – plays with more plausible characters and more convincing arguments on the issue that mattered most to Wilde: what it meant, or should mean, to be a "man" or "woman." Ominously, however, the characters most like Wilde himself, Lord Darlington and Cecil Graham, disappear from the play at the end of Act 3, and by then Darlington himself has already become an apologist for "purity and innocence … everything that we men have lost." In this sense the disappearance of Graham and Darlington also marks the disappearance of the author, Wilde himself, from the final act of his own play.

### *SALOMÉ*: (A)HEAD OF ITS TIME

There was a less accommodating Oscar Wilde than the one who gradually turned down the volume of his criticism of women in the course of rewriting *Lady Windermere's Fan*, which would become one of the most popular and highest-grossing plays on the West End stage in 1892. In the same year he completed work on *Salomé*, the one-act biblical tragedy written in French whose surviving manuscripts show comparatively little evidence of revision of any kind.[37] The French actress Sarah Bernhardt agreed to play the title role, in French, during her London season in the spring of 1892, while *Lady Windermere's Fan* was still playing to packed houses at the St. James's Theatre. But after rehearsals were under way, the official censor, the Examiner of Plays, intervened and banned any public performance of *Salomé* in England, a judgment that was to remain in effect for nearly forty years. The play's combination of biblical and highly erotic content, homosexual as well as heterosexual, accounts for the Examiner of Plays' decision to bar *Salomé* from the stage, even though it was written in a language that most people in an English audience could not understand anyway. Wilde's eroticized and deliberate misreading of a biblical story would have posed no obstacle to the play had it been put up for production in the late twentieth century instead of the late nineteenth. Indeed, *Salomé*'s bold defiance of Victorian dramatic practice in many respects – including its development of character, action, and dialogue – exhibits more commonality with post-1950 theatre than with that of the 1890s. While ahead of its time in these regards, *Salomé* cannot and should not be detached from the context of Wilde's other work as a playwright, for it dramatizes the same thing, albeit in a contrastive mode – the author's anxious regard of "pure" women who possess both strength and power, endanger men, and require to be disciplined in some way to ensure the realization of the masculine ideal of the "Wilde Man."

The question of why Wilde wrote this idiosyncratic drama in French has been variously answered: because it was to be performed by Sarah Bernhardt, who spoke little or no English; because writing and performing *Salomé* in French was calculated to diminish the threat of censorship of a salacious and blasphemous play; or because Wilde wanted to transcend the limitations of thought and feeling that would accompany presenting the work in English to an English audience.[38] But in addition, despite its biblical setting and characters, *Salomé* anticipates late-twentieth-century theatre in presenting a world whose inhabitants are irremediably estranged from each other, their environment, and the language through which they try to express themselves. Nothing quite makes sense in the dramatic landscape of *Salomé*, and above all language fails Wilde's characters as a medium of communication and understanding; their passionate soliloquies go unheard, or rather *as if* unheard, and the meaning and desire invested in their utterances rarely get conveyed. This destabilization of language – emptied of its expressive power and ability to communicate – produces in *Salomé* something like the intellectual and spiritual weightlessness that would later be symptomatic of theatre of the absurd. Jokanaan, locked in Herod's cistern, is not the only "imprisoned" character in *Salomé*; indeed, all of them, including Salomé herself, are hopelessly alienated from each other and the world around them, confined in what Walter Pater had called the prison-house of personality, "through which no real voice has ever pierced on its way to us."[39]

I suggest that writing and performing a play such as this in French, in England, placed Wilde's presumptive audience (or most of it) in the same position of "absurdity" as the dramatis personae of his play – a position in which language fails to communicate meaning, in which dialogue and all forms of connectedness are impossible, and in which settled truths are turned upside-down. In this sense *Salomé* is Wilde's own "theatre of cruelty" in which the audience would be made to experience for itself the alienation and senselessness that plague the characters of the play. To imagine something comparable to the might-have-been production of *Salomé* in London in 1892, one could hardly do better than recall the first London production of *Waiting for Godot* in 1955, written in French but performed in English before a bewildered audience (it had been performed in French before a German audience two years before), many of whom wondered if this disturbing new form of drama was drama at all – or perhaps, as Robert Morley feared, simply "the end of theatre as we know it."[40] Morley's view of *Waiting for Godot* as "the end of theatre" recalls the clever summation of *Salomé* once expressed by Max Beerbohm: "I almost wonder Oscar doesn't dramatize it."[41]

Even if *Salomé* were to have been performed in English in London, the jeweled artifice of Wilde's language, its fantastic repetitions, and its disconnected dialogue would have thrown off an effect akin to a performance in a foreign language. In other words, the effect of estrangement that *Salomé* produces from language itself – from the sound of it, its meaningfulness, and communicative potential – is part of the texture of the play itself, regardless of the language it is performed in or whether the audience is English or French. Similarly, as Philippe Jullian has pointed out, Wilde's use of French seems strange, artificial, and anglicized (although not unpleasing) to a native speaker of French, and in order to capture the true aura of the play, when it is performed in that language, "*Salomé* has to be acted with an English accent."[42]

Richard Dellamora has suggested that *Salomé* was "so sure to enrage English philistines that its conception needed to be translated into – perhaps even to be imagined in – French."[43] There is much to be said for this point of view. Wilde gives us a heroine who lusts after and murders John the Baptist for an erotic frisson, and who traverses both sides of the customary borders of gender, a beautiful and "pure" young woman who also claims possession of masculine power and authority. Salomé's own "masculinity" participates in a homosexual triangle between the Syrian captain who stabs himself to death for love of her and the Page of Herodias who was *his* lover. The passionate language of Salomé's addresses to Jokanaan, in turn, is modeled on the love poetry of the Song of Solomon, except that in the biblical source the passionate speaker is a man extolling the beauty and sexual allure of a woman. Within the frame of this gender shift, Salomé is "like" a man, and Jokanaan like a woman. For Wilde, as we have seen, the author of a true work of art is an actor, and the work itself is his acting out of himself, not as he is, but as he desires to become – a process of theatrical self-realization. Aubrey Beardsley, whose famous black-and-white illustrations of *Salomé* appeared in both the French and English editions of 1893, detected this histrionic presence of Wilde as he sketched scenes from the play, drawing him as the "Woman in the Moon" looking down with a sensual gaze on a feminized and naked man. These gender reversals reach a climax when Salomé kisses and embraces the bloody, severed head of the Prophet after it is brought to her, as demanded, on a silver platter. In this moment of realized desire, sketched by Beardsley in his drawing "The Climax," Wilde's heroine has taken possession of the penis through the symbolic decapitation of John the Baptist; and the erotic satisfaction she receives from his death and dismemberment illustrates the danger to which unmitigated female power and sexuality exposes men.

From this perspective *Salomé* is not so different from Wilde's other plays of the 1890s as it seems on the surface. It is unique in dramatizing a violent clash between men and women, and in Wilde's use of a poetically inflected French that, for all its beauty, calls into question the communicative efficacy of language itself and contributes to the radical alienation of the characters of *Salomé* from each other and the world around them. This effect of estrangement in *Salomé* remarkably anticipates the absurdist dramaturgy of late-twentieth-century theatre, making it one of the most important plays never performed – never in the author's lifetime, that is, except in Paris at the avant-garde Théâtre Libre. Nevertheless, Wilde's one-act tragedy (as he insisted on calling it) is linked to *Lady Windermere's Fan* and all his society dramas not only because of its rich vein of comedy, but also its anxieties about gendered identity, strong women, and a newly powerful feminism that insisted on both "purity" and normative heterosexuality for men. At one level, then, *Salomé* is a play in which these anxieties of gender

Figure 4. Aubrey Beardsley drew Wilde as a self-dramatized
character in *Salomé*, directing a sensual gaze at the unclothed male
in the foreground. (British Library)

take on the dimensions of nightmare, albeit one in which the peaceful
accommodations and compromises of the society comedies lie beyond
reach. Wilde's play therefore exhibits the same political tension as *Lady
Windermere's Fan* and *A Woman of No Importance*, the tension between
Wilde's "decadent" homosexuality on one side and the feminist-identified
New Woman on the other.

Linda Dowling has argued influentially that the "decadent dandy" and
the New Woman, far from being antithetical or even antagonistic, actually

Figure 5. Salomé holds aloft the head of John the Baptist in an early
production of *Salomé*. (New York Public Library)

shared an agenda and were disparaged in similar terms by critics who saw
both movements as dangerous to civilization itself.[44] But while it is true
that both decadents and New Women sought to rearticulate sex and gender
under new regimes of self-development, they did so in radically different

ways. *Salomé* is one of numerous works of the 1890s – not of all them ori-
ented toward homosexuality, such as *Jude the Obscure*, *Dracula*, and *She*
– in which a woman who speaks and acts with power and desire produces
a fatal effect upon men who fall into her orbit. What may be figured in
*Salomé* as an aggressively homosexual dread of women is complicated and
intensified by the narrative dynamic of Wilde's play. That is, Jokanaan,
refusing every seduction that Salomé can imagine, demonstrates the same
conspicuous male chastity that feminists of Wilde's time demanded of
men, and his decapitation/castration at Salomé's order suggests that the
wages of purity is death for men. It also suggests that women (like Salomé
herself) are raging cauldrons of lust and violence behind a mask of virgin-
ity and purity. In this important respect *Salomé* is not so much ahead of its
time as very much *of* it – in its anxious and at the same time exhilarating
resistance to traditional configurations of gender. "Salomé is an Oriental
Hedda Gabler," wrote William Archer in an incisive review of Wilde's play
in 1893; and like Ibsen's, Wilde's reaction to the New Woman of the *fin de
siècle* was both complex and contradictory. Feminism's break with traditional gender roles was in accord, from one point of view, with Wilde's
own vision of flexible and performative genders, but Wilde's vision faded
to nightmare when the displacement of old-fashioned femininity gave rise
to "masculine," death-dealing women like Hedda Gabler and Salomé.[45]

"There are not dead men enough," Salomé grimly mutters at a crucial
moment in the play. Her death wish for men in general is expressed to the
Page of Herodias, lover of the Syrian captain who killed himself in front
of a self-absorbed and inattentive Salomé a few scenes earlier. Salomé's
next words – commanding the Page to "bring me the head of this man,"
Jokanaan, the Prophet – formulate a speech act that turns out to be like all
other expressions of desire in this strangely forward-looking play. Desires
are dead-ends, so remote and out of reach that Herod once asks, "What is
it that I desire? I forget." Desires can be felt, spoken, and forgotten, but not
realized, or if fulfilled in a fashion, with an unexpected whiplash of disap-
pointment or disaster. In *Salomé*, only death can cut through the tangled
web of thwarted desire, failure of language and meaning, estrangement of
people from each other and the world, and panic attacks of personal and
gendered identity. The stage setting is colored with apocalyptic flashes of
stark white, scarlet, and black; the moon, as if in search of death, resembles a globe of blood, the stars seem about to fall from the sky, and the air
is filled with the sound of beating wings.

Jokanaan speaks dire prophecies, yet Herod complains, "I cannot
understand what he saith."[46] Salomé attempts to seduce Jokanaan with

every allurement of poetry and physical passion, but the Prophet hears and sees none of it: "I will not look at thee," he declares; "… I will not listen to thee. I listen but to the voice of God."[47] There is a gulf no less impassable between Herod and Salomé; in a series of increasingly urgent speeches, he offers almost unimaginable riches if she will give up her demand for the head of Jokanaan, but to every such entreaty the Princess stonily replies, "I demand the head of Jokanaan," as if Herod had said nothing at all. "Thou art not listening. Thou art not listening," he complains repetitively, and indeed in this play *no one* listens and speech never breaks out of its self-enclosing circle – for if they listen they do not hear, and no one's voice ever really penetrates the consciousness of another.[48] Always the individual is alienated and alone, and in this cosmic solitude it is possible to make up one's own world and perform one's self with a freedom that is liberating and at the same time fearful. In Wilde's homoerotic retelling of the Salomé story, socially prescribed gender roles fall away – men act "like" women, women become "men." In this scenario an opening is created for someone like Wilde's version of the Judean Princess, an "Oriental Hedda Gabler" who makes men pay dearly when she seizes the phallus and makes her power felt in both physical and emotional registers. In *Salomé*, uniquely among Wilde's plays, the author manipulates the narrative in such a way that it forces a response in kind to the ferocity of the New Woman. "Kill that woman!" cries Herod in the last line of the script – and not just "that woman," I suggest, but all women of the kind.[49]

### REWRITING *SALOMÉ*

A prophetic experiment in drama, *Salomé* looked forward to the theatre of the absurd, the theatre of cruelty, and late-twentieth-century gay theatre, but it was a dead end, theatrically speaking, for Wilde in the 1890s. Although the surviving manuscripts of *Salomé* are strangely unblotted and unmarked by revision, I argue that the major plays that Wilde would yet write – all three of them, beginning with *A Woman of No Importance* – were in themselves revisions of his abortive *Salomé*. In writing *A Woman of No Importance* and the dramas that followed, Wilde was writing more for his own time and place and less for a theatre of the future, producing plays not only written in English but with content that was actually performable under the regime of state censorship that had doomed *Salomé*.

In these later plays he would attempt once again, as in *Lady Windermere's Fan*, to accommodate revolutionary perceptions of gender and identity to the socially conservative medium of West End comedy and heterosexual

romance. Although *A Woman of No Importance* began in its earliest drafts
as a rhetorical and ideological confrontation with an emerging and radical
feminist movement, it developed in its final, much-revised version into a
search for common ground, a hybridized performance of gender which, if
not fully realized in the text of the play, lies just over the horizon, beyond
the final curtain. The marriage of the once-puritanical Hester Worsley
and the bastard son Gerald Arbuthnot will reconfigure traditional understandings of gender, a goal of "Puritan women" and Lord Illingworth
alike. Their marriage will be an accommodation between the excesses of
feminist social purity on one hand and of Wildean dandyism and aestheticism, as embodied in Lord Illingworth, on the other. In *A Woman
of No Importance*, as earlier in *Lady Windermere's Fan*, Wilde was making
conciliatory gestures toward the advocates of purity even as he was resisting them, and in return the play was received with satisfaction in some
quarters where a positive reaction to Wilde could not have been expected,
including religious periodicals.

"You are unjust to women in England," says an assertive young American
to her hosts at a country house shortly after the curtain rises on *A Woman
of No Importance*, "and till you count what is a shame in a woman to be
an infamy in a man, you will always be unjust." Hester Worsley's purity
feminism challenges the double standard by applying the same morality
to men that had always been expected of women. When the name of Lord
Henry Weston comes up in conversation, "a man with a hideous smile and
a hideous past," she insists that her companions bear in mind the outcast
women whose ruin is due to him. Not that his female victims deserve a
better fate – "let all women who have sinned be punished," she declares –
but they should not be the only ones to suffer. "If a man and woman have
sinned," she declares, "let them both go forth into the desert … let them
both be branded … don't punish the one and let the other go free. Don't
have one law for men and another for women." As it is, however, immoral
men are welcomed in the highest society and the best company; "no dinner party," Hester Worsley regrets, is complete without them, while the
woman who has "sinned" is ostracized by everyone.[50]

Her complaint about the way in which "men with a past" are welcomed
into the best homes was a prominent theme of feminist discourse at the
time. In *An Appeal to Men*, for example, Josephine Butler laments that
profligate men are "received in society and entrusted with moral and social
responsibilities, while the lapse of a woman of the humbler classes … is
made the portal for her of a life of misery and shame."[51] In a speech delivered in 1871 to the Ladies' National Association, Butler expresses regret that

the male "black sheep" can enter almost anyone's drawing room "with as fair an exterior as that of any other man." This unequal state of affairs, she reflects, is to a large degree the fault of women themselves, "guilty before God in their weak indulgence to men whom they know to be vicious, and in their cowardly shrinking from the task of discrimination."[52] All the women in *A Woman of No Importance*, with the exception of Hester Worsley and Mrs. Arbuthnot, shrink from the "task of discrimination" in exactly the way that Butler complains of. When Hester complains in Act 2 that Lord Henry Weston is welcome at everyone's dinner parties even though "he has wrecked innocent lives, poisoned lives that were pure,"[53] Lady Hunstanton objects by way of reply, "He is really such good company." Lady Caroline Pontefract admits that her own brother Lord Henry Weston is "infamous, absolutely infamous," but suggests humorously that his moral failings can be overlooked because "he has one of the best cooks in London."[54]

Most of Hester Worsley's declarations at this early point in the play could have been spoken by Josephine Butler and her allies in the Ladies' National Association, campaigning for the abolition of the Contagious Diseases Acts or passage of the Criminal Law Amendment Bill. Wilde's character insists upon the moral accountability of men in a manner not unlike Butler's exhortation to "fallen" *men* in a volume published by the Social Purity League in 1882:

You who have sinned grossly or habitually can never be the same in earthly relations as those who have escaped the deeper pollutions. You are wounded for life; … you will be, even when restored by God, sorrowful men, burdened with bitter memories, weakened through the wearing of heavy chains … You can never become what you were, – *never what you were*."[55]

But Wilde's characterization of the feminism of social purity slides into caricature when he has Mrs. Arbuthnot remark that not only should men and women be "punished" in the same way, but "the children, if there are children, in the same way also." Hester agrees: "Yes, it is right that the sins of the parents should be visited on the children … It is God's law."[56] Although the syphilis epidemic certainly transmitted the sins of the parents to their children, the primitive and retributive morality expressed by Hester Worsley and Mrs. Arbuthnot was far from typical of *fin-de-siècle* feminism. Josephine Butler, for example, instead of condemning "fallen women" with the same severity as Hester Worsley ("Let all women who have sinned be punished"), took up their grievances against the law and the police out of "principles of freedom and of respect for the individual man and woman."[57] Indeed, in Butler's view, society's condemnation of the woman who has "sinned" is extreme; for as she remarks in her *Appeal to Men*, it "drives such a one out of bounds, sets its hell-hounds on the track, and makes recovery all but impossible."[58] From this perspective Hester Worsley appears quite out of harmony with the feminism she espouses when she exclaims, "I don't complain of their punishment. Let all women who have sinned be punished" – although in the first surviving draft Wilde wrote "banished" rather than "punished," in keeping with the lack of humane feeling that he ascribed to Hester in the original version of the play.[59] As for "fallen men," Butler's attitude was far more condemnatory, for she saw that the syphilis epidemic stemmed from their undisciplined behavior, rather than from the prostitutes whom the law blamed – such men, says Butler in her *Appeal to Men*, "disperse plagues and death wherever they move by the very infection of their breath."[60] On the other hand Butler's reaction to the crime and punishment of Wilde himself, as an individual man, would be more sympathetic than judgmental. "I am so sorry for Oscar Wilde," she wrote shortly after his criminal trial and conviction. "I pray for him constantly."[61]

Lord Illingworth in *A Woman of No Importance* is presented as an obvious target of the moral-purity type of feminist – "a bad man," as Mrs. Arbuthnot charges, and of course indispensable at dinner parties and widely admired. He is conceited about having so many "bad" qualities, mocks the idea of moral uprightness and purity that had become the agenda of many feminists, and remarks flippantly at one point that "it is better to be beautiful than to be good."[62] Wilde himself surely agreed with Illingworth on these matters, but Lord Illingworth does *not* have it all his own way in this drama, less and less so as Wilde redrafted the script over time. In the end it is the character known as "the Puritan," the doctrinaire purity feminist Hester Worsley, who comes out best, although chastened and changed. By the final curtain she has had to modify her views on the punishment of sin, and Mrs. Arbuthnot has taught her the value of at least some flexibility where moral codes are concerned. With this modulation of Hester's character, Wilde is formulating new ratios between the puritan morality of Victorian feminists and, by contrast, his own inclination to the amoral aestheticism embodied in Lord Illingworth.

This reading of the play is borne out by early manuscript drafts of *A Woman of No Importance* – manuscripts that have not figured significantly in criticism of the play but reveal Wilde's hesitations and second thoughts about the topic. It seems certain that Wilde was writing within the general context of contemporary feminism from the beginning, for in the earliest known draft of the play, the autograph manuscript entitled

*Mrs. Arbuthnot*, the Liberal politician Mr. Kelvil is inserted early into Act
I to deliver opinions that he continues to express in subsequent versions –
his enthusiasm for the increasing involvement of women in politics and his
approval of the moral dimension that they have brought to political discourse. The "moralisation of politics" through women's participation and
influence was an objective that Wilde himself had endorsed in his own
magazine a few years earlier, but in *A Woman of No Importance* this feminist point of view is given to the fatuous and blinkered politician Kelvil
to espouse. "The growing influence of women is the most reassuring thing
in our political life," Kelvil remarks in the autograph manuscript, adding
approvingly that "women are always on the side of morality."[63] In Kelvil,
Wilde is enacting a parody of himself (not for the first time) – the earlier
self of his feminist phase.

By contrast, the first version of *A Woman of No Importance* introduces
Lord Illingworth as the adversary of Kelvil's point of view – amoral, indif-
ferent to women's growing influence in politics, and skeptical about the
very existence of women like Hester Worsley (called Mabel in this first
draft) and the purity feminists on whom she is modeled. "I don't believe
in the existence of Puritan women," Lord Illingworth confides to Mrs.
Allonby; "there is not a woman in the world who would not be charmed if
one kissed her."[64] But as Wilde revised the play he sharpened its reference
to the social-purity movement in certain respects even as he softened the
play's hostile and at times inaccurate attitude toward it in other revisions.
For example, only in later drafts did Wilde include this exchange between
Lady Stutfield and Mr. Kelvil, the liberal M.P. who is an outspoken advocate of women's rights and social purity – a man on the same side of the
political fence as the National Vigilance Association and Ellice Hopkins's
White Cross Army:

LADY STUTFIELD: And what have you been writing on this morning, Mr. Kelvil?
MR. KELVIL: On the usual subject, Lady Stutfield, on Purity.
LADY STUTFIELD: That must be such a very, very interesting thing to write about.
MR. KELVIL: It is the one subject of really national importance now-a-days, Lady
    Stutfield.[65]

Kelvil, noting in this later draft that he plans to address his constituents
on the subject of purity, then reflects: "I find that the poorer classes of
this country display a marked desire for a higher ethical standard." In this
observation Kelvil follows the lead of purity feminism in its growing solidarity with the working class to counter the resistance often displayed by
those of higher rank. Struggling against opposition from powerful and

well-placed men and women, Josephine Butler was surprised to find how readily the working class was "carried up to the highest standard in judging of a moral question, and how almost universally they acknowledged the authority of the ethical truths which we endeavoured to put before them." Boiler fitters, engine makers, and the like "perfectly understood the message, and acted upon it with intelligence." Nor was their role, as Butler saw it, a subservient one. Working men themselves organized meetings, initiated plans of action which they often headed up, launched petitions to Parliament, and entered into dialogue with politicians standing for election. The politicians they supported were Liberals like Kelvil in Wilde's play, who finds the ethical sense of the "poorer classes" especially congenial to the politics of purity.[66] This element of class antagonism was an important dimension of Wilde's defining conflict with purity advocates, although it has been almost entirely unacknowledged. His dramatic writing on the subject of purity was marked by class tensions, and so were the courtroom trials in which the forces of purity would later hold Wilde to account before the law.

Wilde's rhetoric softened to a significant degree as he revised the play. Early drafts of *A Woman of No Importance* include some very harsh attacks on Hester's puritanism that were later canceled – for example, a passage in which Lord Illingworth argues stridently that the "real enemy of modern life ... is Puritanism, and the Puritan spirit."[67] This speech, deleted from the final version of the play, appears in the licensing typescript prepared just before the play's first production. Lord Illingworth, called Lord Brancaster in this version, offers these comments to Gerald, the new-found son who was born from his seduction of Mrs. Arbuthnot many years ago:

My dear boy, the real enemy of modern life, of every thing that makes life lovely and joyous and coloured for us, is Puritanism, and the Puritan spirit. *There* is the danger that lies ahead of the age, and most of all in England ... Puritanism you will always reject. It is not a creed for a gentleman. And, as a beginning, you will make it your ideal to be a dandy always.[68]

Puritanism, says Lord Brancaster (Illingworth) elsewhere in this speech, is "a creed that starves the body and does not feed the soul," unlike dandyism – which he places in opposition to it as an ideal of masculinity. The entire speech condemning puritanism was eventually cut from the play, its hostile negativism replaced with an affirmation of the ideal of the dandy as a cosmopolitan, modern man who sees life "as it really is," not through the lens of outmoded theories, and who, because he can dominate a London dinner table, "can dominate the world."[69]

Wilde's deletion or revision of broadside attacks on militant reformers occurs again with a passage in which Lord Illingworth vows to "cure" his son of new-found puritan views: "It doesn't run in our family to take the Puritan side of things," he says in a relatively early typescript of the play but not in the final version.[70] Later drafts also modify Hester's rhetoric of strict moral purity, deleting, for example, her Josephine Butler-like description of Lord Henry Weston as "a man who has wrecked innocent lives, and poisoned lives that were pure." Again, in a manuscript of the play when it was still entitled *Mrs. Arbuthnot*, Gerald (called Aleck in this early version) adopts the vocabulary of purity feminism as Mabel (Hester's name in early drafts) appeals to him to "save" her from the sexual advances of Lord Illingworth, who has pursued her into the room. Until restrained by the desperate revelation by his mother that Lord Illingworth is "your own father," the usually mild-mannered Gerald hurls insults and threats that Wilde drew directly from the volcanic rhetoric of purity feminism:

Lord Illingworth, you have insulted the purest thing on God's earth except my mother. You have insulted the woman I love most in the world with my mother. You are infamous. You are foul. You are polluted. As there is a God in heaven I shall kill you ... Don't hold me, mother. Don't hold me. By God, I'll kill him ...[71]

In later revisions, with Aleck renamed Gerald, these repeated references to the keyword of "purity" remained, but the tirade was drained of some of its melodramatic venom with the deletion of "You are infamous. You are foul. You are polluted." These cuts lowered the rhetorical temperature of the play and moderated the polemical tension between Wilde's own position on masculinity and that of the militant feminists whom he was engaging in dialogue in *A Woman of No Importance*. Although Hester Worsley's feminist puritanism is mocked even in the finished text of the play, Wilde's tone is less vehement by far than in earlier versions. For example, Mrs. Allonby in the final, published version can still say of the young American woman that "She is a Puritan," but Wilde drops her sneering follow-up from earlier drafts: " – an out-and-out Puritan – the worst I ever met."[72]

To a large extent, Wilde also moderates his play's conflict with the feminism of social purity through changes that he gradually incorporates into the character of Lord Illingworth, who becomes much less aggressively "bad" and less confrontational in his conduct toward Hester Worsley and Mrs. Arbuthnot. Having cut some of his more strident condemnations of "puritan" women, Wilde prepares for the moment in Act 4 when

Illingworth recognizes that the social-purity feminist Hester Worsley is a "fin-de-siècle person" whose critique of marriage as an institution has surprising affinities with his own views. Also deleted from the final text of the play is Illingworth's strident denunciation of "good" women in answer to Aleck Arbuthnot (Gerald in early drafts), who has just asked him, "there are good women in society, aren't there?": "Oh, lots of them. One doesn't meet them at dinner. At least one shouldn't. Good women are invariably ignorant women. Ignorance is the price a woman pays for being good."

In the typescript Wilde crossed out this passage, and on the verso page wrote out by hand a new version. Aleck's question about whether there are good women in society remains the same, but now Illingworth says simply, "Far too many. Goodness is an admirable thing, I dare say, but it is certainly not becoming." Although the point being made is similar in both versions, the latter concedes something to puritan women ("goodness is an admirable thing") and makes its case less insultingly than before.[73]

Wilde again ratcheted down the conflict between Lord Illingworth and Mrs. Arbuthnot as he rewrote the fourth act. The play still concludes melodramatically in the final version when Mrs. Arbuthnot strikes Lord Illingworth across the face with his own glove, then refers to him as "a man of no importance," just as she had in the earliest surviving drafts of *A Woman of No Importance*. As before, Mrs. Arbuthnot has only moments ago turned down Lord Illingworth's belated proposal of marriage, and, stung by her rejection, he has lashed back with the remark that "It's been an amusing experience to have met amongst people of one's own rank, and treated quite seriously too, one's mistress and one's …" At this point – the point at which Lord Illingworth is about to pronounce his own son a "bastard" – the slap on the face occurs in all versions of the play, but what happens *next* changed significantly as Wilde rewrote the ending. In an early typescript Lord Illingworth responds to Mrs. Arbuthnot's slap with an angry speech that draws attention to her own past: "You are the woman whom I did the honour of asking to be my wife. How foolish the wisest of us are at times. But some day your son may call you by a worse name. He has my blood in his veins as well as yours."

But in the revised version of the scene this mean-spirited attack on Mrs. Arbuthnot is crossed out in pencil. Indeed Lord Illingworth says nothing at all after being slapped, but on the verso page of the typescript Wilde has written a crucial new stage direction: "Lord Illingworth starts. He controls himself, and goes to window and looks out at his son. Sighs, and leaves the room."[74]

Not remorse, exactly, but regret at least, along with recognition by Lord Illingworth that his mode of life has cost him something and that the puritan feminism that he has mocked may have something to say to him after all. Gone is the bitter, confrontational attack on the mother of his son, Mrs. Arbuthnot, with which Lord Illingworth had originally concluded. This difference made for a notable effect in performance. When Beerbohm Tree, as Lord Illingworth, acted this scene in its revised form at the Haymarket Theatre, a critic was struck by the fact that "there was just a look of mingled love and remorse in Mr. Tree's expressive face as he made his exit."[75]

At the beginning of the play Lord Illingworth had declared "I don't believe in the existence of Puritan women," but now their reality has been brought home to him with a slap in the face and the loss of the son he loves. He has an altered understanding of "Puritan women," and the "Puritan women" in the play have changed too – hard at first, exaggeratedly so, compared to their more compassionate real-life models such as Josephine Butler and Millicent Fawcett, they have learned to soften the demands of their austere morality by recognizing, as Hester Worsley says near the end of the play, that "God's only law is love." Mrs. Arbuthnot has administered a slap in the face to the "bad man" who seduced her as a girl and fathered her son, but she no longer sees herself as the woman she described in Act 3, "a woman who drags a chain, like a guilty thing."[76] She has come to the realization that it is only because she *was* seduced as a girl that she gained a son whom she loves more than life – so where is the need for repentance?

Mrs. Bernard Beere, playing the role of Mrs. Arbuthnot, was dressed in black all through *A Woman of No Importance* in the first production, contrasting with the "wonderful evening dress of white satin glittering with silver spangles" worn by Julia Neilson as Hester Worsley.[77] The costume remained the same, but the woman inside it changed. By the end of the play the black dress of Mrs. Arbuthnot has become a badge of defiance, not shame, and rigid categories of good and bad with respect to gender have crumbled. In her self-presentation, this once-puritanical woman changes not only the meaning of "black," but transforms through performance what her life means and who she is. She achieves a virtuosity that even the Wildean dandy, Lord Illingworth, cannot match despite his passion for "style," as he terms it ("A well-tied tie is the first serious step in life").[78] The slap in the face that Lord Illingworth receives suggests that he has failed to invent himself through performance; at the end of the play, as at the beginning, he is a "bad man" in need of correction, something he seems to realize for himself in chastened silence at the end of the final version. Although Lady Hunstanton had flattered Lord Illingworth in Act 3 with the observation that "you always find out that one's most glaring fault is one's important virtue," this talent for self-redefinition belongs more to Mrs. Arbuthnot than to the dandy. She has stepped out of the role of "a woman who drags a chain, like a guilty thing," hiding from the world, and reinvented herself as an assertive, unconventional woman whose so-called sins are her greatest glory. Although still wearing black, she is no longer "a woman of no importance."

Although *A Woman of No Importance* began in its earliest drafts as a rhetorical and ideological confrontation with an emerging and radical feminist movement, it developed in its final version into a search for common ground, a hybridized performance of gender which, if not fully realized in the text of the play, lies just over the horizon, beyond the final curtain. The marriage of the once-puritanical Hester Worsley and the bastard son Gerald Arbuthnot will reconfigure traditional understandings of gender, a goal of "Puritan women" and Lord Illingworth alike. Their marriage will be an accommodation between the excesses of feminist social purity on one hand and of Wildean aestheticism, as embodied in Lord Illingworth, on the other. In *A Woman of No Importance*, as earlier in *Lady Windermere's Fan*, Wilde was making conciliatory gestures toward the advocates of purity even as he was resisting them, and in return the play was received with satisfaction in some quarters where a positive reaction to Wilde could not have been expected. As one religious journal, for example, remarked in its review, "A living sermon is being preached nightly at the Haymarket."[79]

Sir Edward Russell – a leading advocate of social purity, editor of the *Liverpool Daily Post*, and well-known drama critic – confided in a remarkable interview that he was heartened by a "new and stern gospel of absolute purity" in a few modern plays, "a purity that the churches dare not to teach." The churches, Russell explained, were concerned mainly with "technical morality, – the morality of the letter of the Ten Commandments," so that, for example, "they bless all marriages – even the most shameful" and "do not dare – even if they cared – to demand any of the things that really go to make marriage lovely and wedlock pure." Immediately the interviewer thought of the new play by Wilde, and asked: "But the representation of such states of society as that shown in 'A Woman of No Importance' – do you consider it beneficial?" The purity crusader hesitated. "I scarcely know," Russell confessed, then offered the view that perhaps Wilde was on the side of purity after all. "Mr. Wilde satirises the society which he represents, and out of it there grows that wonderful tragedy with its magnificent lesson. Yes, the daring of the play justifies itself, and we are the better for seeing it."[80]

No other play by Wilde received such pious accolades, understandably so, given its surprising accommodation with militant puritanism and the earnest and chaste masculinity that the movement demanded. *A Woman of No Importance* was "pure" Wilde, offering more tokens of reconciliation to social purity and *fin-de-siècle* feminism, and the performance of gender that they advocated, than any other work he would ever write.

# CHAPTER 3

# *Performance anxiety in* An Ideal Husband

The narrative of *An Ideal Husband* (1895), from one point of view, is the story of Oscar Wilde himself – a famous man who seeks to escape the career-ending damage that the exposure of his hidden crime would bring about. Wilde, like his central character Sir Robert Chiltern, was trapped between blackmailers on one side and, on the other, proponents of a puritanical feminism whose agenda for a new masculinity he objected to, and was endangered by.

Wilde's dealings with male prostitutes and blackmailers were putting him at risk, by 1893 or 1894 if not sooner, as a potential victim of a new law that many feminists and their allies in the social-purity movement had successfully pressured Parliament into enacting after years of failure and false starts. Although different from Sir Robert Chiltern in many obvious respects, Wilde uses his main character to map the dimensions of his own developing crisis, caught in a cross-fire between blackmailers and a new ideology whose designed effect was to categorize, punish, and reform such a man as himself. Wilde's attempt to extricate his deeply flawed hero (and himself) from danger is marked by hesitation and evasion, self-contradiction, and wishful thinking that inflict great damage upon the aesthetic integrity of the play as well as the integrity of Wilde's own thought. His unusually laborious rewrites of the play in a series of manuscripts – some of which have scarcely been considered in previous scholarship of *An Ideal Husband* – provide a map of the difficulties, personal and philosophical, that thwarted Wilde's attempts to bring this comedy and his own life to a happy resolution.

But Wilde's crisis of 1894–95 was not only a matter of being besieged by blackmailers and zealous reformers; it was also a crisis of ideas. *An Ideal Husband* raises potentially revolutionary questions without really answering them, especially whether gendered identity is real or in some sense performed, and whether truth itself, of any kind, is "real" or socially constructed. Furthermore, the context of *An Ideal Husband* is in large part the *idea* of context itself, an idea that makes itself felt in this play's pre-occupation with writing and written documents, especially signed ones such as Sir Robert Chiltern's incriminating letter to Baron Arnheim, Lady Chiltern's incriminating letter to Lord Goring, and, by implication, Wilde's own incriminating letters that were already being used against him by blackmailers. What is at issue here, among other things, is the nature of writing, whether it decodes a truth or fixed meaning or whether, in writing, as Jacques Derrida claims, "there are only contexts without any center of absolute anchoring."

If – as Derrida maintains and Wilde, I believe, hoped – the sign can be cut off from any "original meaning" and constraining context, then the incriminating, signed writings of Sir Robert Chiltern and his wife, and therefore of Wilde himself, assume a fluidity that makes it difficult to create a "general now" for those statements and bind the writers to them in any absolute sense.[1] This fluidity of writing suggests something as well about the fluidity of the writer – or the writer's self: that it too, acting through language, will be "without any center of absolute anchoring." In *An Ideal Husband* Oscar Wilde stands at the threshold of new ideas about language and subjectivity, but hesitates to cross it. His numerous revisions and rewritings – far more numerous than for any other of his plays – reveal an irresolute Oscar Wilde, embracing these new possibilities at one moment and then moving on in the next to disentangle his hero by traditional and even reactionary narrative structures from the gathering storm that threatens to engulf him. The result is *An Ideal Husband*, a play full of contradictions, and one whose failure of nerve about embracing what today we could call a performative interpretation of life dooms it to a historically outmoded dramatization of gendered identity.

THE POLITICS OF PROSTITUTION AND *AN IDEAL HUSBAND*

"Robert, how could you have sold yourself for money?" asks Lord Goring of his friend Sir Robert Chiltern in Act 2 of *An Ideal Husband*. A question framed in these words, at this historical moment, would have inescapably referred by implication to those who really did "sell themselves" – the prostitutes at the center of a thirty-year-long "holy rebellion and war" by feminists and others that had rocked the late-Victorian world with challenges to received ideas of morality and gendered identity.[2] The idea of Chiltern selling himself is picked up by his wife when she learns from Mrs. Cheveley that her husband's career was founded on the bribe he received for divulging a Cabinet secret: "You sold yourself for money. Oh!

A common thief were better."[3] Mrs. Cheveley applies similar language to Sir Robert Chiltern when she seeks to blackmail him into support of the fraudulent Argentine Canal Scheme, using a letter in her possession written years ago by Chiltern to the stock-exchange speculator Baron Arnheim, telling him to buy Suez Canal shares, a letter written only days before the government would make public its own purchase. Selling this information to the baron was the turning point in his spectacularly successful career, and now Mrs. Cheveley threatens to expose him unless he speaks in Parliament on behalf of the Argentine Canal Scheme in which she has a financial interest. However, Mrs. Cheveley frames her proposal in terms of a purchase of Chiltern himself: "you have your price, I suppose. Everybody has nowadays. The drawback is that most people are so dreadfully expensive. I know I am."[4]

Mrs. Cheveley's point is not only that Chiltern has sold himself once before, and would again, but that everyone, herself included, would become a prostitute in this fashion if the price were right.

If these characterizations of Chiltern as having "sold yourself for money" invite us, without exactly saying so, to read his behavior in the context of Victorian prostitution, what is the point that Wilde is trying to make with such rhetorical choices? Chiltern is not really a prostitute, for as he more or less accurately protests to his friend Lord Goring, "I did not sell myself for money."[5] But to the considerable extent that he is defined by the rhetoric of prostitution, Chiltern is first of all a *male* prostitute, the type with which Wilde had to do on a regular basis, but also a type largely overlooked by feminist activists who for the last three decades had waged war against state-regulated prostitution as a form of police control over *women's* bodies. Among the direct results of that "Great Crusade" was the enactment of the Criminal Law Amendment Bill in 1885, legislation that introduced new penalties for brothel-keeping and procuring and lowered the age of consent for girls to thirteen. Passage of the bill, along with repeal of the notorious Contagious Diseases Acts, had been at the top of the agenda of militant feminists and their allies in the social-purity movement for years, and it was due to their public campaigns and lobbying efforts in Parliament that the bill was finally enacted. In the moral fervor of the moment, however, the Radical politician Henry Labouchere succeeded in attaching an amendment to the bill which provided legal penalties for "any male, in public or private, committing any act of gross indecency with another male," or "the attempt so to procure."[6] Although recent historiography has demonstrated convincingly that there was little that was new in the Labouchere amendment, its relaxed evidentiary standard and relatively undraconian penalties would make it the most popular mode of prosecuting homosexuals by far in the 1890s.

Indeed, it was this clause – an almost accidental yet ruthlessly logical by-product of the feminist jihad of 1885 – that would begin to complicate Oscar Wilde's life so desperately only a few years later, during the period in which he was writing *An Ideal Husband.* Wilde's problem was not only that his sexual practices were making him vulnerable to police spies and legal prosecution, but they also made him the prey of male prostitutes who sometimes made more money from blackmail than from sex. The Labouchere amendment became known as "the blackmailers' Charter" and as such was responsible by some accounts for creating a whole new industry. In a pamphlet privately printed in 1895 but apparently never offered for sale, the author, sympathetic to Wilde at the time of his criminal trials, charged that in the neighborhood of Piccadilly alone there were twenty or thirty men who typically lured affluent males into having sex with them and then blackmailed them with threats of exposure as offenders against the Labouchere amendment. "They gratefully recognise that they owe their entire existence to that gentleman," states the author, calling himself I. Playfair; "they drink to the health of 'Good old Lab.'"[7] A particularly notable example of the type, according to Playfair, was one "Mr. Burton," who led a gang of youths whom he sent out across London to seduce men into illicit sex, then would visit the victims himself the next morning to explain "Labouchere's clause in all its legal bearings" and name the price of his silence. In open court, in fact, a blackmailer named Burton was briefly mentioned by Wilde's lawyer, Sir Edward Clarke, as the man for whom Fred Atkins – a prostitute and one of Wilde's accusers – actually worked. Atkins sometimes did the blackmailing himself instead of leaving it to Burton the morning after, as pointed out in unfriendly remarks by the anonymous author of *The Trial of Oscar Wilde, from the Shorthand Reports* (1906), the first book about Wilde's trials:

Of all the creatures associated with Wilde in these affairs, this Atkins was the lowest and most contemptible. For some years he had been in the habit of blackmailing men whom he knew to be inclined to perverted sexual vices, and his was a well-known figure up West … He "made up" his eyes and lips, wore corsets, and affected an effeminate air. He was an infallible judge of the class of man he wished to meet and rarely made a mistake … He invariably permitted the beastly act before attempting blackmail, partly because it afforded him a stronger hold over his "victim" and partly because he rejoiced in the disgusting thing for its own sake.[8]

I. Playfair charges that witnesses appearing in court against Wilde included men of this sort who had been bribed to testify – bribed by the Marquess of Queensberry, whose written accusation that Wilde was "posing as a sodomite" set in motion a chain of events leading to the trials. The police, according to Playfair, also prompted the prostitutes as to what type of evidence was wanted against Wilde, and in some recent cases, although perhaps not in Wilde's, had actually ordered male prostitutes "to waylay particular people whom they did not know, (and who were suspected without sufficient evidence), and positively to incite them to the commission of crime," threatening to arrest the prostitutes themselves if they did not.[9]

Such entrapment may not have been practiced upon Wilde because there was no need for it, but the police became involved in another way, according to Lord Alfred Douglas in an article he wrote for the *Mercure de France* in 1895 but was withdrawn due to the intervention of Wilde's friend Robert Sherard. "The blackmailers and the pederasts were approached by detectives," Douglas claims in the suppressed article, "who said to them: 'If you will testify against this man you will have such and such a sum of money and you will be guaranteed not to be prosecuted; if you do not, you will probably be arrested yourselves.'"[10] Douglas charged that his father, the Marquess of Queensberry, had taken his vendetta against Wilde to the highest levels of government, threatening that "unless Oscar Wilde was condemned, new revelations would be made which would incriminate important members of the party in power." Presumably this was a reference to a supposed sexual relationship between the Liberal prime minister, Lord Rosebery, and Douglas's older brother Francis, Viscount Drumlanrig, who had served as the prime minister's private secretary and apparently committed suicide in October 1894, while Wilde was still working on *An Ideal Husband*.[11] Even if Douglas's father was not attempting to blackmail the prime minister, it is certain that blackmail was often resorted to in the 1890s in cases like Wilde's, and it was equally certain, as the extent of sexual blackmailing at the time indicates, that Wilde's offense against the Labouchere clause was by no means unusual. "I know for an absolute fact that the London police has on its books the names of more than 4,000 persons known as habitual pederasts," writes Douglas in his article intended for the *Mercure de France*, "... and many of them occupy the highest and most respected positions in politics, art and society."[12] It was a situation reminiscent of Sir Robert Chiltern's complaint about being blackmailed in *An Ideal Husband* – that although he had done something that most men would call by "ugly names," yet these were "men who every day do something of the same kind themselves ... who, each one of them, have worse secrets in their own lives."[13]

Harassed by blackmailers himself during the period when he was writing and revising *An Ideal Husband*, Wilde increasingly associated Sir Robert Chiltern's predicament with women, and in particular the pressures brought to bear upon him by puritan feminists, women like Chiltern's own wife (or rather, Chiltern's own wife as she turned out after a long series of rewrites by Wilde). The culture of sexual blackmail which was tightening the noose around Wilde from 1893 to 1895 had become a new and profitable enterprise as a direct consequence of the campaigns for passage of the Criminal Law Amendment Bill by activist women like Josephine Butler and their male supporters – W.T. Stead, editor of the *Pall Mall Gazette*; Sir James Stansfield, the Radical parliamentarian; and even some who had little sympathy with feminism or social purity, like Henry Labouchere, but were apparently caught up in the moral excitement and anti-aristocratic sentiment generated by those movements. The pamphleteer I. Playfair, glimpsing a connection between feminist struggles against state-sanctioned prostitution and the dilemma that Wilde faced in the courtroom, notes that "Mrs. Butler and Mr. Stansfield exposed the immoralities and wrongs of the CD Acts," but alleges that they "found nothing there at all so immoral" as the system of sexual blackmail that their efforts ironically brought about and which led to the destruction of Oscar Wilde. Even if not by design, feminists and social-purity activists had created a situation in which the Marquess of Queensberry – despite his own record of domestic violence and adulterous affairs – could bribe prostitutes to testify against Wilde and present himself as a "bright jewel of purity" embarked on a "crusade."[14]

While working on *An Ideal Husband* in 1893–94, Wilde still had a short while to enjoy his liberty, and writing the play became an attempt to defend himself against the militant puritanism that would soon deprive him of everything.

## "THE PROBLEM OF WOMEN"

As the blackmailer Mrs. Cheveley cautions Sir Robert Chiltern, softening him up for extortion: "Remember to what a point your Puritanism in England has brought you. In old days nobody pretended to be a bit better than his neighbours … Nowadays, with our modern mania for morality, everyone has to pose as a paragon of purity, incorruptibility, and all the other seven deadly virtues"[15]

Mrs. Cheveley's catalog of modern morality underlines the point being made in the mid-1890s by Josephine Butler that the purity movement had begun to refract the moral energy that it originally spent almost exclusively on sexual controversies. In a now-rare pamphlet published in 1895, when *An Ideal Husband* was being performed at the Haymarket Theatre, Butler points out with stern disapproval that purity, the word of the moment, had begun to mean many other things besides sexual purity, especially virtue as a more generalized concept that called for temperance and morality in all areas of life. In her pamphlet entitled *An Earnest Appeal*, Butler exhorts her followers to remember the central mission of the movement and "preach the equality of the sexes before the moral law of chastity." By the time Wilde was writing *An Ideal Husband*, therefore, "purity" referred less exclusively to sexual conduct than before and was increasingly being blended with "incorruptibility and all the other seven deadly virtues," as Mrs. Cheveley says.

Although lamented by Butler as a loss of focus, the broadened meaning of "that beautiful word of Purity," as Butler called it, was welcome to other feminists more interested in fostering a civic virtue that transcended sex as such. Millicent Fawcett, for example, imagined that feminine purity could be infused into the male-dominated public sphere with a transformative effect, bringing "true woman's influence on behalf of whatsoever things are true, honest, just, pure, lovely, and of good report to bear upon the conduct of public affairs."[16] Fawcett's description of a purity that resonates with political meaning, without at the same time excluding a sexual field of reference, is exactly the type of purity that Lady Chiltern demands of her politician husband in Wilde's play. It also aptly describes the mission of groups such as the Women's Liberal Association, an affiliate of the Liberal Party. Lady Chiltern is a dedicated member of the Women's Liberal Association in the final draft of *An Ideal Husband* (although not in earlier drafts, in which sexual behavior is more centrally at issue), and in real life its members included Millicent Fawcett as well as Mrs. Oscar Wilde and her close friend, the feminist platform speaker Lady Sandhurst.

Although Mrs. Cheveley understands the social momentum of purity and its widened range of meaning, her perspective on the subject is one of amused skepticism – for her, the mania for purity furnishes a means to extract money from a Liberal politician with a guilty past who supports, and is supported by, progressive women. The perspective of Sir Robert Chiltern's wife, Gertrude, is a different matter, for her ideals of behavior are drawn directly from feminist polemics of the period, some of which, including Millicent Fawcett's, were published in *The Woman's World*, the magazine that Wilde himself edited from 1888 to 1890. Even Josephine Butler, despite her anxieties about the dispersal of meaning around "that beautiful word of Purity," regularly insisted on strenuous virtue for men, a virtue that went beyond sexual good behavior into every aspect of life. As expressed on occasion by Butler, the task was not only to make men pure, in her exclusive sense of the word, but more generally "to elevate the moral tone among men" to such a degree that their virtue was not only strenuous, but practically superhuman – conforming to what Ellice Hopkins, founder of the social-purity White Cross Army, styled "the self-giving manhood" of Christ, the "manhood lifted into God."[17] Such a man would be worthy of worship as well as love, because "pure" in every dimension of life, and as Lady Chiltern expresses it herself, "We women worship when we love; and when we lose our worship, we lose everything." It is important to recognize that for Lady Chiltern, as for other feminists of the time, no other kind of man will do; if Sir Robert turns out to be unworthy of worship, then that unfortunate fact "will kill my love for you."[18]

What Sir Robert Chiltern objects to so vehemently, especially once his crime has been found out, is having been made into an ideal such as this – a specimen of perfected manhood patterned on Christ himself, and therefore requiring worship. It is also important to note that Chiltern sees his wife's demand for an elevated moral tone in men as something more than a personal quirk of hers – it is rather a general attitude of women, or of a large group of them, an aspect of what the new puritanism had brought about. So it is modern women, and not only the particular woman his wife, to whom Chiltern traces his problems:

Women think that they are making ideals of men. What they are making of us are false idols merely. You made your false idol of me, and I had not the courage to come down, show you my wounds, tell you my weaknesses. I was afraid that I might lose your love, as I have lost it now ... Let women make no more ideals of men! Let them not put them on altars and bow before them, or they may ruin other lives as completely as you – whom I have so wildly loved – have ruined mine![19]

It is the idea of perfected manhood "lifted unto God," in the phrase of Ellice Hopkins, that has made Chiltern frantic and spurred him to this rhetorical outburst. Perfected manhood was also the core idea behind the feminist assault on the Contagious Diseases Acts and agitation for passage of the Criminal Law Amendment Bill, measuring men by the standard of "purity, incorruptibility, and all the other seven deadly virtues," as Mrs. Cheveley ironically says. From the viewpoint of men, or rather men like Chiltern and his friend and confidant Lord Goring, the situation had become desperate, both for men and marriage itself. "It is the growth of the moral sense in women that makes marriage such a hopeless, one-sided institution," as Lord Goring says in Act 3.[20]

But women of wit and perception realize the folly of demanding male purity, and such women figure prominently in Wilde's first conception of the play. Beginning with a fragmentary scenario – the first draft of *An Ideal Husband*, which appears to have figured rarely if at all in criticism of the play – there occurs an exchange in which Mabel Chiltern, Lady Chiltern's sister, displays little interest in the ideal man, seeming to prefer one with interesting flaws that he shows no sign of regretting. In this first draft of the play, in which speeches sometimes occur without name-tags to identify the speaker, Mabel Chiltern (called Violet in this earliest version) is addressing the Wildean dandy Lord Goring:

MISS CHILTERN: You are always telling me of your bad qualities, Lord Goring.
[LORD GORING:] I have only told you half of them as yet.
[MISS CHILTERN:] Is the other half very bad?²¹

This conversation, which Wilde altered in various revisions, continues as follows in the next complete draft of the play, an autograph manuscript in the British Library:

LORD GORING: Quite terrible.
MABEL CHILTERN: Do come and tell them to me.
LORD GORING: You will promise not to try and correct me.
MABEL CHILTERN: You know perfectly well that I never correct you. I love your bad qualities.

Wilde has Mabel express herself even more enthusiastically in the licensing manuscript: "I worship your bad qualities."²² But in Wilde's final revision this speech is shortened and toned down in various ways, including with respect to Mabel's enthusiasm for Goring's bad qualities. At the end of a string of rewrites, Mabel says only, "Well, I delight in your bad qualities" – a long way from worshipping or loving them, as before, but consistent with Wilde's overall approach of modulating extreme views, comments, and actions in revising the play.²³ Nevertheless, all through the numerous manuscripts and various stages of revision of *An Ideal Husband*, Mabel Chiltern's coy enthusiasm (indeed, worship, in one version) for a man who is *not* faultless, is being employed as a thematic counterpoint to her sister's demand that Sir Robert Chiltern must embody all the virtues of a right-eous new masculinity in his conduct.

As Wilde was working out an engagement between these two charac-ters in later drafts, Mabel Chiltern is made to react with distaste to the suggestion that Goring ought to make her an "ideal" husband: "It sounds like something in the next world," she says; "he can be what he chooses."²⁴

The point that Wilde is making – that although women have created the notion of ideal men, really clever women understand the absurdity of it – was therefore integral to *An Ideal Husband* as he conceived and wrote it from the ground up. At this earliest point in the textual history of the play, however, Wilde had yet to work out how to win over Lady Chiltern herself to the view that ideal husbands are an absurdity and thus bring the play to a satisfying close in the fourth act. The first draft ends with Chiltern defying Mrs. Chevely's threat of exposure and speaking in the House of Commons against the fraudulent Argentine Canal Scheme in which she is heavily invested, as he does in all subsequent versions of the play; but there is no indication in this earliest version how the breach between the corrupted Chiltern and the wife who demands purity and perfection is to be resolved. It was a problem, indeed, to which he would never find a good solution.

Lady Chiltern's overdeveloped moral sense would eventually be generalized as the problem of women as a gender in *An Ideal Husband*. But earlier drafts are focused on making a very different point – that women are no less fallible than men, and therefore blind at best, or hypocritical at worst, in demanding purity of men. "We all have feet of clay, women as well as men," declares Sir Robert Chiltern in an undated, but early manuscript version of the play.[25] That sentence was altered in revising *An Ideal Husband* to delete any reference at all to women and their own moral failings as being comparable to men's. This particular alteration is one of many that second-guess an impulse to solve what Sir Robert Chiltern once calls "the problem of women" by showing the best of them to be no more pure and moral, sometimes less so, than men.[26] Whereas in early drafts of *An Ideal Husband* the imperfections of men are excused because women have "feet of clay" too, in later drafts women are much less culpable. One effect of these accumulating revisions was that the play over time gravitated toward a time-worn idea about gender that was quintessentially more Victorian than Wildean. Instead of a heroine with grave moral flaws of her own, Lady Chiltern in revision became an icon of almost unsullied if somewhat misguided goodness – in marked contrast to her criminal husband whose successful political career is built on lies and bribery. Wilde's ultimate point is that the good woman should "forgive" and "love" the fallen man, but this alleged redemptive mission of the female is itself part of the quagmire of gender essentialism from which the implausible final act of *An Ideal Husband* could not extricate itself.

"Nobody is incapable of weak action – nobody is incapable of a wrong one," Lord Goring admonishes the "perfect" Lady Chiltern in the first-draft scenario of *An Ideal Husband*. Goring's tactic here is precisely to expose the Victorian fantasy of a pure and perfect womanhood, a task that regrettably takes on diminished importance until it virtually disappears in the final drafts. As Wilde seemed gradually to realize that the thematic exigencies of his play, not to mention his life, required that he resort to mid-Victorian gender stereotypes – pure woman, deeply flawed man – there was no longer any place for scenes that represent Lady Chiltern as capable of sin herself. But it is very different in the first scenario of *An Ideal Husband*, in which Lord Goring, her husband's best friend, rather vainly and abruptly proposes that under certain circumstances she would betray Sir Robert and make love to – himself: "You think you would be quite incapable of taking a sheet of that nice pink notepaper I see on your vanity [?] table and writing to me, something very romantic, 'I love you – I am coming to you.'"

Lady Chiltern rebukes him indignantly in this earliest draft of *An Ideal Husband* – "Lord Goring ... you make love to your friend's wife" – just before Wilde scrawls "Lord Goring is turned out of the house" in a flurry of somewhat disconnected stage directions and dialogue.[27]

Later in the first draft of the play, when Lady Chiltern has actually written the "foolish letter" that Goring accurately predicted she was capable of, she is filled with self-reproach and drops the tone of righteous indignation against her bribe-taking husband. "Each disgraced in the other's eyes," she says remorsefully, "– and I the more to blame."[28] In another early manuscript composed after the first draft, partly typed and partly written in Wilde's hand, Lady Chiltern blames herself more melodramatically: "How mad I was to write that letter! An hour afterwards I could have burned the hand that penned it, burned it for shame!" But on second thought Wilde lined through this speech, canceling it in this little-known typescript in the William Andrews Clark Memorial Library at UCLA.[29] In this early draft of Act 4 – which seems not to have been commented on previously in scholarship, or taken into account in any editions of the play – the deletion suggests that Wilde is already experiencing misgivings about his tactics to this point in dramatizing gender in *An Ideal Husband*.

Those tactics had struck at the core of the feminist argument for a new kind of masculinity, pure and perfect – the argument, as Josephine Butler and others framed it, that men should be held to the same austere standard of conduct to which men hold women. Wilde's first thought was to dramatize a rebuttal to the effect that women – even the best and purest, the Lady Chilterns of the world – were themselves no better, perhaps worse, than the men they blindly found fault with. That is the point he wanted to make with Lady Chiltern's speech of self-recognition in the first draft – "Each disgraced in the other's eyes – and I the more to blame."[30] In the later and largely overlooked typescript draft of Act 4 at UCLA, this realization by the "good" woman of her own sin remains in the text and motivates Lady Chiltern's distracted wish to burn her own hand "for shame" because it had penned a romantic letter to her husband's friend. But this entire line of thought and dialogue was eventually deleted as Wilde proceeded with revisions of the play. So was Lady Chiltern's harsh declaration of personal and perhaps sexual freedom in the first draft when she learns of her husband's crime, telling him that "I consider myself no longer bound to you in any way. I claim the right … to live as I choose."[31]

As Wilde rewrote *An Ideal Husband*, therefore, Lady Chiltern becomes progressively milder and less culpable as he gradually abandons his original plan to expose a good woman's own moral failings in order to discredit her call for a pure and perfect masculinity. Perhaps he had come to recognize that the real issue was not whether a woman like Lady Chiltern was imperfect herself, or even hypocritical, but whether her agenda for a rigorously moral revision of manhood had any merit of its own. Whereas in the first draft Lady Chiltern writes to Goring, "I love you. I trust you. I am coming to you,"[32] her note becomes much less self-incriminating in a later manuscript version, which survives in the final version as well. "I trust you," she now writes, "I want you. I am coming to you."[33] Nevertheless, when Goring reads this later and significantly revised version of the note, he reflects to himself that the "little trap" he has laid for her will surely "teach her a salutary lesson." But even this vague imputation that Lady Chiltern is guilty of something that requires a "lesson" from Goring would be deleted in months to come. In the licensing typescript dated January 2, 1895, only one day before the first production, Goring's reaction to the note from Lady Chiltern is further moderated: "Upon my word," he says, reading it, "I'll give her a good lecture, make her stand by her husband, and send her home."[34] In this comparatively late version of the text, Lady Chiltern's note on pink paper is no longer an invitation to adultery, but simply the demonstration of a rule of thumb that, as Goring says in the licensing manuscript, "immaculate people do very foolish things sometimes." By the time Wilde revised the play for book publication, his final version of *An Ideal Husband*, even Goring's slam at "immaculate people" who do unspecified "foolish things" would be cut, to be replaced by speech more pertinent to the play's adjusted thematic focus – not the hypocrisy of good women any longer, but the absurdity of the new morality for men: "Well, I will make her stand by her husband. That is the only thing for her to do. That is the only thing for any woman to do. It is the growth of the moral sense in women that makes marriage such a hopeless, one-sided institution."[35]

As for Lady Chiltern, she no longer reproaches herself for writing what was originally, in the first draft, an adulterous proposal to Goring. Instead, in later versions, she blames her husband's would-be blackmailer, Mrs. Cheveley, for putting a romantic interpretation on the revised note when she chanced to find and read it. Goring himself, the recipient of the letter, corroborates this milder view of what had been a "mad letter" in the first draft, actually calling Lady Chiltern's revised note to him "a very beautiful, womanly letter, asking me for my help." When Lady Chiltern learns in the final version that Mrs. Cheveley is in possession of the letter and has misconstrued the note as a love letter, she cries out to Goring, in all innocence: "Oh! Not that! Not that! If I – in trouble, and wanting your help, trusting you, propose to come and see you … that you may advise me … assist me … oh! are there women as horrible as that?"[36] But not only has Mrs. Cheveley intercepted the letter and put "a certain construction" on it, she has sent it to Sir Robert as well. Threatened with exposure, Lady Chiltern responds with rhetorically violent outbursts in earlier drafts, a reaction entirely inconsistent with the gentler, more "womanly" characterization of Lady Chiltern that Wilde would later adopt as he revised. For example, in a manuscript revision dated March 10, 1894, still more than eight months before the first production at the Haymarket Theatre, Lady Chiltern shows the dark side of her character that Wilde gradually erased as he worked on the play. "What did you make me do?" she cries out to Goring. "Why did you let her take it [the letter]? You should have killed her first. Why didn't you kill her?"[37]

This homicidal rhetoric is dropped in the final version of *An Ideal Husband*, where an irreproachable Lady Chiltern decides to tell her husband about the letter even though there is no practical need to do so. When he finally receives and reads the "I want you" letter, Sir Robert erroneously assumes his wife addressed it to him, not Goring, for there is no addressee's name at the top of the note. Safe now from exposure, Lady Chiltern, after some hesitation, tells her husband the truth – i.e., the note on pink paper was sent to Goring, but of course in all innocence. At the end of the final version of *An Ideal Husband*, therefore, Lady Chiltern has lived up to the ideal of perfection that she has demanded of others, guilty of little more than a bad prose style in the letter she wrote to Goring. The only thing that can make her better is a more tolerant attitude toward men, whose natural imperfections (in this play at least) can only be redeemed by the love and forgiveness of a good woman like herself.

There *are* bad women in the multiply revised *An Ideal Husband*, but they no longer include, as they did in earlier drafts, women like Lady Chiltern. As he reworked his play from draft to draft, Wilde gradually canceled most of the material that emphasized the moral turpitude of self-anointed and hypocritical "good" women – material that would have taken *An Ideal Husband* in a far different direction had it remained in the script. Wilde would focus instead on discrediting the radical reinterpretation of manhood put forward by Lady Chiltern. But he did not, or perhaps could not, put forward any clearly articulated alternative of his own to counter the pure and perfect masculinity of *fin-de-siècle* feminism. Lacking one, he fell back on the conventional and self-serving idea of gendered identity that, as Josephine Butler lamented, gave men wide latitude for conduct on the presumption they were by nature impure and corrupt. From this arch-Victorian point of view, anathema to feminists and social-purity groups, women are by nature the ministering angels to men, redeeming them with an inexhaustible supply of forgiveness and love. *An Ideal Husband* would run aground on the shoals of this essentialism of gender in its disastrous final act.

## THE LAST ACT: "TRUTH" VERSUS PERFORMANCE

The more Wilde worked on *An Ideal Husband*, therefore, the more firmly entrenched in the text was what the play refers to as the "true character" and "real self" of individuals. Lady Chiltern became less flawed and more and more the idealized Victorian woman as Wilde revised; and once she understands, in the final version of the play, her allegedly "true" identity as a woman, she realizes at the same time that her mission in life is to redeem through blind love and forgiveness the inevitably baser male, her husband. The main counterforce against this essentialism of personal and gender identity, especially in early drafts of the play, is the notorious Mrs. Cheveley, and to a lesser extent, in one of his contradictory moods, Lord Goring. Although he becomes the enforcer of conventional male and female gender identities in Act 4, Goring is capable at moments of a more flexible view of what is real and true. "Vulgarity is the conduct of other people," he says in Act 3 of the published play, and "falsehoods the truths of other people."[38]

This perception that "truth" is a matter of individual perception – a view entirely at odds with Goring's sanctimonious speeches in the final act of the play – usually emanates in *An Ideal Husband* from Mrs. Cheveley, who is regrettably absent from the last act. For her, life is a performative event, and everything one is, does, or expresses is an act. Knowing some-thing about Sir Robert Chiltern's past, she perceives that his "ideal" qual-ity as a husband and politician is a "pose," as she says, not real at all, and that the stern morality preached by purity feminists and others is an act rather than the expression of truth. Indeed, according to Mrs. Cheveley, "everyone has to pose as a paragon of purity" or else be crushed in the machinery of modern morality.[39]

By contrast, Lady Chiltern, until she is disillusioned in the matter, regards her husband as being of "an upright nature," one whose "ideal" qualities are no pose, but an essential part of himself. It is his "real self," says Lady Chiltern, and the "purer aims and higher ideals" that he has brought into political life are the inevitable outcome of his core being, as she states in the final version of the play. Her view correlates nicely with Chiltern's own pronouncement that "a political life is a noble career!" For Mrs. Cheveley, however, politics itself is a show, "a clever game," as she explains to Chiltern, perhaps "more ... becoming" than other pursuits, but containing nothing fundamentally true or inherently noble.[40] Not only politics and morality, but also individual attitudes and outlooks are dramatic presentations of the self to the world. Optimism as well as pes-simism, says Mrs. Cheveley in response to a question from Chiltern, "are both of them merely poses." This exchange follows:

CHILTERN: You prefer to be natural?
MRS. CHEVELEY: Sometimes. But it is such a difficult pose to keep up.[41]

In a prompt-book Wilde expresses with even more emphasis the idea that "being natural" is itself a pose; "it is," he has Mrs. Cheveley say, "the most artificial pose of all."[42] Both versions underline Mrs. Cheveley's belief that everything we do and say – even what is performed "in the mode of belief," as Judith Butler has put it – is after all enmeshed in a network of "gestures, movements, and enactments of various kinds" with which we build up the *illusion* of a genuine and natural selfhood.[43]

Nevertheless, the revisions of *An Ideal Husband* were sometimes exe-cuted in a way that toned down or eliminated some of the most forceful expressions of the performativity of the self. In an early version of the play, for example, this exchange appears between Mrs. Cheveley and Sir Robert Chiltern on the topic of self-realization through an almost theatrical type of enactment:

MRS. CHEVELEY: I wanted immensely to meet you, and to ask you to do some-
　　thing for me.
CHILTERN: What?
MRS. CHEVELEY: I can't tell you just now! There are either too many people pre-
　　sent or too few. I don't know which.
CHILTERN: You are particular about an audience.
MRS. CHEVELEY: Ah! To be without an audience, is like being without a looking
　　glass. One can't understand oneself. [44]

These deleted passages would have sharpened the audience's sense of
Mrs. Cheveley's view of the self as artificial and theatrical. It is a view
that rules out the kind of authentic subjectivity invoked by Lady Chiltern
when, in the earliest complete version of the play, she refers deprecatingly
to Mrs. Cheveley's "true character," believing it to be evil. Mrs. Cheveley's
response once again calls into question the whole concept of a fixed and
known identity. "One's true character," she retorts, "is what one wishes to
be, more than what one is."[45] Her lines, unfortunately deleted from the play
later on, take us to the threshold of postmodernity and a view of the self
as dramatic artifice. Wilde's editing-out of some of Mrs. Cheveley's more
daring formulations of this kind suggests a reluctance to fully embrace his
own and his characters' innovative thinking about the performed nature
of the self and the world containing it.

Wilde diluted this performative view of life as he revised *An Ideal
Husband* over a period of months, tightening the focus on Lady Chiltern's
feminism and the threat it represented to men. To this end, Wilde's final
revisions of the play for book publication in 1899 made explicit for the
first time the feminist politics of Lady Chiltern, which in earlier drafts
was implied rather than named. As Wilde increasingly associated her with
purity feminism, he abandoned the strategy in early drafts of making
Lady Chiltern seem a hypocrite, as impure sexually as her husband had
proved to be politically – someone whose claims to "purity" do not prevent her from writing love letters to her husband's best friend and seeking
an affair with him. Yet even in the earliest versions of *An Ideal Husband*,
for all her hypocrisy, Lady Chiltern's emphasis upon a pure standard of
morality for men as well as women and her efforts to influence political
life for the better align her with contemporary feminists such as Josephine
Butler, Millicent Fawcett, and Lady Sandhurst, the friend and political
mentor of Wilde's wife Constance. Lady Chiltern exercises her woman's
influence primarily upon her husband in early drafts, encouraging him
to bring into political life "a nobler atmosphere, a finer attitude towards

life, a freer air of purer aims and higher ideals."[46] Throughout the textual history of *An Ideal Husband*, indeed, Lady Chiltern acts in the spirit of Josephine Butler's admonition that "women should be politicians" – in the sense of engaging with the serious issues of the day so that public opinion could be "purified," as Butler said, "as it should be."

But not until Wilde's final revision of the play does Lady Chiltern heed Butler's crucially related advice, shared by most feminists of the time, that for women to be "politicians" in the full sense they had to work for women's right to vote and hold political office, and "when they got it, it would have a perceptible effect upon Parliament."[47] Like Butler as well – not to mention Wilde's own wife – Lady Chiltern in the final version of *An Ideal Husband* is an active member of the Women's Liberal Association, which advocated women's suffrage along with other feminist causes. In earlier versions of the play Lady Chiltern has just returned home from the park when she enters in Act 2, but in Wilde's last revision, now the canonical text of the play, she has "just come from the Woman's Liberal Association" where Sir Robert's name was loudly applauded and the discussion centered on such matters as "the Parliamentary Franchise" for women. In this final version of *An Ideal Husband* Lady Chiltern stands shoulder to shoulder with feminists of the day on a broad range of issues, including some contested within the movement itself – not only purity for men, but "Factory Acts, Female Inspectors, the Eight Hours' Bill, the Parliamentary Franchise … everything, in fact, that you would find thoroughly uninteresting," as she patiently explains to an obtuse Lord Goring.[48] With her activist political and moral views and her role in the Women's Liberal Association, Lady Chiltern is a profile of *fin-de-siècle* feminism in the final revision of *An Ideal Husband* as well as a strong woman in her own right – at least she is all of this until the unlikely, unworthy last act of Wilde's play.

Wilde revised the play to make Lady Chiltern a card-carrying purity feminist when he was preparing *An Ideal Husband* for book publication, a process of revision that began in 1897 after his release from prison. Since Wilde's own copy of the script had disappeared in the court-ordered sale of his property after his arrest, he asked his publisher, Leonard Smithers, to procure a copy from Lewis Waller, the actor who played the part of Chiltern at the Haymarket Theatre. Working from this typescript, now held by Texas Christian University as an uncataloged item in its Special Collections, Wilde revised the play heavily in his own hand, adding elaborate stage directions, altering the action in at least one important respect, and making explicit the feminist affiliations of Lady Chiltern. Few people have seen this crucial revised typescript, which is clearly the missing link between earlier manuscript drafts of the play and the form it took for book publication in 1899. In all, this overlooked typescript of *An Ideal Husband* contains approximately thirty-five pages of revision in Wilde's handwriting, including some passages marked "Note to the Printer – n.b." in order to keep clear the sequencing of typed and handwritten material in preparing the draft for publication. The addition of the material in which Wilde draws out the connection of Lady Chiltern with the Women's Liberal Association is handwritten on the verso of a typescript page in Act 2.[49] The Texas Christian typescript also contains, in the form of typed copy, a key scene that does not appear in the licensing manuscript and that Wilde claimed was added immediately before the first production – the scene in which Lord Goring gains the upper hand over Mrs. Cheveley by enticing her to put on a stolen brooch that she is then unable to remove. This order of composition suggests that the Texas Christian typescript is very late indeed in Wilde's chain of revision, with the typescript coming after the licensing manuscript but before the first production of the play, and his later autograph revisions being added in 1898–99.

After Act 2 ends with Lady Chiltern vehemently denouncing her husband as if he were a male prostitute, accusing him of having "put yourself up to sale," we see no more of her until near the end of the play in Act 4. Her long absence is surprising in view of the fact that her program for lifting men to a higher moral level is the central thematic problem of *An Ideal Husband*. When she finally does reappear in the last act, her attitude to her husband – indeed her attitude to lifting men to a higher level – undergoes changes that are unaccountable. The last time we saw her, she was pushing Chiltern away from her and exclaiming, "Don't come near me. Don't touch me. I feel as if you have soiled me forever."[50] Now, when Lady Chiltern belatedly appears again, she learns from Lord Goring that he has seized and burned the incriminating letter with which Mrs. Cheveley had hoped to blackmail Sir Robert Chiltern, and she blandly approves of Goring's act because as a result "Robert is safe" – it will protect her guilty husband from exposure. What has happened to her feminist devotion to civic virtue and accountability in public life, her ferocious anger only hours ago at her husband for taking a bribe, and her revulsion at the mere thought of his proximity? Is the Lady Chiltern of Act 1 the same woman who now addresses Goring, praising him for destroying the blackmail letter that could expose her husband's crime? "What a good friend you are to him – to us!" she gushes, entirely out of character for one who was, the last time we saw her, only yesterday, so "pitiless in her perfection

– cold and stern and without mercy" and utterly disdainful of her criminal husband.[51]

Indeed, the increasingly permissive attitude of Lady Chiltern toward her errant spouse is her defining attribute in Act 4, and it is a tolerance grotesquely out of tune with the purity feminism that Wilde, in revising the play, made the hallmark of her character instead of the cynical façade it was in the early drafts. Now that her virtue is sincere rather than hypocritical, what are we to make of the scenes in which Lady Chiltern betrays her own most deeply held principles and in so doing brings her story, and that of the larger drama, to a happy ending? With respect, however, to the final and now-accepted text of the play, it could have been worse. In an early version of a lamentable moment in the fourth act, Goring tries to dissuade Lady Chiltern from requiring that Chiltern leave public life because of the secret crime in his past. Until Wilde revised it for book publication, Goring began his reactionary diatribe on gender with comments that would have seemed reprehensible, indeed comically archaic, to a feminist like Lady Chiltern in the 1890s:

GORING: Be content if you can keep your husband's love. Don't sacrifice him to gratify the vanity of a high moral tone!

LADY CHILTERN: Is this the philosophy you are going to teach your wife when you marry?

GORING: Certainly ... I think that women are simply made to love and to be loved, and if I ever do some weak or wrong thing, I will expect from my wife pity, gentleness, kindness, forgiveness.

LADY CHILTERN: You think me hard and unwomanly, then?

GORING: I think you hard but not unwomanly ...

LADY CHILTERN: You think that Robert wishes to continue in public life, having done what he has done?

GORING: A strong man thinks only about his future. A weak man only about his past. [52]

Wilde deleted these lines in the final version of the play, probably because they so heavy-handedly and undramatically express a conventional understanding of gender that was coming under heavy fire from feminists in the 1890s, and had been a target in Wilde's own magazine a few years earlier.

Although no one could regret the deletion of such a passage, its omission meant that what follows in this same crucial conversation between Goring and Lady Chiltern became more absurd than it was before. In its final form, Lord Goring's complacently Victorian lecture on the "true" nature of men and women is so abrupt in its brevity, and the revolution it produces in Lady Chiltern's thinking so profound yet unmotivated, that the result, dramatically speaking, is simply incredible. Goring expounds on his essentialist views of gender as follows in the final version of the play:

Women are not meant to judge us, but to forgive us when we need forgiveness. Pardon, not punishment, is their mission … A man's life is of more value than a woman's. It has larger issues, wider scope, greater ambitions. A woman's life revolves in curves of emotions. It is upon lines of intellect that a man's life progresses. A woman who can keep a man's love, and love him in return, has done all the world wants of women, or should want of them.[53]

It is not as if these retrograde opinions are news to Lady Chiltern – far from it, for her brand of radical feminism was founded upon a complete and conscious repudiation of them. But now, as Goring runs through the litany of an old-fashioned gender ideology based on what *men* "need," Lady Chiltern is left abjectly speechless and shaken, converted in an instant – in less than a page of dialogue in typescript – to the very views that she has devoted her life to resisting. So when her husband enters the scene to show her his letter of resignation from public life, a letter she insisted he write in expiation, she tears it up and repeats Goring's exhortation about the fixed natures of women and men almost word for word: "A man's life is of more value than a woman's," and so on to the bitter end, noting finally that "I have just learnt this, and much else with it, from Lord Goring." Then, in words more or less her own, but still parroting Goring's ideas, Lady Chiltern concludes, "Men easily forget. And I forgive. That is how women help the world. I see that now." It is hard to believe that she really does, or that Wilde did either. Indeed, this improbable scene does not appear in the first draft of the play at all; it was added later, as Wilde struggled with little success to bring the play to some kind of satisfying closure.[54] Recent critics of Wilde have been creative in trying to find something between the lines of this regrettable scene that will exculpate him from the gender essentialism and misogynist politics that bring about narrative closure in *An Ideal Husband*. Richard Dellamora, for example, deals interestingly with some of the social purity backgrounds of the play; but when confronted with Lady Chiltern's parroted declaration that "a man's life is of more value than a woman's," he simply declares it an instance of "reverse discourse" in which Wilde's objective is to satirize aristocratic and middle-class culture within the conventions of social comedy. Such a leap of political faith in Wilde is impressive, especially coming from one of his most astute critics, but it bears little relationship to what is going on in Act 4 of *An Ideal Husband*.[55]

From the beginning of its textual history, however, *An Ideal Husband* was at odds with itself on the key thematic question of gendered identity, and it remained so at the end. In its final form the play veers crazily between Goring's proclamation of a core, essentialized manhood and womanhood on one hand, and on the other a sense of identity (advanced mainly by Mrs. Cheveley) that is *performed* rather than "real" or natural – a sustained enactment without which there would be no gender and no identity at all. For Mrs. Cheveley, being "moral" and being "natural" are merely poses – regulatory fictions, as Judith Butler calls them, rather than expressions of any deep-seated truth – and in this theatre of identity one may claim the improvisational freedom to define oneself, or at least to exercise limited control over who and what one is working toward, in Mrs. Cheveley's phrase, "what one wishes to be." The crucial exchange between Goring and Lady Chiltern in Act 4 about what women are "meant" to do, and what men "need," almost mortally wounds *An Ideal Husband* by invoking self-serving concepts of gendered identity that feminists and their allies had convincingly discredited over the previous twenty-five years or so. But those outmoded concepts do not prevail unchallenged at the end of the play; rather, they persist in tension with a more performative interpretation of identity that Wilde erratically felt his way toward as he wrote and rewrote this play so marked by his own hesitations and second thoughts.

LIVING BETWEEN QUOTATION MARKS

One of the remarkable features of the narrative of *An Ideal Husband* is the crucial importance it gives to letters, notes, and written signatures – not merely because they *are* so prominent in the action, but because they function to open a perspective on personal identity different from, and irreconcilable with, the complacent preachments of Goring to Lady Chiltern on the fixed natures of men and women. Both Sir Robert Chiltern and Lady Chiltern have signed their name to letters which place them in a position of guilt – Chiltern's letter to Baron Arnheim in which he sold a state secret, and himself, "for money," and Lady Chiltern's letter on pink paper to Goring, which seems (more so in some drafts than others) to be a betrayal of her husband.

A crucial question posed by *An Ideal Husband* is whether these incriminating, signed documents communicate a pure meaning or truth, reproducing their content and what they communicate about their authors in a perpetual "now." As Jacques Derrida has said, signed documents are characteristically used to "tether" the writer to his or her statement in the present, to attach statement to source, and to reproduce statement and source under conditions of "rigorous purity." Of this supposed pure reproducibility of statement and source, Derrida asks: "Is there such a thing? … Are there signatures?" His answer is yes, but not in the pure form that might be supposed. The blackmail perpetrated upon Chiltern testifies to the existence and potency of signatures, as does, by the same token, the blackmail being practiced upon Wilde himself in 1894 – by male prostitutes who used his love letters to Lord Alfred Douglas to extort money from him, the price of keeping him out of reach, for the moment, of the Criminal Law Amendment Act. In the play, furthermore, Lady Chiltern's note to Goring is used against her in an effort to wreck her marriage by revealing, through her signature affixed to a piece of writing, that her goodness is merely a pose and her real character something quite different.

Viewed in this way, *An Ideal Husband* works toward Derrida's tentative acknowledgment of the existence of signatures insofar as they bind an individual in the present to his or her written statement in the past, thus attaching statement to source and defining each in terms of the other. If this were not so, blackmail would be implausible at best, or pointless. But as to the larger question of what truth or meaning is conveyed by signatures, Wilde – uncannily like Derrida a century later – moves beyond the question of the existence of signatures to consider to what extent they really bind the signer to the statement and whether, therefore, the signer can execute a break with the context of the statement and engender a new context for both the statement and the source. On this point Wilde says yes, moving intuitively in *An Ideal Husband* toward the same response that Derrida would offer much later in "Signature Event Context." The "very structure of the written," as Derrida expresses it, is that every sign breaks with the context that "organizes the moment of its inscription," and this is so because every sign is citational, "put between quotation marks," and consequently no potential exists in written communication for the decoding of absolute truth or meaning. Rather, writing provides only "contexts without any center of absolute anchoring." Such a view strictly limits the extent to which an individual can be tied to a written statement that he or she has signed. Writing itself, therefore, can be cut off from any "original meaning" or "constraining context" that organized its actual composition.[56]

In *An Ideal Husband* this destabilizing outlook on writing, and on the relation between statement and source, is realized dramatically through the letters penned by Sir Robert Chiltern and Lady Chiltern. The blackmail and threats against husband and wife are founded on their signed writings, believed to have the capacity to puncture their enactments of strict morality so as to reveal sordid real selves behind the masquerade. At issue, then, is whether the writers can be tethered to, and thus defined by, their signed writings from the past. There is no doubt about such matters on the part of Lady Chiltern in the first act: "One's past is what one is," she asserts confidently but unreflectively, in answer to her husband's suggestion that Mrs. Cheveley may have changed for the better since she knew her years ago.[57] As events transpire in her life and in her husband's, however, the error of that point of view is exposed. Her own potentially incriminating note to Goring is read by her husband with an interpretation quite different from Mrs. Cheveley's – not as a betrayal, but as evidence of her love and need for him. In its break with its original meaning and context, Lady Chiltern's note realizes in action Derrida's point about the structure of writing in general; every sign, he argues, can be "put between quotation marks ... and engender infinitely new contexts in an absolutely nonsaturable fashion."[58]

Like Lady Chiltern's note, the dishonorable letter by which her husband sold a Cabinet secret does *not*, as the play turns out, define the "real self" of the writer by chaining the statement to him, its source, in a perpetual now. Lady Chiltern acts on the assumption that her husband's letter to Baron Arnheim has corrupted him forever, and on that basis pushes him away with the command "Don't come near me. Don't touch me." But Chiltern's address to Parliament, in which he condemns the Argentine Canal project in spite of Mrs. Cheveley's blackmailing threats, demonstrates the reverse of his wife's maxim that "one's past is what one is." His incriminating letter to the baron is in the process of engendering new contexts, and its having been cut off from its original meaning is signified in the third act when Goring takes the letter from Mrs. Cheveley and burns it to ashes over a lamp.

One measure of the internal contradictions which beset *An Ideal Husband* is that the character most associated with a view of the self as performance rather than reality – Mrs. Cheveley – is also the character who tries to enforce through her blackmailing and threats a general "now" for these incriminating letters. She attempts to bind the Chilterns in perpetuity to their signed writings, which would thus become a kind of code to decipher the meaning or truth of their lives. Writing under the pressure of a personal crisis similar in some respects to Sir Robert Chiltern's, and without any map of postmodern theory to guide him, Wilde uses the device of signed letters in *An Ideal Husband* to work toward the realization that there is no such thing as what Derrida would later call "the pure reproducibility of a pure event," and thus the signer or source of a statement cannot be attached to it forever as if that statement were the repository of settled meaning and truth. This insight into language as being capable of breaking with its original meaning and engendering new contexts, and new identities for the speaker or writer, was to form the basis of Wilde's next and greatest play, *The Importance of Being Earnest*, which he was already at work on while revising *An Ideal Husband*.

Wilde's laborious revisions of *An Ideal Husband* were determined in part by his complicated task of discovering how to resist the radical feminist redefinition of masculinity – a redefinition along the lines of a new puritanism which endangered him personally and which he opposed philosophically – without at the same time falling back upon the conventional idea of natural and immutable gendered identities for men and women. In this regard *An Ideal Husband* fails egregiously, as the fourth act makes painfully clear when Goring teaches Lady Chiltern what "real" manhood and womanhood are. Standing in unresolved tension with that uninspired scene is Wilde's treatment of writing and signatures, an aspect of the play that leads in the direction of a postmodern understanding of identity and language – their condition, as Derrida says, of being constituted as "only contexts without any center of absolute anchoring," unstable in themselves and in relation to each other.

### WRITING THE FOURTH ACT OF WILDE'S LIFE

The burning of one signed, incriminating document and the changing, unstable meaning of another create an opening for Lady Chiltern and Sir Robert to reinvent themselves at the end of *An Ideal Husband* and escape the doom that Lady Chiltern had pronounced as general truth in Act 2: "One's past is what one is." But in composing the last act of his play, Wilde was also writing, or trying to write, a comic resolution for his own life, one that would free him from his past too. Like Sir Robert Chiltern, Wilde was being blackmailed over his criminal behavior, and while he was writing and revising *An Ideal Husband* stood on the brink of exposure no less than the "ideal husband" of his play. Like Lady Chiltern, he had written compromising letters that had fallen into the wrong hands, and consequently what he had conceived as the delightful comedy of his life was in danger of turning into grotesque tragedy. Wilde would be unable in the months ahead to extricate himself from the web of secret crime, blackmail, and puritanical justice that he saved Sir Robert Chiltern from in the fourth act of his play, however unconvincingly.

Even in the play, however, Wilde's forced happy ending defies belief and exacts great damage upon it, both intellectual and aesthetic. Sir Robert

Chiltern is able to guard his guilty secret and keep up the act of honorable public servant – at a higher level, now that he has been appointed to the Cabinet – only because his wife has betrayed her own most deeply held principles in a conversion that takes only a minute or so to work itself out in Act 4. Lady Chiltern's rigid purity feminism demands "a high moral tone" for men and women alike, but a few smooth words from Lord Goring persuade her that men are by nature deeply flawed; and because their lives are "of more value than a woman's," her highest mission as a woman, she suddenly realizes, is to forgive and love the erring but large-minded male. What we are left with, incredibly for a writer of Wilde's views, is a Victorian essentialism of gender in which the double standard of morality is revived and Lady Chiltern, "the white image of all good things" whom, as her husband says, sin cannot touch, abdicates her feminist convictions to become a ministering angel to her morally wounded husband.

Wilde's unusually tortured revisions of *An Ideal Husband* had been taking the play down this wrong turn for months before he finished rewriting it. Lost in the shuffle as he brought the play to closure was Mrs. Cheveley, the most Wildean character of the drama, the one for whom identity (and everything else) is inevitably *performed* in a world devoid of fixed truth and value. Her view that morality is simply an "attitude" and that one's character is not given, but more a matter of "what one wishes," would have had a wide and fertile field in which to operate in Act 4. Mrs. Cheveley's performative view of life, although toned down in revision, was Wilde's own. But as with his own life when it mattered most, Wilde did not, or could not, save his play with such an interpretation of so-called reality. Mrs. Cheveley makes no appearance at all in Act 4, having disappeared from the play unceremoniously along with the unconventional ideas that were more Wilde's own than were the melodramatic, retrograde ones he called upon to force a happy ending and bring down the final curtain on *An Ideal Husband.*

# CHAPTER 4

# Performativity and history

## Oscar Wilde and *The Importance of Being Earnest*

In his hostile review of the first production of *The Importance of Being Earnest*, Bernard Shaw found no authentic "being" in its characters; they failed to instill any "belief in the humanity of the play."[1] But what Shaw interpreted to be the failure of *Earnest* – the absence of a characterological reality in which he could believe – is from another perspective the main point and chief interest of Oscar Wilde's play. A character such as Jack Worthing, with his tenuous hold on personal and social identity, cannot be expected to inspire "belief," if we use that word in Shaw's bedrock sense. Jack represents not the reality but the contingency of the self, exposing it as the product of an array of textual, ritual, and theatrical practices. "Being Earnest" in this attenuated sense creates an opportunity for Wilde to call into question the essential reality not only of a masquerader such as Jack Worthing, but all personal identity, and in particular the gendered identity of men – thus creating an opportunity to disturb and rearticulate these fundamental concepts.

By renaming the play *The Importance of Being Earnest* just before its first production and reintroducing the phrase at the final curtain, Wilde signaled his concern with what it meant to *be* someone, particularly in relation to culturally scripted cues like those embedded in the term "earnest." My study of the surviving manuscripts of the play indicates that this central issue of self-performance became clearer and better-defined to Wilde himself as he revised *Earnest* over a period of months in 1894 and 1895. In the process Wilde's play became a turning point in Victorian thinking about subjectivity, for as it developed from a crude scenario to the first edition, *Earnest* focused more and more intently upon personal identity as a matter of performance and textuality rather than natural fact, and explored and refined tactics for self-fashioning in light of that recognition.

In its final form, *The Importance of Being Earnest* is a textual crossroads where performativity and history meet. Jack Worthing undertakes the renegotiation of his identity to become "E(a)rnest" in a particular time and place; and his tagline utterance at the final curtain – "I now realize for the first time in my life the vital Importance of Being Earnest" – contains a residuum of meanings that, in some cases, can mean little to us today. What it signified for Jack to become "Earnest" *and* "Ernest" is the product of several discourses of social change in the 1890s, notably those of feminism, the social-purity movement, and an emerging gay culture with which Jack himself is implicitly affiliated. The word *performativity* was not in the vocabulary of any of these discourses, nor in Wilde's, but what the word has come to suggest operates powerfully in Wilde's play, where these competing rhetorics of social change not only intersect, they collide. For at issue in *The Importance of Being Earnest* are two main tendencies of current thinking about performativity: (1) the idea that language can produce, not only describe, reality, and (2) the concept of social life as a performance, a repertoire of speech, gestures, and rituals that constitute a theatrical "act" rather than express any extra-discursive, core truth.[2] The crux of the play is whether Jack Worthing can autonomously enact himself through language and theatricality. Jack's dilemma – "I don't know who I really am" – provides an opportunity for self-definition, although in the end Jack reinvents himself within and through what he has opposed all along. Finally he is defined by his social and historical context as much as, or more than, he defines himself.

## JACK WORTHING AND THE ANTHROPOLOGY OF PERFORMANCE

Jack Worthing is posed at the threshhold of the social world, having precipitated a crisis by his alienated behavior and status. As Lady Bracknell puts it to him, Jack's very existence affronts "the ordinary decencies of family life" and "reminds one of the worst excesses of the French Revolution." What alarms Lady Bracknell is Jack's deficiency in the performance of social rituals that simultaneously confer an authorized identity upon individuals, telling them "who" they are, yet limiting individuality by claiming them as society's own to control. Unable to prove himself named in this essential way, Jack appears to Lady Bracknell not as a socialized human being, but a kind of parcel, "born, or at any rate bred, in a handbag," occupying a liminal zone in which he makes up his own name and status to please himself, unconstrained by the rites of passage of the world around him.[3]

As Barbara Meyerhoff has expressed it, these rites of passage are "constructed performances," occurring at moments of high anxiety, such as birth, marriage, and death. They are dramatic events that "announce our separateness and individuality and at the same time remind us vividly that we belong to our group and cannot conceive of an existence apart from it." While all societies attempt to absorb the individual and shape the creature into a bona fide, self-regulating member, they never succeed entirely. "No society," as Meyerhoff says, "has failed to generate a few people who are innovators, poets, madmen, deviants, skeptics, artists, revolutionaries, and intellectuals."⁴ Jack Worthing is this type of disruptive, unregulated person, as Lady Bracknell instantly perceives. With respect to three of the constructed performances that impose order on the social world – birth, marriage, and death – Jack acts outside and against the authorized script for all three. He has omitted essential rituals (naming, and with it integration into the Family); he plans to marry Gwendolen in defiance of the forms of betrothal, kill his "brother" Ernest, and be baptized and give the name Ernest to himself in comic disregard of the protocols by which society identifies its members. Evading or deforming the rituals that enforce social identity and confer selfhood, Jack is situated at the margins of his world, displaying no "humanity," as Shaw said, no selfhood in which anyone could believe – not even Jack himself. "I don't actually know who I am," he confesses.⁵ Any self he inhabits in this void, whether "Jack" or "Ernest," will be a theatrical act rather than an expression of core identity. But is Jack different in this respect from anyone else?

"The basic stuff of social life is performance," writes Victor Turner in *The Anthropology of Performance*. "Self is presented through the performance of roles ... [and] through performance that breaks roles."⁶ In several ways Jack "breaks" the role of someone asking the family of a young woman for her hand in marriage – he is already engaged to Gwendolen Moncrieff when he asks permission from Lady Bracknell, and his name does not appear on her "list" of eligible young men; moreover, he cannot respond as expected to ritual questions about his parents and origins. In each of these cases Jack fails to present himself in relation to the textual directives of "society," as Lady Bracknell calls it, which prompts her to sense in him a threat to order, "a contempt for the ordinary decencies of family life." The script for self-identification upon which Lady Bracknell insists has the function of instilling stability and meaning through banishment of the disruptive, chaotic element that Jack represents. As Sally Moore and Barbara Meyerhoff have pointed out, all rules, laws, and customs are part of a dramatic process of ritual whose purpose is to veil the abyss underlying social life: "Every ceremony is par excellence a dramatic statement against indeterminacy in some field of human affairs. Through order, formality, and repetition it seeks to state that the cosmos and social world . . . are orderly and explicable and for the moment fixed . . . Ritual is a declaration of form against indeterminacy."[7]

From the perspective of this secular ritual of meaning-making, someone like Lady Bracknell, despite her insistence upon rigid principles and established categories, is no less a "performer" than Jack Worthing, because all social and personal identity, all meaning and order, are performed, not "real." Unaware of the performativity of all social life, Lady Bracknell's complaint about Jack is the same as Shaw's – he lacks real humanity, a selfhood in which others can believe. So she denies Jack "a body that matters," in Judith Butler's phrase, or rather denies him any human body at all. Mistaken as an infant for a manuscript of fiction and left in a handbag in the cloakroom of Victoria Station, Jack appears to Lady Bracknell to have no claim at all to bodily or social existence: "You can hardly imagine that I and Lord Bracknell would dream of allowing our only daughter – a girl brought up with the utmost care – to marry into a cloak-room, and form an alliance with a parcel?"[8]

This pronouncement exiling Jack from the realm of the human is decisive and barely contested in the final version of *Earnest*, but in earlier versions Jack talks back, with emphasis, and the force of Lady Bracknell's remark is diminished. In the holograph draft of the play, Jack "*starts indignantly*" and testily complains of Lady Bracknell's characterization of him as a parcel: "I was in a carpet-bag. That is quite a different thing." He then proceeds to deny emphatically the importance of having any family at all.[9] The final version, by contrast, presents a more subdued Jack, his complaints reduced to a murmur. Lady Bracknell, the voice of "society," excludes Jack from human sodality with a force that is crucial at this pivotal moment in the play, and the "*majestic indignation*" which she is supposed to display in the scene is borne out. The effect of this final version of the "parcel" scene is to emphasize, more emphatically than earlier versions, the power that social ritual exerts over the individual who attempts to improvise independently of it.

Even when the rules are enforced as sternly as Lady Bracknell could wish, there still remains some indeterminacy that social ritual aims to eliminate. It is this aspect of social performance that Victor Turner emphasizes – unscripted and disruptive, as opposed to the "role-playing sequence in an institutionalized or 'corporate group' context." This spontaneous acting erupts from the surface of the normative role-playing of social life and precipitates a crisis, as Jack does in Wilde's play when he breaches the correct performance of identity as Lady Bracknell and her world have defined and tried to fix it. "Social drama" is the name that Turner gives to this crisis of broken roles, and it arises in Wilde's play from the collision between Lady Bracknell's institutionalized performance of ritual and Jack's spontaneous acting. *The Importance of Being Earnest* is shaped by the crises of this "social drama," but in addition interprets it and assigns meaning to it, and in this processural operation becomes a performance in its own right. The play becomes part of the performative dynamic of life.

### HISTORICIZING *EARNEST*'S "SOCIAL DRAMA"

In Victor Turner's vocabulary, the so-called "cultural performative genres" – theatre, film, fiction, etc. – imitate social drama and interpret it, welding together a system of "consensual meaning" by processing social performance into constructions of "reality."[10] *The Importance of Being Earnest*, however, is a particularly striking example of a work belonging to the cultural performative genres because of its unusually knowing and purposeful engagement with the performativity of social life. More strikingly still, the play lifts the veil which the dramatic processes of social life aim to keep in place – the veil concealing the abyss of indeterminacy that, as Moore and Meyerhoff argue, lies just beneath all ritual declarations of an orderly and explicable world. Seeing *The Importance of Being Earnest* as a specimen of the cultural performative genres, one remarkably conscious of its participation in the performative dynamic that organizes society, exposes the weakness of Shaw's denunciation of the play as deficient in humanity and reality. From this perspective, *Earnest* could scarcely be more "human" or more real, for characters like Jack Worthing and Lady Bracknell not only exemplify, but compound, the performative constructions of life.

They do so, in large part, through their engagement with language and textuality, for in *The Importance of Being Earnest* the linchpin of performance is words themselves. It is language – names, speech, written texts – that in the world of Wilde's play is the fountainhead of personal identity, its source and at the same time the power that limits and constrains the enactment of self. Although the names of some of the dramatis personae changed as the play was written and rewritten, the earliest surviving lines of dialogue that Wilde wrote for *Earnest* – in a manuscript notebook brought to light by Peter Raby, entitled *The Guardian* – show clearly that the nucleus of his original idea was the name Ernest itself, coupled with the idea that ceremony might have the power to determine a child's future. "Beautiful name, Ernest. I couldn't love anybody who wasn't named Ernest –," says the earliest incarnation of Gwendolen, in

Wilde's manuscript notebook. "Oh, don't say that Gwendolen," responds the character who would become Jack Worthing. "Is a man's whole future to depend upon the [baptismal] font?"[11] He mentions other names, Geoffrey and John, that in his opinion ought to be as acceptable as Ernest, but Gwendolen is inflexible, as she remains throughout all manuscript, typescript, and printed texts of *Earnest*. From beginning to end of the textual history of Wilde's play, it is important that men be named "Ernest" – no other name will do. Interestingly, however, this was not the case in an early scenario that Wilde wrote in a letter to George Alexander, manager of the St. James's Theatre and the original Jack Worthing. This scenario, discovered by Peter Raby in the Wilde archive at UCLA, contains a sketch of many of the play's eventual incidents and characters, but the name Ernest is, at this early date, not part of Wilde's conception of the play.[12]

This self-presentation through naming in *Earnest* is for the most part gendered masculine, and for Wilde's purposes, as for Gwendolen's, no name but Ernest was acceptable. Although the word had subcultural, sexual connotations, the authorized meanings of "earnest" in the 1890s had incorporated diverse but intertwined associations with sobriety, restraint, fair dealing, straightforwardness, abstemiousness, and at the most general level an undifferentiated but active virtue. The word was most often applied to men, but was sometimes attached to women, and used by women, to model a quality of "being earnest" that men could and should conform themselves to. When he was editor of the *Woman's World*, Wilde himself commissioned articles that applied the term "earnest" to women in this manner – for example, a profile of Lady Margaret Sandhurst, the feminist platform speaker and close friend of Wilde's wife, Constance. Lady Sandhurst was a major figure in the Women's Liberal Association who encouraged Constance Wilde to join the movement, which she did, becoming a "leading light" in the Chelsea branch.[13] "Moral earnestness" is cited in the article in Wilde's magazine as the "keynote of Lady Sandhurst's character" and the force behind her support for women's voting rights and increased occupational opportunities, as well as her establishment of a home for poor, sick children. "There may be few Liberals among ladies of position," notes the *Woman's World*, "but they are nearly always earnest and determined in their politics."[14] Two of these earnest women were Lady Sandhurst and Mrs. Oscar Wilde.

For men and their world, this phenomenon of earnest womanhood had consequences. Frederick Dolman, the author of the piece in Wilde's magazine, portrays Lady Sandhurst as "a living witness to the introduction of women's influence into the affairs of the State." This intrusion of earnest women into the male-gendered public sphere would, as the article suggests, transform "the State" and, potentially, the conditions of masculinity itself, making the state and the men who governed it as "earnest" as women like Lady Sandhurst.[15]

Feminists such as Lady Sandhurst and her protégée Constance Wilde, who spoke at meetings and wrote in the late 1880s on "rational dress" for women, belonged to a more moderate side of the movement than the one led by Josephine Butler, the most outspoken and influential woman activist of her time. Butler, who mobilized the Ladies' National Association to lead the fight against the Contagious Diseases Acts of the 1860s, was not only more militant, but more focused upon dismantling the double standard of sexual morality for women and men. Legislated in response to the Victorian syphilis epidemic, the Contagious Diseases Acts had brought into existence a "diabolical triple power" of doctors, magistrates, and police whose purpose, as Butler relentlessly proclaimed, was to place working-class women under surveillance by detaining them without trial for three months or longer and subjecting them to involuntary internal examination if police believed them to be prostitutes infected with syphilis.[16] For the Ladies' National Association and allied "purity" groups such as the Social Purity Alliance and National Vigilance Association, the root of the problem was men themselves and the prevailing belief that men, being brutes by nature, required a regulated but legalized system of prostitution to satisfy their lust and spare so-called good women, who would otherwise become their victims. Butler wanted to end the "government by police" that she claimed the CD Acts had brought about; and to do so, she said, she and her allies "were compelled to lay the axe to the root of the whole congeries of doctrines as to the necessity of vice, the impossibility of male chastity, and the creation of woman as a mere vessel of dishonour for the brutal instincts of man."[17] Thus was normative masculinity, as defined by Victorian law and custom, exposed in "the great crusade" of Josephine Butler as a fiction rather than an expression of biological or any other natural fact.[18] "This double standard [of morality for the sexes] is man's invention, for his own base convenience," Butler writes in her scarcely remembered *Appeal to Men*, published for the Social Purity Alliance in 1882. It is not female prostitutes who are mainly responsible for the syphilis epidemic, she argues, but "the male tyrant" who claims sexual freedom as his natural right. "Such men dispense plagues and death wherever they move by the very infection of their breath."[19] Only in the unparalleled collection of rare feminist and social-purity propaganda in the Women's Library, London, can the vehemence and extent of this rhetoric be documented.[20] Its target was men like Wilde, who conducted their lives with disdain for the new ideal of earnestness and "purity."

The new masculinity that Butler advocated would be defined by the same domestic ideology that governed women throughout the Victorian period. "The great thing that has to be done is to create a pure moral tone among men," Butler asserted. "It will be our duty to require sternly of men that they be pure; to demand it of them as they have hitherto demanded it of us." Men's sphere was to be the home, as much as women's; and women would be as free to enter public life as men were. Speaking in 1888 to the Women's Liberal Association – the feminist organization with which Constance Wilde and Lady Sandhurst were also affiliated – Butler declared, according to the WLA pamphlet in which her talk was summarized in the third person: "women should be politicians ... [and] Liberal women must work for the Parliamentary vote. When they got it, it would have a perceptible effect upon Parliament ... woman's sphere was in the home ... but it was the same for a man."[21]

This feminist move to domesticate the male provides the atmosphere in which Gwendolen Moncrieff remarks to Cecily Cardew in *The Importance of Being Earnest*: "The home seems to me to be the proper sphere for the man," citing her own father Lord Bracknell as an example of a man so absorbed by domesticity that "outside the family circle" he is "entirely unknown."[22] The invisible and ineffectual Lord Bracknell forms part of Wilde's commentary on this new masculinity; confined within a new gender script authored by women, such men barely exist in their own right. Lord Bracknell's absence, in fact, gives Jack no choice but to ask Lady Bracknell for Gwendolen's hand in marriage, although custom dictated that such appeals be made to the father of the intended bride. But even if Lord Bracknell had been there to ask, it would have made no difference, as Lady Brancaster (Lady Bracknell's original name) observes in an early manuscript of the play. "Lord Brancaster is in the habit of agreeing with me on all points," she asserts. "It is the keynote of his character," and therefore his consent to the marriage of Cecily Cardew and Algernon Moncrieff, to which Jack strongly objects, is sure to be a formality.[23]

But it was not enough for feminists and social-purity workers to produce domesticated men like Lord Bracknell. For Josephine Butler and likeminded people, the task of morally earnest women was to expose Victorian masculinity, as it was usually understood, as a kind of masquerade, one patched together by men with "beautiful language" and "subtle arguments" to justify their policing of women on one hand, and through that, the indulgence of "their own selfish interests and degraded passions."[24] In her fascinating pamphlet of 1895, *A Letter of Earnest Appeal*, Butler claims the term "earnest" for her own agenda, rejecting the morality which allows free sexual indulgence to men as part of the nature of things, but also resisting what she saw as a drift in her own feminist brigades toward campaigning for a generalized virtue or "moral earnestness" of the kind associated with Lady Sandhurst in the magazine Wilde edited. For Butler, the core issue continued to be the sexual exploitation of women by men who justified their behavior by laying claim to an essentialist masculinity that made it necessary. To dilute this central issue by amalgamating it into a concern for moral earnestness in a broader sense, she insisted, would be a mistake. What Butler was advocating in *A Letter of Earnest Appeal*, published at the moment of the arrest and conviction of Wilde for gross indecency, was the refocusing of reform efforts on "that gigantic evil of modern days," the regulation and control of women's bodies by men pretending to act in the name of morality and nature. To secure victory on this point, men would have to become as "pure" – sexually pure – as women.

To a large extent Josephine Butler in 1895 was the victim of her own success, her "holy war" having produced an earthquake of conscience resulting in the repeal of the Contagious Diseases Acts in 1886 and the passage, in 1885, of the Criminal Law Amendment Bill under which Wilde would be indicted and convicted. That legislation enacted stiff penalties for the prostitution of children, raised the age of consent for girls, and – in an amendment offered by the Liberal politician and journalist Henry Labouchere – specified criminal penalties for a new crime, gross indecency between men. In the *Earnest Appeal*, addressed to an international federation of her supporters and co-workers, Butler nostalgically rehearses those great victories, pointing out with emphasis that the main supporters of the Criminal Law Amendment Bill "were chiefly, if not entirely, our own prominent workers," collaborating with W.T. Stead in his journalistic exposure of child prostitution and with "good men" in Parliament to mobilize support there and among the public for the new law.[25] With his love for young men and boys, Oscar Wilde was in the cross-hairs of that law.

Butler's *Earnest Appeal* therefore refocuses the word "earnest" in a strategic way, using it to question social constructions of gender and insist upon male sexual purity as the foundation for a thorough revision of gendered identity. This radical deployment of the word was significantly different from the "moral earnestness" associated with moderate feminists like Lady Sandhurst and Constance Wilde, even though reformers and moralists

with conflicting perspectives could agree that it was important for a man
to be earnest. The word was used to advocate sexual purity in men, male
domesticity and submission to "feminine" ideals, moral rectitude in both
public and private life, and, increasingly toward the end of the century,
an ideal of masculinity founded upon Jesus Christ himself. Much of this
layered resonance in the word "earnest" was captured by W. Davenport
Adams in his *Book of Earnest Lives*, a popular inspirational volume of short
biographies that went to a seventh edition in 1894. Although none of the
"earnest lives" recounted by Adams are contemporary ones, they form, as
he says, a "company of educational reformers, of Christian missionaries,
of philanthropists, of Good Samaritans; men and women who have dedicated their lives to the great work of making their fellow-creatures better,
purer, happier." The inclusion of "purer" as an attribute of these "earnest
lives" is an interesting choice, because by 1894 the "beautiful word" of *purity*, as Josephine Butler called it, had inescapable associations with the alliance of feminists and other reformers who fought against the Contagious
Diseases Acts, agitated for passage of the Criminal Law Amendment Bill,
and demanded a single standard of sexual morality for men and women
alike. Most of Adams's "earnest lives" were men's, and their manhood was
of a special type, lived in imitation of Christ, "unostentatiously, but earn-
estly, following in the footsteps of the Great Samaritan."[26]

     Adams's promotion of a Christ-like earnestness in men is imbued with
the rhetorical aura of Josephine Butler and, especially, Ellice Hopkins,
founder of the White Cross Army. On Hopkins's political agenda, the
teaching of Christ-like "true manliness" was at the top of the list – what
she described as "the self-giving manhood of Him who is the prince of
passion and the Lord of love, the manhood lifted into God." Members
of her far-flung White Cross Army, the heavily working-class movement
led by Hopkins, pledged themselves "to maintain the law of purity as
equally binding upon men and women," one of the five "Obligations"
of all those who belonged to the organization. Her book *The Power of
Womanhood* holds up the ideal of the "True Man," constituted "at least
as much" by purity as by traditional male virtues such as "truth and
courage"; and for Ellice Hopkins the model of the "True Man" is Christ
himself.[27]

     The manhood of Christ is manhood without sex, and in *The Importance
of Being Earnest* it is Canon Chasuble ("I am a celibate, madam") whom
Wilde employs to mock the new gospel of manliness that policed male
sexuality and theorized an ideal of "True Man" in the image of Christ.[28]
Chasuble's comic and finally unsuccessful attempt to repress his own

sexuality is a reminder that male purity was a factor to be reckoned with in the larger field of meaning that by 1895 was attached to "being earnest" as an ideal of masculinity. Like the prophet Jokaanan in Wilde's anti-biblical drama, *Salomé*, Canon Chasuble is so excessively devoted to sexual purity that he becomes a mockery of the masculine ideal that was being aggressively put forward by Josephine Butler, Ellice Hopkins, and their coalition of feminists and social-purity workers.

In high contrast to Chasuble's inflexible purity, Wilde deposits into *Earnest* some hints of his own sexual practices, not only impure, but illegal ones. These references were obscure enough to go unnoticed or at least unremarked by the censor, audiences, and the press – for example, his including among the props a signed cigarette case like those he gave young male prostitutes, or locating Algernon's rooms on Half Moon Street, the site of a homosexual ménage well-known to him. Some have speculated that the name "earnest" itself was an allusion to the term "uranist," which was being used in scientific journals and elsewhere in the 1890s to identify "congenital inverts," as those attracted to members of their own sex were now being called.[29] If so, few in the audience could have been in on the joke, for if such an allusion were widely understood, the play, like *Salomé*, would not have been licensed for performance by the Lord Chamberlain's office. In any case, as we have seen, the name Ernest was used by Wilde from his earliest manuscript jottings in reference to a *woman's* ideal of what a man should be – i.e., Gwendolen's "ideal" of marrying a man named Ernest, a sly and significant misreading of the ideal upheld by women in the feminist and purity movements of a new manhood that would be defined by the evolving concept of earnestness. Wilde's play resists the new manhood by countering it with performativity. Algernon Moncrieff's "Bunburying," suggestive of anal sex, and the insurgent double life of Jack as Ernest, which undermines all sanctioned versions of earnestness, produce a reversal of supposedly real masculinity that suggests without actually stating a gay, or proto-gay, subtext.

By the mid-1890s, moreover, there was already precedent for doubling the terms "Earnest" and "Ernest" into a coded allusion to same-sex passion, a precedent with links directly to Wilde and his lover Lord Alfred Douglas. A volume of homoerotic poems in the Pre-Raphaelite style entitled *Love in Earnest* (1892), written by John Gambril Nicholson, consists of ardent love poetry with titles such as "Forbidden Love" and "Secret Love." *Love in Earnest* frequently breaks into praise of the beauty of young men, but its title is most striking in relation to a poem entitled "Of Boys' Names." For the poet, as for Gwendolen in *The Importance of Being*

*Earnest*, the sheer magic of the name Ernest makes all other men's names pale by comparison:

> Cyril is lordly, Stephen crowned
> With deathless wreaths of asphodel,
> Oliver whispers peace profound,
> Herbert takes arms his foes to quell,
> Eustace with sheaves is laden well,
> Christopher has a noble [?] fame,
> And Michael storms the gates of Hell,
> But Ernest sets my heart a-flame.[30]

J.F.G. Nicholson, the author of the poems, was also the author of a story that appeared in the notorious and only edition of the Oxford undergraduate magazine, the *Chameleon*, edited by Douglas's friend John Francis Bloxam and used against Wilde as evidence of gross indecency in his trials. Wilde contributed his "Phrases and Philosophies for the Use of the Young" to the *Chameleon*, where it shared space with homoerotic poems and stories and Douglas's fateful poem "The Two Loves." But even if Wilde knew Nicholson's "uranian" writing, it is not mainly a question of *Love in Earnest* having influenced *The Importance of Being Earnest*, notwithstanding Nicholson's wordplay linking "Earnest" with "Ernest" in the context of same-sex passion. The point is rather that *Love in Earnest* provides strong evidence of the growing contestation in the 1890s around the concept of "being earnest" as a standard for masculine behavior and identity. The poems in *Love in Earnest*, unlike Wilde's play, contain open, indeed *earnest* declarations of homosexual love, and no mockery or sabotage of earnestness as such. They do not challenge the concept of "earnest" manhood, but rather claim a place for homoerotic passion within it.

Alan Sinfield has argued that *The Importance of Being Earnest* is not a play explicitly about homosexuality, because as a category of sex and gender identity it was still in the process of formation and therefore not accessible to Wilde or his audience.[31] Whether *Earnest* is "about" homosexuality or not, some recent research makes clear that there was certainly a flourishing homosexual subculture in London (and elsewhere) in the 1890s, and that Wilde and his contemporaries were equipped with an interpretive framework enabling them to "read" homosexuality in life and representations of it on stage, even if theatrical depictions of homosexuality were necessarily inexplicit under the watchful eye of state censorship. In *The Importance of Being Earnest*, Jack Worthing's origins, cloaked in secrecy and a suggestion of sexual indiscretion, are traced to a vaguely detailed incident involving a handbag and a bassinet at Victoria Station, a significant metropolitan locale under the circumstances. As Matt Cook has recently shown, urban train stations such as Victoria had already become notorious meeting places for homosexuals, attracted by the distinctly modern experience of close contact with anonymous strangers, "forced proximity to unknown men," and a sense of transition and flux that was experienced by some as a disruption of the social order and suggestive of impropriety. The late-Victorian gay subculture was both distinct and various, including well-known rendezvous sites such as the cloakrooms and toilets of train stations, recognized "cruising" areas such as parts of Oxford Street and Piccadilly; a niche publishing industry for homosexual readers who purchased and read fiction like *Sins of the Cities of the Plains* (1881); theatres, music halls, and gay bars where cross-dressed prostitutes prowled for homosexual clients; and "Molly houses" such as the infamous Cleveland Street brothel whose proprietors sent runners into Piccadilly Circus to hand out printed cards advertising the house. This *fin-de-siècle* homosexual scene forms part of the ambience of *The Importance of Being Earnest* – resonating, as we have seen, in the word "earnest" itself; in Miss Prism's references to unsavory young men in the Piccadilly area; and in Wilde's conspicuously situating Jack's chambers at the Albany, off Piccadilly, where George Ives lived and associated with his Order of the Chaerona, a shadowy fraternity whose members, as Matt Cook points out, "drew on Hellenism to understand and legitimate their desires."[32]

If *The Importance of Being Earnest* is on one level a play about homosexuality, it is also, as its eventual title indicates, about "being earnest." By 1895 "earnestness" had become an increasingly complicated and controversial idea that bore with special force upon masculinity as a gendered identity – including, but by no means limited to, masculine sexuality. The term "earnest" was being invoked as a text for what it meant to be a man; and it is one of the great comic effects of the play that this term, so laden with meaning and authority, is turned inside-out by Wilde to become an empty signifier, null and void. Gwendolen Fairfax and Cecily Cardew have an ideal, as they frequently insist, but it is the ideal of marrying a man named Ernest, not the ideal of earnestness as the defining principle of male conduct and character. As the play develops from this premise of emptiness in the word itself, the concept of "being Earnest" is vaporized in wordplay; there is no real Earnest/Ernest at all, only an act, Jack Worthing's and Algernon Moncrieff's theatrical pretense of "being Earnest." Exposing earnest manhood as a performative rather than "real" entity, Wilde clears the stage for the enactment of something very different, turning the ideal of "being Earnest" against itself.

## PERFORMING *E(A)RNEST*

What makes *The Importance of Being Earnest* not just a delightful play, but an important one – a turning point in Wilde's career and a landmark in late-Victorian thinking about subjectivity – is that it recognizes and strategizes who we are as the work of dramatic artifice rather than as natural fact. The idea of a "genuine self," in Matthew Arnold's nostalgic phrase, gives way, and the subject begins to appear as the product of textual and ritual practices that are performed rather than natural. What happens in the play – and this has contributed to its dismissal by Shaw and many critics as a failure of realism – is that Jack Worthing, after merely pretending to be "Ernest," actually becomes Ernest just before the final curtain drops. But this narrative development also exemplifies, and complicates, a type of reality created by "performative utterance," as J.L. Austin terms it in *How to Do Things with Words*. Pronouncing himself to be "Ernest" is actually, or is part of, the action that remakes Jack as Earnest – just as a phrase such as "I take this woman to be my lawful wedded wife" is not a description of getting married but the actual doing of it. But at second glance, Jack's performance as Ernest does not neatly fit Austin's model of performative language, for "our performative utterances ... are to be understood as issued in ordinary circumstances," or they become void. The "ordinary circumstances" which are necessary for the production of genuine speech acts, Austin claims, exclude the whole realm of the theatrical, for an actor – pretending, speaking lines from a script – uses language in specious ways, "not seriously, but in ways *parasitic* upon its normal use."[33] Jack's pose as Ernest not only occurs in a stage play, but even in that environment is so theatrically insincere, so scripted (as Jack himself reluctantly admits to Algernon), that its deployment of language clearly fits Austin's category of *parasitic* utterance that is unserious, a quotation rather than a "pure" performative that makes something happen.

Secondly, although the act of naming forms one of Austin's most prominent examples of performative speech, he is careful to exclude naming practices which run counter to accepted procedures, and would nullify the speech act, as in the case of baptizing a dog or christening a child if the person performing the baptism is not authorized to do it. Jack Worthing in Wilde's play attempts to name himself, and to do so outside the accepted ritual practices that ordinarily confer personal identity upon someone. Yet in spite of these "infelicities," as Austin calls them – the violation of rituals of naming, and Jack's unserious use of language (like an actor's) in naming himself Ernest – something does happen to make him Ernest after all. Moreover, Jack could never have become Ernest without first playing the role – could not have recognized himself as such, nor could others, including Gwendolen, and there could have been no Act 3 in which his new identity as Ernest becomes official. In other words, Jack's role-playing as Ernest preceded and enabled the "reality" of his being Ernest, and any other sequence is unimaginable within the world of the play.

With Austin's help, we can go some distance, but only so far, toward an interpretation of *Earnest*. It will be useful now to consider Jacques Derrida's objection to Austin's exclusion of theatrical speech from the domain of the performative on the grounds that it is unserious because derived from a script. For Derrida, unlike Austin, there can be no such thing as a "pure" speech act that is an original statement-event, because all performative statements – such as naming a person or a ship, or saying "I do" to become married – are embedded in context, a pre-existing ritual or verbal formula, which lies outside the self and the intention of the speaker. Even performative speech events, therefore, can be seen as citational, or placed within quotation marks – scripted like (even if not exactly like) an actor's speech. The result is *différance*, "the irreducible absence of intention or assistance from the performative statement" in producing a speech act.[34] If true, Derrida's hypothesis would doom Jack's performance as Ernest to failure, the same failure that awaits every attempt at performativity – that is, its containment and limitation by the citational context that frames it. At the same time, however, an opportunity presents itself: if all performative acts are impure and citational, unserious in Austin's sense of the term, then Jack's identity as a person named Jack is contingent too, a quotation. Indeed, Jack was given the surname Worthing because his benefactor was carrying a railway ticket to the seaside town of Worthing when he "found" him in Victoria Station. Jack's supposedly real identity is a quotation of a ticket on the Brighton line; and if he were to carry out his plan to be baptized as Ernest to make the name "really" his own, it would be extracted from a different text – the ritual of baptism as written in the Prayer Book.

As it turns out, Jack only pretends to be Ernest, without benefit of clergy, but even this act is likewise determined by text and context – in this instance, Gwendolen's extraordinary remarks on the meaning and aura of the name of Ernest: "It is a divine name. It has a music of its own. It produces vibrations."[35] Extraordinary, yes, but Gwendolen's remarks on being Ernest/Earnest are citations of prior texts too. In proclaiming E(a)rnest a "divine" name, Gwendolen enters the contextual field of feminists and purity reformers who exalted earnest manhood as an imitation of the divine "true Man," Christ. In a starkly different register, however, her pronouncement that the name has a unique "music" and produces "vibrations" belongs to the textual realm of J.G.F. Nicholson's *Love in Earnest*, in which the name Ernest is coded with homoerotic passion and a superior *music* that drowns out the music of all other male names:

> One name can make my pulses bound,
> No peer it owns, nor parallel,
> By it is Vivian's sweetness drowned,
> And Roland, full as organ-swell;
> Though Frank may ring like silver bell,
> And Cecil softer music claim,
> They cannot work the miracle, –
> 'Tis Ernest sets my heart a-flame.[36]

Names are texts, whether verbal or musical, and one's identity the enactment of them. Furthermore, as the textuality of the name "Ernest" makes clear, all texts are unstable; they are freighted with mixed and even contradictory meanings that will inevitably complicate, or doom, any attempt at autonomous self-fashioning. If all identity is a performance, some space may exist for Jack to perform himself as Ernest; but if Derrida is right, that performance will also be traceable to a context that precedes and partly determines it. In order to be Ernest, therefore, Jack may also have to become, at least to some extent, "earnest" too.

"Performativity is thus not a singular 'act,'" as Judith Butler writes in *Bodies That Matter*, "for it is always a reiteration of a norm or set of norms."[37] It is always derivative and therefore always has historical precedent, even if, as Butler suggests, "its historicity remains dissimulated." By these terms, Jack Worthing's becoming Ernest in Wilde's play cannot be entirely the effect of his originating will, although his intention is not at all irrelevant. Rather, his new identity as Ernest is partly or even largely derived from a pre-existing context that implicates the rebellious Jack in the structures of power and convention. This ironic turn of events might be explained by the iterability of all performative speech, including Jack's own act as Ernest. If so, his being Ernest is the product, in some measure, of the very norms of earnestness that Jack has sought to resist in his act of self-reinvention.

As Butler puts it, "There is no power that acts, but only a reiterated acting that is power in its persistence and instability."[38] Building on a foundation laid by J.L. Austin and Victor Turner, among others, she argues that in performing the rituals of social life – whether baptism or marriage or an action in court or merely gestures and movements – we are engaged, usually unawares, in a "stylized repetition of acts" that really constitutes our

identity as individuals. As in Victor Turner's anthropology of performance, we re-enact a set of meanings already established, thus bending to
the corporate will and underwriting dominant conventions – ones that
guarantee production and consumption of material goods, for example,
or ensure cultural survival (such as the heterosexual imperative). Unlike
the theatre, however, where there is an actor behind the role, distinct from
the role he or she is playing, there is no "real self" behind this performance in life; rather, the self is precisely what is constituted by and through
the "regulatory fiction" of the performance. In the end, however, the self
is not passively scripted, or not entirely so, for its performative character
can provide the basis for contesting the terms of social ritual. If those who
fail to enact their gender "right" are regularly punished, as Butler argues,
perhaps the individual can still claim some improvisational freedom, just
as a script can be enacted in a theatre in different ways by various actors in
various productions, thereby producing different meanings.[39] This zone of
performative freedom would exist within a restricted space, inhibited by
directives written, as it were, into the cultural script.

   Although this conception of performativity owes an obvious debt to
Turner, Austin, and Derrida, its history can be traced further – to Oscar
Wilde – the Wilde of *The Importance of Being Earnest*, especially, and of
*De Profundis*. In the latter work, staring at the dead-end of his life from
a prison cell, Wilde meditates upon human subjectivity as a kind of puppet-theatre, but one in which the puppets have passions, and even a kind
of "freedom" despite their lack of control. It is "the paradox of life," he
remarks.[40] From one point of view, postmodern theories of performance
are an elaborate footnote to the life and writing of Wilde, who was perhaps among the first to experience life in their terms, although he did so
without the benefit of a pre-existing structure of theory. Performativity as
we now think of it came to Wilde and his dramatic characters intuitively,
pulsing with their own thoughts and feelings, rather than as a developed
system of thought, although Wilde himself was moving in that direction
in *The Importance of Being Earnest* and in his courtroom and prison experiences immediately thereafter.

   Jack Worthing and other characters in *The Importance of Being Earnest*
are puppets in the performative sense of the term that Wilde invokes in *De
Profundis*. Although lacking the freedom to become authors of their own
scripts, these passionate puppets speak and act with an intentionality that,
as Derrida puts it, "will have its place, but from this place it will no longer
be able to govern the entire scene and the entire system of utterances."[41]
What these puppets with passionate intentions *can* do, according to Wilde

in *De Profundis*, is introduce new elements of plot "in what they are presenting," which makes for, as he says, "the paradox of life." It is also the
paradox of some recent theories of performativity in their negotiation for
some degree of improvisational freedom for individual actors confronted
with a script that was already written and rehearsed when they came on
the scene. Finally, it is the paradox that lies at the core of *The Importance of
Being Earnest*, organizing a network of seeming contraditions and bringing the play to equivocal closure with Jack actually becoming Ernest, but
not exactly on his own terms, for he has had to learn the "vital Importance
of being Earnest" as well.

These performative failures and accomplishments begin to crystallize
in the final act of the play when we learn for the first time that Miss Prism
took out a male infant in a perambulator twenty-eight years ago and never
returned, although the baby buggy itself was discovered a few weeks later,
containing the manuscript of a work of fiction where the missing baby had
been. Miss Prism, "in a moment of mental abstraction," had placed her
unpublished melodrama in the bassinet, and put the baby in her handbag,
which she left behind in Victoria Station. As the current possessor of the
handbag, Jack Worthing now realizes that he was the mislaid infant and
embraces Miss Prism as his mother, exclaiming "I was the baby you placed
in it." But Miss Prism is unmarried, a regrettable fact that prompts Jack
to paraphrase Christ, when asked for a judgment on the woman taken
in adultery: "after all, who has the right to cast a stone against one who
has suffered? Cannot repentance wipe out an act of folly? … Why should
there be one law for men, and another for women?"[42]

This situation comically dramatizes a central theme of the militant
feminists and purity workers led by Josephine Butler and Ellice Hopkins,
who offered shelter, forgiveness, and rehabilitation to "fallen women" and
condemned all efforts by men to punish them, most notoriously by means
of the Contagious Diseases Acts. Indeed, feminists often cited Christ's tolerance toward the woman taken in adultery as the correct attitude to take.
Josephine Butler, for example, in a much-noted speech to students at the
University of Cambridge, took John 8:7 as her text – "He that is without sin among you, let him cast the first stone at her" – and made it the
centerpiece of her attack on the double standard of sexual morality that
has "more or less coloured and shaped the whole of our social life."[43] By
asking "who has the right to cast a stone?" and exhibiting misdirected tolerance toward Miss Prism as a "fallen woman," Jack slips briefly (and ludi-
crously – that is the point) into the language and role of the "True Man,"

Christ, the model that Josephine Butler and Ellice Hopkins proposed for a new masculinity that would redress longstanding inequities by establishing, to paraphrase Jack, "one law" for both men and women. Jack's act as Ernest, which began as a cover for getting into "dreadful scrapes" in town, draws to a close with quotations of Christ and the Victorian reformers of gender who were demanding of men "precisely the same chastity" that was required of women.

Jack's quotation of Christ in the heat of his identity crisis draws attention to the fact that subjectivity in *Earnest* is a matter of textuality rather than of an internal or core reality. In infancy, Jack was displaced in his perambulator by the manuscript of a melodramatic novel written by Miss Prism, who could not tell the difference between a boy and a book – suggesting that from the beginning Jack's identity was textual, performative rather than natural or "real." Prism's momentary mix up of baby and manuscript not only emphasizes the textuality of the self, but demonstrates that this textuality is so thoroughly concealed from our everyday consciousness that confusing a manuscript and a baby can only seem an outrageous breach of common sense and decorum – something for which, as Miss Prism says, "I never can forgive myself."⁴⁴ In earlier versions of the play, including the licensing manuscript approved by the censor just before the first production of *Earnest*, the infant's textualized identity is given an additional flourish of emphasis. Wilde writes in this early draft of Act 3 that a few weeks after the baby was mislaid, Lady Brancaster (as Lady Bracknell is called in this draft) imagines that the baby "was probably left at the offices of one of those publishers who do not return rejected contributions unless accompanied by stamps." She adds, "I have no doubt that that unfortunate child is at the present moment lying in the waste paper basket of some large commercial [publishing] house."⁴⁵ Perhaps Wilde canceled this passage because it belabored what had already been established, namely that Jack's life is a text – or "a mere mode of fiction," as Wilde would soon describe his own attitude toward life while serving two years at hard labor.⁴⁶

Attempts at autonomous self-fashioning always loop Jack into a text of which he is not the author, whether that text is the ritual of baptism as scripted in the Prayer Book or the word "earnest" itself, with its growing repertoire of meanings that he is unable to transcend or control. This pattern continues to the climactic moment in Act 3 when Jack consults the Army Lists and is officially renamed. Rushing to the bookcase, he *"tears the books out,"* ransacking them for some basis of his identity as Ernest. In an earlier draft of the play, underlining the textual nature of this crisis, Jack also distributes various other books to be searched by Cecily Cardew, Miss Prism, Canon Chasuble, and Lady Bracknell – including railway guides, price lists, and even Robert Hichens's novel *The Green Carnation*, a fictional book about Wilde himself and thus part of the problematic of his own identity.⁴⁷ When Jack finds himself cited as "Ernest John Moncrieff" in the Army Lists, he has not only been renamed but written into an official text that is sanctioned by society. For Jack, who as Lady Bracknell's nephew is now situated inside her orbit of "good society" instead of outside, the point is that "I always told you … my name was Ernest, didn't I? Well, it is Ernest after all. I mean it naturally is Ernest."⁴⁸

Derrida believed that no performative could succeed if it did not repeat a coded precedent, similar to, if not the same as, an actor performing in a play. Building on this point, Judith Butler argues in *Bodies That Matter* that performativity is not an act by which subjects bring into being what they name, for all acting is reiteration – it controls us, as much as, or more than, the other way round. The concluding scenes of *The Importance of Being Earnest* move toward a similar understanding: life is a fiction, as Wilde would later write, but at the same time, all text is context. All identities, including the one Jack has performed as Ernest, are formed under these limitations, and so Jack's identity as Ernest already existed, in a sense, before he came on the scene. Indeed, his name was in the Army Lists before he was born. Jack has become Ernest, as he desired, but to do so he has had to act out, or cite, his textual origins, which are numerous, unstable, and contradictory. They include the rhetoric of feminism and social purity; the Prayer Book and Bible; the homoerotic "music" coded into the name E(a)rnest itself; the melodramatic novel that took Jack's place in the perambulator; the journal of Gwendolen, who by writing him as "Ernest" lays claim to Jack's future; and the official publication on the bookshelf that Jack consults to bring the play to a supposedly happy conclusion.

*The Importance of Being Earnest* is postmodern *avant la lettre*, but at the same time explodes the assumption, prominent in contemporary performance studies, that masquerade releases one from customary and essentialist versions of subjectivity – which are themselves performed. The contextualization of the name "Ernest" helps to account for the conventional destination at which the rebel associated by Lady Bracknell with the French Revolution, class conflict, and anarchist's bombs finally arrives. Although his posing as Ernest has been mostly in conflict with all the authorized meanings of "earnest," Jack in his new identity as "Ernest John Moncrieff" bears the name of the Father, and his lies have become convoluted earnestness. Jack, as Wilde persists in calling him in the stage directions, ends up an engaged man about to be married, a legitimized aristocrat, and the product, through his military father, of British imperialism in India. Like a character in a melodramatic novel, Jack has risen above his marginal position – suddenly transformed by miraculous disclosures of who he "naturally" is – and as a result his rebellious, proto-gay performativity has been neutralized. How appropriate, then, that Miss Prism had difficulty in distinguishing the infant Jack from a character in her own manuscript of melodramatic romance. Instead of liberating him, Jack's derivative self-performance naturalizes him into the Family and the cultural system of which it forms the core.

Yet Jack has also become what he designed himself to be; and his rebellious ways have not only contributed to his identity-formation as Ernest, but some trace of them, at least, will survive it. "Gwendolen," he remarks as the newly certified Ernest, "it is a terrible thing for a man to find out suddenly that all his life he has been speaking nothing but the truth. Can you forgive me?" She can, "for I feel that you are sure to change."[49] Moreover, as we have seen, the homoerotic music of the name Ernest can be heard between the lines of the play from beginning to end. Although pure performativity may be impossible, Jack has accomplished something after all. As Ernest, he will live the paradox of freedom coexisting with constraint, simultaneously a puppet and yet an actor with some limited range for improvisation. As Wilde himself would soon express it in his long letter from prison: "puppets themselves have passions. They will bring a new plot into what they are presenting ... to be entirely free, and at the same time entirely dominated by law, is the eternal paradox of human life that we realize at every moment."

Meanwhile, Algernon Moncrieff, with his own desire to become Ernest, is left hanging at the end of the play, the question of his identity unresolved. The doubling of "Ernest" and "earnest" onto two characters, Algy as well as Jack, demonstrates that it is a performance for *men* which is at stake in the play, and that "the vital Importance of Being Earnest" is not unique to Jack Worthing. But it is not clear how, or whether, Algy's aspirations to become Ernest are going to be fulfilled, even though in the diaries of Cecily Cardew his identity as Ernest was already textualized, waiting for him to "cite" it. At any rate, Wilde does not follow Algy's story further, allowing the curtain to drop just there – perhaps because the story has already been told. That is, Jack has already experienced the limits of individualized performativity – a thwarted actor inhabiting a script that is not, after all, a text of his own writing. Wilde would end his life as a similarly thwarted performer, feeling that after his release from prison he would have no choice but to "alter my name into some other name"[30] – and did so, more than once – with results not less but much more problematic than they were for Jack Worthing.

CHAPTER 5

# The "lost" transcript, sexual acting, and the meaning of Wilde's trials

After *The Importance of Being Earnest* went dark prematurely, closed in response to the outcry that followed its author's arrest for gross indecency, the only play of Oscar Wilde still running in London was the drama of his own life, as he came to understand it in more than metaphorical terms. In this "hideous tragedy," as Wilde would refer to it in prison after three courtroom trials, both plot and character eluded his authorial control, lurching toward a coarse and brutal catastrophe.[1] The mythic prestige that has accrued to the trials in recent years is based on the view that they were not primarily about sexual transgressions, but Foucauldian innovations of personal and group identity, a historic "specification of individuals" which Wilde inaugurated in the courtroom.[2] But as Wilde experienced them, and indeed as they really were, the trials and what followed in his life were less an occasion for iconic identity-formation than self-repression; not the self-authored poem Wilde wanted his life to be, but a puppet-play revolving around "sodomitic" sex and texts. The recent discovery of the lost transcript of one of the trials, along with other archival evidence, makes clear that Wilde's trials were sex trials, contrary to what has become our accepted understanding of them. The lost transcript, although it has been little commented upon to date, will in due course transform our understanding of the trials and of Wilde himself, even as it discloses in surprising and important ways the performativity of sex and texts in which both sides of the case were engaged.

MISREADING THE TRIALS A CENTURY LATER

To read Wilde's trials and imprisonment as *he* did – not merely as tragedy, but a sordid, ignoble one with Wilde himself as the mockery of a tragic hero – runs strongly against the grain of much recent and important scholarship. The tendency of this scholarship has been to invest the trials with large-scale cultural significance, making Wilde in his ordeal the martyred inaugurator of a new gender identity. As Ed Cohen expresses it in *Talk on the Wilde Side*, the prosecution of Wilde on charges of gross indecency "played no small part in crystallizing the concept of 'male homosexuality' in the Victorian sexual imagination." Wilde was characterized in the trials, according to Cohen, as "a kind of sexual actor without explicitly referring to the specificity of his sexual acts," resulting in a reinterpretation of sex that was founded upon the personality of an individual rather than upon a particular sexual behavior. Cohen's argument, which has been influential in its portrayal of the trials as key to the emergence of homosexuality as a new characterological category, is based in part on the belief that lawyers "undertook to impress upon the court *not* that Wilde had engaged in any specific sexual acts," but that he had demonstrated instead a tendency toward "non-normative" relationships more generally. Newspapers, Cohen emphasizes, reproduced this representation of Wilde by publishing reports of the trials "without explicitly referring to the specificity of his sexual acts, and thereby brought into being a new constellation of sexual meanings predicated upon 'personality' and not practices."[3] Similarly, Stephen Arata, relying on newspaper reports of the trials, claims that the focus of Wilde's trials "was less on what he did than on what he was." The evidence for such a view, as Arata notes, is that "press accounts never named and seldom even alluded to the specific sexual acts Wilde was charged with."[4]

But the aversion of Victorian journalism to sexual explicitness was not unique to Wilde's case – indeed, it was inevitable, manifesting itself whenever Victorian journalists wrote about sex, which as a practical matter they were compelled to do without writing about specific sexual acts. For example, William Stead's notorious series on child prostitution, which ran in the *Pall Mall Gazette* a decade before Wilde's trials and set the stage for them, generated a scandal about men legally buying girls as young as thirteen for sex, but in language that provided little or no specificity about any sexual acts involved.[5] A similar reticence marked the newspaper coverage of homosexual sex in the Cleveland Street scandal of 1889, six years before Wilde's arrest for gross indecency. The Cleveland Street affair concerned a male brothel in the West End where aristocratic, homosexual men paid for sex with working-class boys; it resulted in charges of gross indecency against some of the principals in the case, but the most highly placed, including Lord Arthur Somerset and the Earl of Euston, escaped prosecution. Stead's *Pall Mall Gazette* reported these events aggressively, alleging an official cover-up that allowed socially prominent figures in the case to avoid trial, but discussed the actual sexual details of the scandal in very discreet terms. Breaking the story on September 11, 1889, Stead's newspaper identified only "a criminal charge of a very disgraceful nature" lodged against two defendants who had been committed for trial in the case. In its own report, the *Times* described the charges in general terms as well – "conspiring to induce boys to go into a house in Cleveland Street" – and alluded to "evidence we cannot report."[6] The *North London Press*, whose bold reporting (bold for the time) put it on the wrong side of a libel action in the Cleveland Street scandal, referred to the male brothel euphemistically as "a den of infamy," and to acts of gross indecency as "unutterable" and "nameless crimes."[7]

Not just Wilde's, but any homosexual case at the time, would have been, and was, heavily censored in journalistic accounts. In view of this standard of reticence, it seems implausible that the lack of specific reference to sexual acts in newspaper accounts of Wilde's trials could have been responsible to any significant degree, in itself, for the formation of a new, male homosexual identity that did not depend for its existence upon particular sexual acts. As Sean Brady has recently pointed out, furthermore, there was actually less specific detail presented in articles about sodomy in the 1860s than much earlier in the century, due in part to the anxiety with which newspaper writers and editors reacted to the Obscene Publications Act of 1857. Clearly, as Brady claims, "Sex and sexuality between men posed such a threat to British masculinity that any recognition of their existence was destablilising."[8] Knowledge of homosexuality was widespread but tacit, and homosexual self-realization was influenced more by the unspeakability of the concept, producing a closeted identity, than by any intentional effort by the state to construct a new category of "The Homosexual."

Some recent historiography provides us with a new way of understanding the reticence surrounding homosexual scandals of the period, including the Cleveland Street affair and the trials of Wilde. In the Cleveland Street matter, for example, Henry Labouchere, author of the amendment on gross indecency, charged authorities with a cover-up when they failed to arrest and prosecute aristocratic men involved in the scandal. But in an important and richly detailed study of the prosecution of homosexual offenses in the Victorian period, H.G. Cocks concludes that the press, police, and courts maintained a convention of silence on such matters. The social and specifically legal agenda gave high priority to controlling scandal by limiting the extent of public knowledge about the practice of sodomy and other homosexual offenses. While this social policy had the effect of insulating privileged men from publicity and prosecution, the larger and primary objective was to control public discourse and, through silence, both marginalize and minimize sexually deviant behavior. Even when a newspaper prided itself upon reporting what was going on in this sensitive area, as the *North London Press* clearly did in its coverage of the Cleveland Street scandal, this compact of silence made it impossible to identify the crime at issue – i.e., sodomy – and the newspaper was left with no resource but to fall back on euphemistic formulas such as "nameless offences." The consequence of such practices was a form of journalistic and legal discourse in Victorian England that simultaneously referred to male–male desire and yet "tried to cover all traces of its existence with circumlocution and evasion," as Cocks argues.[9] The proceedings of homosexual criminal cases were not even recorded in the official records of the Central Criminal Court, although the proceedings of other criminal trials were summarized in these volumes in great detail. That is why, until recently, there has been no true account of what happened and was said in the courtroom in the trials of Oscar Wilde. Male homosexuality was not an unfamiliar concept to the Victorians, but it was a sexual and gender category defined by its very unspeakability.

What now seems clear, in short, is that journalistic and legal reticence about homosexual acts was a strategically important facet of the Victorian social agenda, and thus the absence of sexual detail in journalistic accounts of Wilde's case does not in itself mean that the trials were about the construction of a gay identity and not primarily about sex. Many critics who do not make that particular argument, however, still regard Wilde's trials as a historical turning point for gender identity, the site where homosexuality was invented. Jeffrey Weeks, in his influential *Sex, Politics and Society*, represents the downfall of Oscar Wilde as "a most significant event for it created a public image of the homosexual" – whereas before the trials, in this view, "there was no sense of homosexuality as an identity." Weeks argues that Wilde, through his trials and imprisonment, was responsible for "creating a new community of knowledge, if not of life and feeling, amongst many men with homosexual leanings."[10] Similarly, Eve Kosofsky Sedgwick identifies Wilde in *Epistemology of the Closet* as "the very embodiment of ... a new turn-of-the-century homosexual identity and fate."[11] Alan Sinfield argues in *The Wilde Century* that the trials contributed significantly to the Foucauldian moment in which the "homosexual" materialized – a "new kind of person," not merely a sodomite, but a mosaic of personality generated by Wilde's trials in which male same-sex love was subsumed in an array of subversive attributes including aestheticism, effeminacy, and dandyism.[12] Even Sinfield's nuanced appraisal of the significance of Wilde's case is primarily retrospective, mapping Foucault's arguments about the "proliferation of sexualities" in the nineteenth century upon the specific site of the trials.

Moe Meyer puts this case in its most extreme form in *The Politics and Poetics of Camp*, arguing that Wilde entered the trials without a "homosexual social identity" because none existed at the time of his arrest in April 1895. Yet, according to this reductive argument, the jail sentence given Wilde at the end of the third trial could only be meted out to an individual "inscribed as a homosexual." This was, for Meyer, the moment that homosexuality came into being as a social identity: "I suggest," he writes, "that between the close of his libel suit against Queensberry on April 5, 1895 and the close of the State's case against him on May 25, The Homosexual was discursively produced." In other words, Meyer continues, "Wilde entered the court as a run-of-the-mill sodomite, but exited as the first homosexual." By this view, Wilde's trials established a "signifying code" for the homosexual, and having done so in a few weeks of April and May 1895, it became possible to convict Wilde – not of sexual crimes, but of perverse "signifying."[13] Meyer's argument is unusual only because of the rhetorical extremity with which it states its case that Wilde's trials were instrumental to the formation of a homosexual identity. Like most such claims, it is very short on historical evidence and long on Foucauldian speculation. Arguments of this type, nevertheless, have given Wilde's trials an assigned meaning and triumphal importance that has been extremely influential. But while this meaning has been imposed upon the trials in recent years, and has indeed become widely accepted, it is not an interpretation that would have made coherent sense to Wilde at the time, and the arguments supporting it lose much of their force when the trials are viewed in the context of their historical moment.

Indeed, H.G. Cocks and others have argued recently that signifying systems identifying homosexuality were already well-established and readily understood by the public long before Wilde's trials. Leisured inactivity, lack of moral purpose, inattention to duty, and giving in to one's "selfish passions and base desires of any sort," as Cocks expresses it, were widely considered unmanly and implied possible deviation from normative male sexuality. Moreover, what was considered "effeminacy" throughout the nineteenth century provided a means for recognizing those inclined to commit "nameless offences," as street terms such as "Molly houses," "Mary Annes," and "Margeries" suggest. This association of effeminacy with homosexuality is reflected in court records where cross-dressing was at issue, as in the well-known scandal involving the female impersonators

Ernest Boulton and Frederick Park in 1869–70. There can be no doubt that Boulton and Park were guilty of sodomy as charged – or at least there was no doubt in the mind of the judge, who observed that their women's attire demonstrated an "unnatural and detestable connection" between the two men, a relationship that the prosecutor described as "unnaturally analogous to that of husband and wife." Some have attributed the acquittal of Boulton and Park to the lack of an interpretive apparatus enabling the Victorians to recognize homosexuality, but as Cocks argues convincingly, it was really a lack of physical evidence that led to the dismissal of charges. Convictions for sodomy were notoriously difficult to obtain because of the evidentiary requirement that both anal penetration and "emission" be proved to have taken place.[14]

In view of this recent historiography, it has become difficult to maintain the view that Boulton and Park were acquitted in 1870 because there would be no, or barely no, public understanding of homosexuality until the trials of Wilde twenty-five years later. Cocks has shown in his elaborate and careful study of court cases involving homosexuality in the mid nineteenth century that trials for sodomy were numerous before the notorious Boulton and Park proceedings in 1870, averaging in fact sixty indictments a year in the 1860s, more than in the 1890s. Of course the availability of the new gross indecency law, with its less elaborate evidentiary requirements and less draconian penalties, ensured that homosexual offenses would be prosecuted increasingly under the 1885 statute and less and less under the old sodomy laws.

Moreover, as Matt Cook points out, the Offences Against the Person Act of 1861 already included *attempted* sodomy and the vaguely conceived act of "indecent assault" as legal categories under which homosexual offenses could be recognized and prosecuted, short of the commission of sodomy itself. Criminalizing a variety of homosexual acts without bothering to name them, the Offences Against the Person Act was legislated three-and-a-half decades before Wilde's trials on charges of so-called "gross indecency." In this context, it is now more difficult than ever to accept the claims of Weeks, Cohen, and others that the Criminal Law Amendment Act of 1885, which created the vaguely configured law against "gross indecency," was really a decisive historical shift that produced, in the form of Wilde's trials, a public identification of "The Homosexual" that was clearly differentiated for the first time from the act of sodomy itself.[15] In short, Clause 11 of the Criminal Law Amendment Act, the so-called "Labouchere Amendment," is less historically important than we have been led to believe in much influential scholarship. It surely did not, in itself, produce the large-scale classification of a homosexual "species" that has been supposed, although it *was* a law that exacted a devastating toll upon Oscar Wilde personally – and not only him, but hundreds of others in the 1890s.

This book is not the first, therefore, to call into question some of the scholarly mythology surrounding the trials of Oscar Wilde. The work of H.G. Cocks, Matt Cook, and Sean Brady, among others, has already cast serious doubt on the view that the trials at the Old Bailey were the Bethlehem where "The Homosexual" was born. Long before Wilde's arrest and conviction in 1895, homosexuality was already differentiated from the act of sodomy as such and was generally and even legally recognized by characterological attributes such as "effeminacy." The statute on gross indecency under which Wilde was convicted was newly enacted, but not decisive; he could also have been prosecuted not only under the old sodomy laws, but also the 1861 Offences Against the Person Act which comprehended all manner of physical contact and gestural behavior in its scope, although no less vaguely articulated than in the Criminal Law Amendment Act under which Wilde was indicted and convicted. Even so, it is helpful to bear in mind Joseph Bristow's nuanced and elegant argument in *Effeminate England* for the historical importance of the "gross indecency" statute and Wilde's trials as part of the long evolvement of homosexuality and what it was coming to "mean" over time. In Bristow's view, affirming the insights of Mary Poovey in *Uneven Developments*, sexual and gender categories do not change or form overnight; they develop, not in a coherent or suddenly completed manner, but "unevenly," taking one shape after another as part of a long process.[16] As Poovey puts it, sexual and gender ideology is "always under construction," and in this light Wilde's trials and the powerful impression they made on Victorian society, and continue to make on us today, are part of a transformative process that is more subtle, and certainly more gradual, than the increasingly implausible scenario that Wilde entered the courtroom in 1895 as a mere "sodomite" and exited as the "first Homosexual."[17]

Wilde's trials, as they actually happened, had much more to do with "sodomy and other acts of gross indecency," as court documents expressed it in Wilde's case, than with what Weeks calls "a new community" and Sinfield terms the "new kind of person" supposed to be modeled on Wilde. Moreover, the recently discovered transcript of the libel trial provides irrefutable evidence against the argument that Wilde was *not* accused of having "engaged in any specific sexual acts," and other evidence points in the same direction. In leaving a note with the porter at Wilde's club – "To

Oscar Wilde, posing as a somdomite" – the Marquess of Queensberry was uttering (although misspelling) a sexual term "not to be spoken among Christians," according to Coke's *Institutes of the Laws of England*, and certainly not to be named in the press or even, except when necessary, courtrooms.[18] The note written by Queensberry, the father of Wilde's lover Lord Alfred Douglas, was therefore an extreme provocation, one to which Wilde responded by suing for criminal libel.[19] Because Queensberry's task as defendant in the libel trial was to prove that Wilde was indeed "posing as a sodomite," the use of the forbidden word was practically unavoidable in arguments and testimony; indeed, it is now undeniable that it was invoked repeatedly, not only by Queensberry's counsel, but on occasion by Wilde himself and other principals in the case. This fact, borne out in the newly available transcript of the libel trial, suggests that the silence of the Victorian press on the subject of sodomy and other sexual acts was more the result of a consistent, longstanding practice of censoring homosexually specific details than the first sign that a gay sensibility transcending particular sexual acts was being born.

### THE "LOST" TRANSCRIPT OF WILDE'S TRIAL

The provenance of the recently discovered transcript of Wilde's first courtroom trial is shrouded in mystery, and its immense importance to the future of Wilde studies requires that the mystery be addressed, particularly in view of the fact that some scholars have yet to be convinced of its authenticity. The transcript, whose existence was previously unknown except to a few people, turned up when an individual who insists on remaining anonymous brought it to the British Library, stuffed in carrier bags, for an exhibition on the centenary of Wilde's death in 2000. At that time the transcript came to the attention of Merlin Holland, the grandson of Wilde and editor of his correspondence, who immediately understood its significance. Holland obtained permission from the donor of the manuscript to publish it on condition that the identity of the donor would remain a secret. The transcript later appeared in book form, edited by Holland, in 2003 in England, in 2004 in America, and the transcript itself was given on permanent loan to the British Library with a strict condition of anonymity. The British Library accepted permanent loan of the transcript after being satisfied of its authenticity and with the recognition that divulging the identity of the donor could lead to removal of the transcript and its return to private hands, with incalculable loss not only to the library but to scholarship. Who was the donor who "owned"

the transcript? Where had it been all these years? These questions cannot be answered, although the answers are known. In general terms, it
can be said that the transcript was not an official court document, but
was commissioned by someone with a vital stake in the trial, someone
who required a close monitoring of everything that was said in the courtroom. Afterwards, the transcript, having been privately commissioned,
remained in private hands without being auctioned or otherwise sold off.
Furthermore, permanent deposit of the transcript in the British Library
under condition of anonymity was directly connected with the potentially
great market value of the document and a desire to ensure that it would
not be sold and perhaps lost to this and future generations of scholars.[20] As
of this writing, however, the newly published transcript has been mainly
discussed in book reviews, appreciatively but superficially for the most
part, without recognition of the fundamental ways in which it will transform our understanding of Wilde and his trials.

The holograph trial transcript, now one of the top-security items in
the British Library, has been seen first-hand by very few people. When
I examined it in the course of researching this book, its authenticity was
immediately evident, from the transcription of the police court hearing
of March 9, 1895 to the verbatim report of the three-day trial of April
3–5, a report that differs fundamentally from the abbreviated and heavily censored accounts previously available. As H.G. Cocks points out in
*Nameless Offences*, official transcripts were not produced for homosexual
sex trials in the Victorian period and are omitted from the Old Bailey
sessions papers, except for a bare mention of the verdict; Wilde's case was
entirely typical in being "blacked out" in this way, although the usual
brief mention in the sessions papers occurred.[21] The absence of official
records in cases such as Wilde's was part of the Victorian compact of
silence on homosexuality, and such prosecutions were the result of a
social policy that distanced and erased homosexuality from the cultural
record even as homosexual men were targeted for surveillance and, where
possible, harsh punishment.

Based on my own examination of the transcript, I can state confidently
that it has been edited to a high standard by Merlin Holland for book
publication. But while scrupulously accurate in editing the courtroom
proceedings, Holland has omitted some of the "framing" material in the
original documents that would have provided key information toward
answering two crucial questions: Where did the transcript come from?
Why, and for whom, was it produced? This is not the place to go into a
detailed textual analysis of the transcript, but it is important to note that

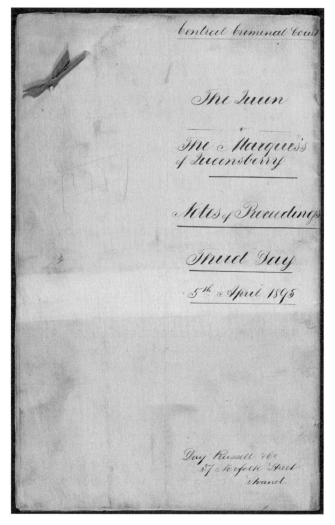

Figure 6a. Photograph of the recently discovered transcript of Oscar
Wilde's first courtroom trial. (British Library)

the framing materials of these documents, such as notations on the outer
wrappers, contain answers to these fundamental questions and provide an
explanation of the role that they played in the trial – and thus a rationale
for their existence and function.

The title pages of the separate police court hearing and trial transcripts
reveal that the firm of Day, Russell & Co., 37 Norfolk Street, Strand,

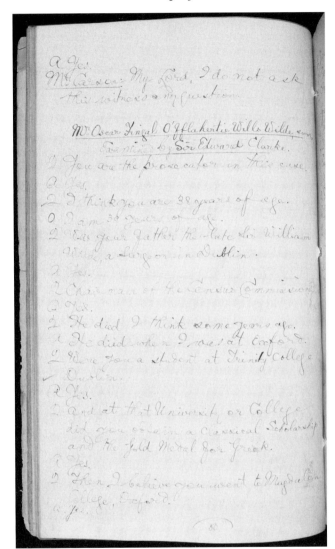

Figure 6b. Photograph of the recently discovered transcript of Oscar Wilde's first courtroom trial. (British Library)

prepared the holograph transcript from shorthand notes taken by another private firm. Charles Russell himself is mentioned in the transcript title pages as having "instructed" Queensberry's lawyers, Edward Carson, C.F. Gill, and A.E. Gill, in the preparation of their case for the defense. Russell and his associates assisted with taking down depositions, filing Queensberry's "plea of justification," and – as the trial transcript makes clear – preparing and transmitting to the defense team the longhand transcription of shorthand notes from the hearing and trial. News reports by the BBC and others have inaccurately characterized the transcript as a "shorthand report," whereas in fact it is a longhand transcription from shorthand notes whose whereabouts remain unknown, if indeed they still exist. Inscriptions on the fly-leaves and title pages of the several portions of the longhand transcript reveal that one copy of the proceedings went to Queensberry's lead defense lawyer, Edward Carson, and another to his associate A.E. Gill, both of whose names are inscribed in script on the cover sheets. The copies designated for Gill are frequently marked with red pencil in the margins, drawing attention to important exchanges in the hearing and trial – including those having to do, for example, with the admissibility of contested evidence. The longhand trial transcript, in other words, was prepared for the day-to-day use of Queensberry's lawyers as they assembled and presented the case for his defense against Wilde's charge of criminal libel.

Given this etiology of the long-lost trial transcript, the vital issue of its significance can now be addressed – it will inevitably and fundamentally alter the way we understand Wilde and his trials. It will no longer be possible to maintain that Wilde's adversaries in court "did not overtly charge him with sexual transgressions," or that anything other than sexual behavior was at the heart of his case.[22] Not only does the longhand transcript make clear that sodomy and other sexual acts were the central issue in the libel trial, the first of Wilde's three trials, but other, long-neglected archival resources provide additional evidence of the crucial role that sexual behavior played in the second and third trials in which Wilde was accused of gross indecency. This is not to say that the legal system had overcome its anxieties about naming or discussing sodomy; far from it, for the predictable absence of a full, official transcript of the proceedings explains why Queensberry's legal team needed to hire shorthand writers from a private firm to give them access to a day-by-day record of the trial.[23] What was too lurid for even the law reports to publish was certainly out of the question for the press to report; no Victorian newspaper would – or could – have published the sexually explicit details contained in the transcript of the first trial. It was on the same principle that the press did not publish explicit sexual detail in connection with the Cleveland Street scandal that preceded Wilde's case by six years, and the *Pall Mall Gazette* did not refer to specific sexual acts in W.T. Stead's important series of articles on child prostitution in 1885. However, the recently discovered transcript of the libel trial makes transparently clear that Wilde's trial was above all a sex trial.

In prison, Wilde would recognize himself, indeed most of humanity, as actors bound to a script that left little room for improvisation and self-definition. There was no discernable "real" self to refer to, only an enactment imposed by external forces in the puppet-theatre of life, as he came to view it. The external forces that inhibited Wilde's self-definition in this way were numerous and powerful, but all of them were set in motion by a new law forbidding gross indecency between men – a law whose very meaning was uncertain in Wilde's time, and is perhaps even more so today. The crisis of meaning in the term "gross indecency" was influenced by a crisis in masculine subjectivity itself, as the origins and early implementation of the law on gross indecency indicate. And gross indecency was all about sex, even if what it had to say about sex was radically inconclusive.

The law under which Wilde was prosecuted – section 11 of the Criminal Law Amendment Act of 1885, criminalizing gross indecency between men – was legislated in the midst of widespread, contentious debate over what should be considered "true" manhood. Drafted as a last-minute amendment by the Radical M.P. Henry Labouchere, who was inspired by a private dossier on homosexual activities in London that W.T. Stead had provided him as agitation for passage of the Act reached fever pitch, the statute forbade "any male, in public or private, committing any act of gross indecency with another male."[24] Section 11, however, did not say what exactly constituted gross indecency. It was a short segment of a multifaceted piece of sex legislation resulting from a long and hard-fought campaign by feminist and social-purity reformers to protect proletarian girls from sexual predators. In this "holy war," as its feminist leader Josephine Butler called it in her polemic *An Earnest Appeal*, another and profounder aim was to rouse the consciences of men "as by earthquake shock" and put an end to the double standard of morality, not by lowering the standard of conduct for women but by raising the expectations for men.[25] "That beautiful word of Purity," as Josephine Butler called it, was the battle cry of this holy war, which would be won only when the "law of purity" was equally applied to men and women.[26]

A product of the developing controversy over what it meant to be a "man," the law on gross indecency was so new – enacted only ten years before Wilde was arrested for violating it – and so imprecise in its language that an important part of the proceedings against him was to determine exactly what gross indecency was. Legal experts themselves were perplexed, but pointed out at the time that the new law was radically different from the existing law on indecency, for Henry Labouchere had written a statute that only males could be charged with violating, whether in public or private. As Frederick Mead and A.H. Bodkin pointed out in their legal handbook published soon after passage of the new law, the old law on indecency applied equally to men and women and stipulated that an indecent act could occur only when committed in a public place in the presence of other persons.[27] The more private the act, the less certain would be its supposed indecency. Indeed, according to Sir James Fitzjames Stephen's authoritative *Digest of Criminal Law*, the old law on indecency could be violated only when a so-called indecent act was perpetrated in such specifically non-private spaces as "the inside of an omnibus ... the roof of a house visible from the back windows of several houses ... the inside of a urinal open to the public," etc.[28] By defining gross indecency as occurring "in public or private," section 11 of the Criminal Law Amendment Act was equipped with a flexibility that invited state control over male behavior to a somewhat greater extent than before – in the matter of "indecency," that is; sodomy itself had long been a felony, of course, whether done in public or private. That is an important caveat, and one often lost sight of in scholarly discussions of gross indecency; i.e., the 1885 statute was not the first law to target homosexual acts that were committed in private and consensually. Few could be arrested and prosecuted for sodomy if the law applied only to acts committed in public view; the difficulty was to secure the needed evidence of anal penetration and "emission" regarding acts that were done in private in the first place.

But despite clear differences between the new law of gross indecency and old-fashioned indecency, the fact is that no generally acknowledged meaning of the newer term, gross indecency, existed by 1895. This indeterminacy did not prevent Henry Labouchere, author of the law on gross indecency, from declaring in his magazine *Truth* at the end of the third trial, "the verdict of the jury in the case of Wilde ... was amply justified by the evidence set before it." Writing only days after Wilde's conviction, Labouchere makes no attempt to explain the meaning of gross indecency or identify any behavior by Wilde that constituted it, saying only that "Wilde and [co-defendant Alfred] Taylor were tried on a clause in the Criminal Law Amendment Act which I had inserted in order to render it possible for the law to take cognisance of proceedings like theirs."[29] The vagueness with which Labouchere expressed himself as to the meaning of gross indecency after Wilde's trials – "these iniquities," "proceedings like theirs," etc. – was also characteristic of pronouncements on the subject in legal publications that were not so limited by the self-censorship that made sex unprintable in Victorian newspapers and magazines. As one legal analyst, R.W. Burnie, wrote in 1885, Labouchere's amendment had produced a "class of newly created offences" – a welcome development, Burnie asserts in his commentary, because "there were many outrages on decency which could not be dealt with under the former statutes against unnatural acts."

This claim – that the new law on gross indecency would enable prosecution of "outrages" that previously "could not be dealt with" – was precisely the same justification for it that Labouchere offered in the aftermath of Wilde's conviction. Moreover, as recent historical work by H.G. Cocks and others has shown, it was not really true, since there was hardly any form of male–male sexual contact that could not be prosecuted under existing laws concerning sodomy, attempted sodomy, and "offences against the person." But in Burnie's legal commentary of 1885, just as in Labouchere's article in *Truth* a decade later, the "offences" and "outrages on decency" that could at last be prosecuted as gross indecency are never named or even indirectly identified. Burnie's now-rare book – its full title is *The Criminal Law Amendement Act, 1885: With Introduction, Commentary, and Forms of Indictments* – functioned at the time as a practical guidebook to all aspects of the new law. But nowhere in his discussion of gross indecency does Burnie offer any clue as to what it is, or how to recognize it.[30] These contradictions are further evidence that the late Victorians were well aware of homosexuality, but labored ingeniously to find ways of referring to it while simultaneously covering all traces of its existence with either artful circumlocutions or a cloak of silence. It was a situation certain to bewilder even those who were well-informed on the subject.

Indeed, in addition to Burnie's, several other commentaries on the Criminal Law Amendment Act were published between the passage of the bill and Wilde's prosecution ten years later, usually with the purpose of interpreting the statute for police and lawyers. One of these – written by an Inner Temple barrister and a police court magistrate – went through many editions after its first appearance in 1885, and emphasized the problematic aspects of section 11 of the Act. The authors, Frederick Mead and Archibald H. Bodkin, admit that it is by no means clear what constitutes gross indecency, citing in their 1890 edition a courtroom trial to illustrate the point: "For instance, in a recent case tried at the Central Criminal

Court, among other facts it was proved that two male persons kissed each other under circumstances which showed that the act was immoral and unnatural; this, though clearly indecent, could hardly be called 'an act of gross indecency,' within the meaning of this section."[31]

Not only did it require a trial to determine that men kissing each other was "clearly indecent" – yet not *grossly* indecent "within the meaning of this section" – but in other respects the new law under which Wilde was accused was confusing to legal scholars. For example, wrote Mead and Bodkin in their 1890 edition, "It is difficult to understand why the section is limited to conjoint acts by two or more persons and to male persons." Their observation got at the heart of the matter, for under the new law it was impossible for a man to act indecently on his own, alone, or with a woman – he could only be prosecuted for "committing any act of gross indecency with another male," as the law expressed it. Even though "indecent" kissing between men had been held not to be an act of *gross* indecency, it remained certain, the authors emphasized, that one could be guilty of gross indecency without "sufficiently direct connection with a more abominable crime" – in other words, without committing the act of sodomy itself.[32] In this analysis from their long-forgotten legal handbook published five years before Wilde's trials, Mead and Bodkin make clear that they cannot identify a particular sexual act that by definition counted as gross indecency, yet everything in their spectrum of possibilities was sexual behavior of some type.

Indeed, a great variety of specific sexual behavior gradually came to be admitted as evidence of gross indecency – including, in various times and places, mutual masturbation, oral sex, placing one's hands on the "private parts" of another man, and sodomy itself.[33] Furthermore, allegations of each of these sexual activities were allowed as evidence in Wilde's own trials, even though misleading and inaccurate accounts of the proceedings have obscured this fact. The key component of gross indecency, then, was sexual behavior, and this was true even if the behavior was only intended or proposed, and could not be shown to have taken place – just as "attempted sodomy" had long been a charge brought against men who demonstrated an effort or intent to commit sodomy, but could not be shown to have actually done it. This principle of intent was borne out in Wilde's case when he was accused of soliciting certain boys and young men for sodomy over a period of years but not of consummating the act with them. Intent, as opposed to actual behavior, continued to be applied in cases after Wilde's. For example, a defendant was convicted of gross indecency in 1922 for telephoning a man he thought to be a procurer and asking "if he could have two boys at 10 shillings each that evening" – even though no boys were provided or even approached.[34] Moreover, a case heard in 1954 – little more than a decade before the law on gross indecency, after much agitation, was finally repealed – made clear that an act of gross indecency could be consummated even when the participants in the act did not touch each other. Two men were found by police in a shed making "indecent exhibitions" to each other without establishing physical contact. On appeal, the verdict of guilty of gross indecency was upheld.[35]

In addition to premeditating or committing a range of sexual acts, what might be termed "atmospheric" details could also become important if somehow connected to implied sexual behavior that suggested gross indecency. For example, although unreported in nearly all accounts of Wilde's trials, the presence of face powder on the pillows of his rooms at the Savoy Hotel was used as evidence against him in the third and final trial, in which he was at last found guilty of gross indecency. Stylistic details such as these, when framed in a sexual context, continued to be important in gross-indecency cases after Wilde. In 1918, a man's possession of two powder puffs was allowed as evidence in his trial for gross indecency on the testimony of two boys who said he accosted them in a public urinal. "It is well-known," stated the appellate judgment against him, "... that persons who commit abominable crimes or acts of gross indecency with male persons make use of appliances such as powder and powder-puffs."[36]

Although prosecutions of gross indecency soared in the 1890s, while prosecutions of sodomy dropped off dramatically, it is important to recognize that the focus of the gross indecency statute was the prosecution of various types of sexual behavior between men. The silence of the statute as to what that behavior consisted of, in specific terms, does not mean that the focus was being shifted from specific sex acts to the classfication of a homosexual "type" of person. As we have seen, Victorians were already well-equipped to recognize homosexuality as a characterological type, but they were not prepared to talk about it except when absolutely necessary – and even then, as in court proceedings, the talk was shrouded in euphemism and withheld as much as possible from the public. Part of the inestimably great value of the lost and now recovered transcript of Wilde's first trial is that it breaks through that veil of silence and allows us a glimpse of homosexual culture. The Victorian code of silence on this matter, therefore, hardly means that homosexuality did not exist before Wilde – and the fact that so many scholars today believe that Wilde was the "first Homosexual" is testimony to the power of a social policy of silence whose entire point and purpose was to erase all traces of the existence of homosexuality even while policing it. The lost transcript of Wilde's trial breaks that silence at last, allowing us to read between the lines of the vaguely written law on gross indecency and other legal and social texts designed to control homosexuality while at the same refusing to recognize its existence.

Labouchere's gross indecency amendment to the Criminal Law Amendment Act did not, therefore, produce the revolutionary effect that has often been claimed – the effect, that is, of criminalizing for the first time a set of male–male behaviors that had nothing to do with sodomy or with sex as such, but much to do with specifying and outlawing a stylistics of living that we now call homosexuality. In reality, the law on gross indecency neither enlarged the scope of the law in this area nor introduced anything new. H.G. Cocks's remarkable archival work in court records shows that by the beginning of the nineteenth century almost any advance or condition of intimacy between men could be prosecuted as an attempt to commit sodomy, including "a great variety of sexual acts, overtures, and invitations."[37] This fact does not mean that everyone agreed on what was illegal and what was not in same-sex relations – indeed, the unspeakability of homosexuality as an open secret made it likely that even legal commentators and lawyers would be uncertain and even bewildered when addressing this subject, as indeed they often were when writing about the meaning of gross indecency after Parliament's enactment of the new law.

Even Henry Labouchere, author of the gross indecency statute, was clueless at the time of Wilde's trials about the extent and nature of the implementation of the law he had written a decade ago. Labouchere was under the mistaken impression that prosecutions for gross indecency were infrequent by 1895, so much so that the law was in danger, he said, of becoming a "dead letter."[38] The truth of the matter was very different: in 1895 in London, according to the annual report of the Metropolitan Police to Parliament, arrests and convictions for gross indecency were far more numerous than for any other category of homosexual offense: thirty-five arrests and twenty-eight convictions, numbers that were slightly lower but still comparable to two years earlier (forty-two arrests, twenty-one convictions in 1893). In 1898, however, in the wake of Wilde's trials, the number of committals and convictions reached a high-water mark (fifty-two arrests, thirty convictions). The numbers of arrests and convictions for gross indecency had indeed been gradually on the rise since the year after the law's enactment in 1885, when only two people were charged in London and neither convicted. In the meantime, sodomy and attempted sodomy prosecutions fell off dramatically in the city; in 1895 there were only three prosecutions for sodomy and six for "intent to commit sodomy."[39] As Wilde's case dramatically illustrates – now that we can see what actually transpired in the first trial, thanks to the recently recovered trial transcript – gross indecency cases allowed prosecutors to cite a range of sexual, gestural, and even verbal behavior as evidence against the defendant. Indeed, the charges could, and did in Wilde's case, include accusations of both sodomy and attempted sodomy as part of the evidence that gross indecency had occurred. Some key factors that influenced the popularity of charging someone with gross indecency instead of sodomy included the fact that the evidentiary standard for gross indecency was much less stringent than for sodomy. In addition, the comparatively light sentence for gross indecency (a maximum of two years in prison at hard labor) made it more likely that juries would convict a defendant than if he were facing the much harsher penalties for sodomy (even though it had not been a capital crime since 1861) – as the roughly 50 percent conviction rate in gross indecency cases in the 1890s suggests.

Of the hundreds of gross indecency cases tried in the 1890s in London alone, is it really true or even plausible that Wilde's was so distinctly different that it resulted in the consolidation of a new gender concept and social identity, "The Homosexual," as many now assume? Indeed, can we even be sure that Wilde's case was instrumental in defining and consolidating the much less important concept of gross indecency? The answer to both questions is demonstrably no – we have no idea what happened in the overwhelming majority of late-Victorian prosecutions for gross indecency, given the Victorian code of silence that governed discourse on all levels about homosexuality, and until very recently we could have only a distorted, house-of-mirrors view of what happened in Wilde's trials. Perhaps all that we can safely say is that it was clear, by the end of the proceedings against Wilde, that a conviction on charges of gross indecency would require evidence of specific sexual acts, or intended acts, between males, ranging from sodomy to at least certain kinds of touching and self-display. Although "lifestyle" issues could be considered, such as a man wearing face powder or carrying powder-puffs, these atmospherics of self-presentation would have to be connected to what was centrally at stake – the sexual behavior of the defendant. Gross indecency was a sex crime – not a Foucauldian "specification of individuals," and it was not the first law on the books to be concerned with a variety of homosexual acts, whether done in public or in private.

THE SEX CRIMES OF OSCAR WILDE: THE FIRST TRIAL

Queensberry's counsel framed his defense in explicitly sexual language, even before the trial began, in the so-called "plea of justification." This pre-trial pleading argued that the alleged libel of Wilde was in fact the truth and published for the public benefit, and at the same time provided Carson with a map for his presentation in *Wilde* v. *Queensberry* over three days in April 1895. Filed in the Central Criminal Court ten days before the trial convened, the plea of justification was preceded by an indictment of Queensberry for libeling Wilde, one framed explicitly in terms of sodomy. The indictment found that Queensberry had written and published "a false scandalous malicious and defamatory libel in the form of a card … 'For Oscar Wilde posing as somdomite' meaning thereby that the said Oscar Fingal O'fflahertie Wills Wilde had committed and was in the habit of committing the abominable crime of buggery with mankind."[40]

Queensberry's plea of justification responded to the indictment in kind, providing the names of young men whom Wilde was alleged to have solicited for sodomy, and with whom he was said to have committed other sexual acts. For example, in February and May 1892 at the Albermarle Hotel, according to Queensberry's plea of justification, Wilde "did solicit and incite one Edward Shelley to commit sodomy and other acts of gross indecency and … did then indecently assault and commit acts of gross indecency and immorality with the said Edward Shelley." The language of Queensberry's plea confirms that sodomy was one of many sexual acts upon which the charge of gross indecency against Wilde was founded, even though the other acts were not specified. The plea of justification continued with a compilation of men and boys with whom "Wilde had committed the offences aforementioned and the said sodomitical practices for a long time with impunity and without detection." When Wilde saw the contents of the plea of justification, he had to have known, at that moment, that although he was the nominal prosecutor in the libel trial, he would become the defendant in reality and the case against him would be founded on his sex life, whose details Queensberry and the spies employed by him had ascertained.

In several instances Queensberry's plea of justification states that Wilde solicited a particular male for "sodomy and other acts of gross indecency," then adds, ambiguously as to sodomy, that he "did then and there commit the said other acts of gross indecency and immorality."[41] But what other sexual "acts" was the plea of justification referring to? The answer is evident in the uncensored transcript, which makes clear for the first time the centrality of sexual behavior to the libel trial. Among much explicit testimony that was not included or bowdlerized in earlier accounts of the trial is Edward Carson's interrogation of Wilde about his conduct with Alfred Wood:

CARSON: Did you ever have any immoral practices with Wood?
WILDE: Never in my life.
CARSON: Did you ever open his trousers?
WILDE: Oh, no!
CARSON: Put your hand upon his person?
WILDE: Never.
CARSON: Did you ever put your person between his legs?
WILDE: Never.
CARSON: You say that?
WILDE: Yes.
CARSON: I say to you that several nights in Tite Street you did that.[42]

Also omitted in earlier accounts of the libel trial were the sexual acts attributed to Wilde as Carson's questioning turned to Edward Shelley, referring to an evening in February 1892 when the eighteen-year-old Shelley visited Wilde's rooms at the Albermarle Hotel:

CARSON: Did he stay all night and leave the next morning at eight o'clock?
WILDE: No.
CARSON: What?
WILDE: Certainly not with me; I say no.
CARSON: Did you commence, when he was in the sitting room, embracing him?
WILDE: Certainly not.
CARSON: Did you ever embrace him?
WILDE: Never.
CARSON: Did you kiss him?
WILDE: Never.
CARSON: Did you put your hand on his person?
WILDE: Never.
CARSON: And then bring him into your bedroom?
WILDE: Never.
CARSON: Sleep in the same bed with him all night?
WILDE: Never.
CARSON: Each of you having taken off all your clothes, did you take his person in your hand in bed?

Later, Carson turned his attention to Wilde's relationship with Ernest Scarfe:

CARSON: Did you ever kiss him?
WILDE: Never in my life.

CARSON: Or caress him in any way?
WILDE: No.[43]

Then, Carson moved on Walter Grainger, "about sixteen," a servant of Lord Alfred Douglas who visited Wilde in Goring:

CARSON: Did you ask him to come into your bedroom?
WILDE: Never in my life.
CARSON: Or into your bed?
WILDE: No.[44]

Finally, Carson disclosed his plan to call various witnesses who would testify about Wilde's sexual behavior, including Charles Parker, one of Wilde's proletarian "victims" named in Queensberry's plea of justification – "he will tell you how he was brought to bed by Mr. Wilde and he will tell you of the shocking immoralities which he was led to perpetrate on that occasion." The masseur at the Savoy Hotel, a man named Migge, "will tell you that he was astonished upon going unexpectedly one morning into Mr. Wilde's room to find a boy lying in his bed. And the servants, some of them in the same hotel, will be brought and they will tell you the disgusting filth in which they found the bedclothes on more than one occasion."[45] At this critical juncture, with witnesses like Parker and Migge ready to testify, Wilde consulted with his lawyer and acquiesced in a verdict of "not guilty" on his charge of libel against Queensberry. In view of this development, the judge pronounced it unnecessary to listen further to "prurient details which can have no bearing upon the matter which is already concluded by the assent of the prosecutor to an adverse verdict."[46] By consenting to a not-guilty verdict for Queensberry in the libel trial, Wilde was therefore able to head off the disclosure of even more "prurient details" about his sexual activity than had already been presented. But there were too many already, as the uncensored transcript finally makes clear, and within three weeks he had been arrested and put on trial for gross indecency.

### THE SEX CRIMES OF OSCAR WILDE: THE SECOND AND THIRD TRIALS

Although there are no known surviving transcripts of the ensuing criminal trials – the first of which ended in a hung jury, the second in Wilde's conviction – it is inescapably clear that specific sexual acts were at the heart of the case in these proceedings too. The centrality of sex in the criminal trials, however, was carefully obscured in H. Montgomery Hyde's first edition of

Figure 7. Wilde appears subdued and thoughtful as sketched from a side view in the courtroom by an unidentified artist in 1895. (Uncataloged item in the Clark Memorial Library, UCLA)

the standard account of the trials, *The Trials of Oscar Wilde* (1948), which omitted all reference to sodomy and other specific sexual acts. In later editions of his book on the trials, beginning in 1962, Hyde enlarged his narrative to include some, but not nearly all, of the sexually explicit material he had found in *The Trial of Oscar Wilde: From the Shorthand Reports*, a rare, privately printed volume of 1906 that is closer in time to the trials than any other book-length account, and much more straightforward in its presentation of sexual detail.[47] Yet *Shorthand Reports* has been cited rarely in accounts of Wilde's trials. Michael Foldy, for example, does not mention the book at all in his recent *Trials of Oscar Wilde*, and Ed Cohen refers to it only once in *Talk on the Wilde Side*, dismissing it as only another account of the trials compiled from newspaper reports – a claim that cannot be reconciled with the raw language and graphic detail of *Shorthand Reports*.[48] None of this sexual detail appears in Montgomery Hyde's primary source, the shamelessly sanitized *Oscar Wilde: Three Times Tried*, edited by Christopher Millard ("Stuart Mason") and first published in 1912. But in later editions of his own now-canonical book, Hyde relies on *Shorthand Reports* considerably, quoting word-for-word much of the narrative summary and testimony he found there, a small portion of it quite sexual, but never identifying *Shorthand Reports* as his source. For example, Hyde in later editions of his book follows *Shorthand Reports* in reporting Charles Parker's testimony that Wilde "committed the act of sodomy upon me," paying him £2 afterward.[49] According to Hyde in 1962 and later editions, again duplicating the 1906 *Shorthand Reports*, Charles Parker states, "I was asked by Wilde to imagine that I was a woman and that he was my lover. I had to keep up this illusion. I used to sit on his knees and he used to play with my privates as a man might amuse himself with a girl."[50] In Hyde's revised account, nearly all of this sexually explicit detail occurs in the course of narrating Wilde's first criminal trial – rather than the second one, in which he was found guilty – and in the context of an examination of Charles Parker conducted by prosecuting attorney Charles Gill.

Although there are a few sexual references in his revised account of the trials, all derived from the 1906 *Shorthand Reports*, Hyde self-censors many sexual details that he found in the much earlier narrative. Consequently, the sexual content of the criminal proceedings remains muted and distorted in spite of Hyde's claim in the preface to later editions that he had corrected the "discretion" that marred the first edition of his *Trials of Oscar Wilde*. In Hyde's account, for example, Alfred Wood testifies that he and Wilde would put their hands inside each other's trousers, but "it was a long time … before I would allow him to actually do the act of indecency." In the more explicit *Shorthand Reports*, however, Wood says, "It was a long time … before I would allow him to actually do the act of sodomy."[51] In addition, although Hyde reports that staff members at the Savoy Hotel saw Wilde in bed with an unnamed "boy" and stated that the bedsheets in his room were "stained in a peculiar way," he omits the vivid testimony quoted in *Shorthand Reports*, attributed to Emily Becca of the Savoy: "The bed-linen was stained. The colour was brown. The towels were similarly discoloured. One of the pillows was marked with face-powder. There was excrement in one of the utensils in the bedroom."[52]

Not only is the *Shorthand Reports* version more sexually specific than Hyde's narrative, it provides a disarmingly frank explanation that could allow no doubt about what was being referred to in such passages: "It may be explained here … that the sodomistic act has much the same effect as an enema inserted up the rectum. There is an almost immediate discharge, though not, of course, to the extent caused by the enema operation."[53]

This passage alone should put to rest the widespread notion that the word "sodomy" itself may have had a range of possible references and lacked any agreed-upon, specific, sexual meaning. While gross indecency remained unspecified in statutory language for as long as it existed, sodomy itself was very precisely defined in law: "Every one commits the felony called sodomy ... who (a.) Carnally knows any animal; or, (b.) Being a male, carnally knows any man or any woman (*per anum*)."[54]

Hyde also omits from his account of the third trial the sexually detailed summary he found in *Shorthand Reports* of the testimony of Edward Shelley, an employee of the publisher John Lane who had become involved with Wilde. Whereas Hyde reports vaguely, "according to his [Shelley's] story Wilde had forced him to commit indecencies with him on two separate occasions," the account in the 1906 narrative is far more specific as to the sexual activity that was alleged to have occurred:

The witness had been subjected by the prisoner to attempts at improper conduct. Oscar had, to be plain, on several occasions, placed his hand on the private parts of the witness and sought to put his, witness's, hand in the same indelicate position as regards Wilde's own person. Witness resented these acts at the time; had told Wilde not to be "a beast", and the latter expressed his sorrow. "But I am so fond of you, Edward," he had said.[55]

With regard to the second trial, Hyde omits the sexually explicit portion of the opening statement of prosecutor Charles Gill, who arose "amidst a breathless silence," according to the 1906 *Shorthand Reports*, to accuse Wilde of employing Alfred Taylor to put him in touch with "a number of young men who were in the habit of giving their bodies, or selling them, to other men for the purpose of sodomy." When Wilde visited Taylor's dark, perfumed rooms on Little College Street, "on nearly every occasion ... a young man was present with whom he committed the act of sodomy. The names of various young men connected with these facts were mentioned in turn."[56]

What is remarkable about the 1906 *Shorthand Reports* and the newly discovered transcript of the first trial is the extent to which, considered together, they reveal that all three trials were focused intently on specific sexual acts by Wilde and on investing the vaguely conceived and tentative concept of gross indecency with detailed sexual content – far more so than has been acknowledged in scholarship to date. These accounts of the proceedings portray Wilde as being on trial pre-eminently for sex crimes, and they provide rich and specific detail about the actual behavior that was supposed to have constituted his guilt – although the dearth of precedent meant that Wilde's case was functioning to some extent as the proving ground for what actually would constitute gross indecency. Influential arguments that the trials were primarily about a new homosexual identity, and only vaguely or incidentally about sex, do not accurately reflect what happened in the courtroom. To see Wilde and his ordeal as the crucible of gay sensibility is surely a good thing if it has produced "homosexuality as an identity," in Jeffrey Weeks's phrase, or been instrumental in producing it – but it now seems clear that this myth-ologizing of the man and his trials cannot be supported by a record of the events as they actually occurred in court and, later, prison. The problem has been compounded by the fact that our knowledge of Wilde's trials has been formed by accounts that are deliberately inaccurate.

If the trials were not the enactment of a new homosexual identity, des-pite what has been made of them a century later, they were clearly an enactment of the meaning of gross indecency. Given the puzzlement of Victorian legal commentators about what gross indecency really was, Wilde's trials, along with some others before and after that we know much less about, were likely part of a process that attached tangible meaning to the concept. One cannot say of Wilde's case that any one sexual act con-stituted gross indecency, but one can say with certainty that a number of specific sexual acts were crucially at issue – not only, or mainly, Wilde's unconventional style in other areas of his life, such as frequenting incense-permeated rooms and associating with young men far beneath him on the social scale. As Wilde's case and others suggest, the statute on gross indecency was, or came to be, concerned mainly with a range of sexual traffic between men; yet, even though it was one of numerous sex laws consolidated in the Criminal Law Amendment Act, the statute on gross indecency had nothing specific to say about sex at all. Against this back-ground of a law so inexplicit in its language, so notoriously problematic with respect to what it actually "meant," the trials of Oscar Wilde can be perceived as a dramatic event, although not the only one of its kind, in which the actors produced and refined the effectual meaning of gross indecency. The term, as its significance took shape in the proceedings at the Old Bailey, had everything to do with sex, and sex in turn had every-thing to do with texts and performance.

### SEX AND TEXTS IN THE TRIALS OF WILDE

With the publication of the lost transcript of Wilde's first trial, we can appreciate for the first time how extensively and crucially these proceed-ings revolved around not only sexuality, but also textuality – around novels, letters, and poems that were portrayed in the courtroom as theatri-cal sites where Wilde became visible as a bad actor, performing or "posing" sodomy and gross indecency in, or through, texts that he wrote or was associated with. These written texts were interpreted as staging areas where the histrionic presence of Wilde could be observed, but they also reinforced the foundation of the case against him – a case that was all about sex, even when the lawyers talked about texts. At issue were texts in which sodomy and gross indecency were said to be "posed" or performed, and that struck at the heart of what it meant, or was supposed to mean, to be a man. This vital linkage of sex, texts, and performance in the actual trials is obscured in the heavily censored accounts of the proceedings provided by Montgomery Hyde and others. But the newly discovered trial transcript enables us to see clearly that certain texts were represented on one hand as sites of sodomy and other forms of criminal sexuality, and simultaneously, of Wildean self-performance.

For example, in twenty-five pages of the uncensored transcript – some 10,000 words – defense attorney Edward Carson attempts to justify Queensberry's libel of Wilde ("posing as a sodomite") by examining lengthy passages from *The Picture of Dorian Gray*. Carson's motive was to represent Wilde's novel as having "a sodomitical tendency," then to build on that point by arguing that, as its author, Wilde was, de facto, "posing" or performing sodomy and thereby justifying Queensberry's alleged libel. The *Dorian Gray* element of the trial is much shorter in Montgomery Hyde's standard account in *The Trials of Oscar Wilde* – less than one-fourth as long as the transcript's – and it includes no mention of sodomy at all, or of any other specific sexual act.[57] In the actual trial, however, Carson's examination of Wilde regarding *Dorian Gray* was focused on establishing it as a novel about sodomy: "You left it open to be inferred, I take it, that the sins of Dorian Gray, some of them, may have been sodomy?" Wilde responded evasively, so Carson redirected his question in terms of the novel as a whole: "I take it that some people upon reading the book, at all events, might think that it did deal with sodomy?" "Some people might think so," replied Wilde, who then conceded in his own words that he had made at least one revision with the aim of dispelling "the impression that the sin of Dorian Gray was sodomy."[58]

After an adjournment for lunch, Carson resumed his interrogation along the same lines, establishing the "sodomitical" character of *Dorian Gray* to justify, in due course, Queensberry's allegation that its author was "posing as a sodomite": "The affection and love that is pictured of the artist [Basil Hallward] towards Dorian Gray in this book of yours might lead an ordinary individual to believe it had a sodomitical tendency, might it not?"

Figure 8. An early French edition of *The Picture of Dorian Gray*
(Paris: Charles Charrington, 1908) visualizes the key moment in
which Dorian stabs himself in the heart in the act of stabbing his
own portrait, changing places for the second time in the novel with
the posed representation of himself. (British Library)

To demonstrate the point, Carson read extensively from the novel,
including the following passage in which Basil Hallward, as Carson put it,
"confesses his love to Dorian Gray":

it is quite true that I have worshipped you with far more romance of feeling than
a man usually gives to a friend. Somehow, I had never loved a woman ... I quite
admit that I adored you madly, extravagantly, absurdly. I was jealous of everyone
to whom you spoke. I wanted to have you all to myself. I was only happy when I

was with you … I grew afraid that the world would know of my idolatry … One day I determined to paint a wonderful portrait of you … It is my masterpiece. But as I worked at it, every flake and film of colour seemed to me to reveal my secret. I grew afraid that the world would know of my idolatry. I felt, Dorian, that I had told too much. It was then that I resolved never to allow the picture to be exhibited.

Characterizing this passage as the description of an unnatural feeling "of one man towards another," Carson sought to clinch his argument by drawing a direct connection between the feelings expressed in the text and those of the author himself. Only a brief and modified version of the following exchange appears in Hyde's self-censored account of the trials, thus short-circuiting the connection that Carson was trying to make between Wilde's sexuality and the text of *Dorian Gray.* "Have you yourself ever had that feeling towards a young man? … Is it an incident in your life?" When Wilde evaded the question, Carson asked it again – in the lost transcript of the trial, that is, but not in Hyde's or other accounts: "Is it an incident in your life … Have you ever adored a young man, some twenty-one years younger than yourself, madly?" Carson then continued to press the point, with an urgency and focus not to be found in Hyde's or other narratives of the trial, as follows: "I want an answer to this simple question. Have you ever felt that feeling of adoring madly a beautiful male person many years younger than yourself?"

After Wilde professed to loud laughter that "I have never given adoration to anybody except myself," Carson persisted: "'I quite admit that I adored you madly.' Have you ever had that experience towards a beautiful male person many years younger than yourself? … you never had that feeling that you depict there?" Wilde coolly resisted these attempts to interpret *Dorian Gray* as the dramatic enactment of his own "sodomitic" feelings – "No," he responded, "it was borrowed from Shakespeare I regret to say."[59]

Wilde's reference to Shakespeare seemed to distract Carson for the moment from his pursuit of the main point, that *Dorian Gray* was the acting out in textual form of Wilde's own grossly indecent desires. He was reminded of "The Portrait of Mr. W.H.," Wilde's essay on Shakespeare's sonnets as a coded expression of same-sex love, but until the recent appearance of the trial transcript the sexually specific nature of the ensuing exchange was unknown to us:

CARSON: I believe you have written an article pointing out that Shakespeare's sonnets were practically sodomitical.
WILDE: On the contrary, Mr Carson, I wrote an article to prove that they were not so.

In his canonical narrative of the trials, Hyde substitutes "suggestive of unnatural vice" for "sodomitical," then abruptly concludes this exchange on Shakespeare's sonnets by claiming: "This reply appeared to satisfy Carson, as he returned to his reading of *Dorian Gray*."[60] In reality, however, as the newly discovered transcript shows, Carson was far from satisfied with Wilde's explanation, and continued to pursue the issue relentlessly:

CARSON: You did write an article to prove that they were not sodomitical?
WILDE: Yes, the statement had been made against Shakespeare by Hallam the historian, and by others ...
CARSON: In your opinion, they were not sodomitical?
WILDE: Certainly not.
CARSON: I suppose in that article you dealt fully with the subject?
WILDE: With the Shakespeare sonnets?
CARSON: With the question of sodomy.
WILDE: No, except that I said I object to the shameful perversion put on Shakespeare's sonnets by Hallam ...
CARSON: [returning to the subject of *Dorian Gray*]: "I grew afraid that the world would know of my idolatry." Why should he [Basil Hallward] grow afraid that the world should know of it? Was it anything to be concealed?
WILDE: Yes, because there are people in the world who cannot understand the intense devotion and affection and admiration that an artist can feel for a wonderful and beautiful person ...
CARSON: And these unfortunate people who have not that high understanding that you have, might put it down to something wrong?
WILDE: Undoubtedly.
CARSON: And sodomitical?
WILDE: Hallam had done it about Shakespeare.
CARSON: And sodomitical?
WILDE: To any point they choose ... [61]

Although temporarily sidetracked from his point that the text of *Dorian Gray* became a stage for Wilde's own performance as a sodomite, Carson had seized an opportunity to pair the novel with "Mr. W.H." and thus expand the list of Wilde's writings which were, in the counsel's terminology, "sodomitical" forms of self-presentation.

Then, however, Carson turned the court's attention to the portion of *Dorian Gray* in which Dorian is corrupted by the "yellow book" given him by Lord Henry Wotton. Picking up on Wilde's comment that the poisonous yellow book was "suggested" to him by Joris-Karl Huysmans's *A Rebours*, Carson laid the foundation for his argument by trying to maneuver Wilde into acknowledging that it was a book about sodomy. The following exchange between Carson and Wilde appears in the newly available transcript, but is omitted in all previous narratives of the trial:

CARSON: Now, that book that you say you referred to there, *A Rebours*, was that an immoral book … Was it a book, sir, dealing with undisguised sodomy?
WILDE: *A Rebours*?
CARSON: Yes.
WILDE: Most certainly not.
CARSON: Let me read to you.
WILDE: You must remember, Mr Carson – I wish distinctly to state that while the suggestion … of a young man taking up a book in a yellow cover and having his life influenced by it – while that to a certain degree suggested to me that I might write a book like *A Rebours*, on the other hand when I quote from the book … and allude to passages in the book, those passages do not occur in the book. It was merely what I imagined …
CARSON: Was *A Rebours* a sodomitical book?
WILDE: *A Rebours*?
CARSON: Yes.
WILDE: No.
CARSON: Now just take the book in your hand.
WILDE: You must describe to me what you mean by a sodomitical book.
CARSON: You don't know?
WILDE: I don't know.

At this point, however, Wilde's attorney, Sir Edward Clarke, began to object that Wilde was being cross-examined on the contents of a book that was not, by his own account, the yellow book referred to in *Dorian Gray*. "It was merely a motive," chimed in Wilde. "There is the difference."[62] There ensued a heated debate, unknown until the discovery of the trial transcript, over whether the fictional text by Huysmans had anything to do with the alleged libel of Wilde's "posing as a sodomite." For his part, Wilde asserted, "I don't think you have a right to cross-examine me on the work of another artist – I entirely decline to – I will not give my opinion." Sir Edward Clarke, his attorney, added:

I submit that while it is perfectly open to my learned friend – and perfectly fair – that upon any language of his own, Mr. Wilde should be cross-examined as severely as my learned friend may choose, upon the language of another person – which he has never adopted or repeated in any way whatever – I submit that my learned friend is not entitled to read that in court for whatever purpose he desires so to use it, because it is not relevant and cannot be relevant to any question in this case.

Despite these protestations, what mattered to Carson was that when writing the yellow-book episode of *Dorian Gray* "the book you had in your mind was

*A Rebours* ... a book that dealt with sodomitical incidents." Then, Carson appealed directly to the judge, insisting that Wilde's "posing as a sodomite" was directly linked to this fictional text written by someone else:

> Surely, my lord, where the issue here is whether Mr. Wilde was posing as a sod-omite, which is the justification pleaded here – I have the right to show when he was publishing that book he had in his mind a novel, which according to the extract that I have was plainly a novel which would lead to and teach sodomitical practices? My lord, surely I ought to be allowed to ask the witness and to test the witness as to whether the book was of that descripton?[63]

Proposing in effect that Wilde was inhabited by a "sodomitical novel," for *A Rebours* was "in his mind," Carson was suggesting that he performed or "posed" this textualized version of himself in the yellow-book episode of *Dorian Gray*. Carson hoped to demonstrate that while on one hand Wilde could be said to be "posing as a sodomite" because of his self-representation in so-called sodomitic works he had actually written, such as *Dorian Gray*, on the other hand his posing as a sodomite was compounded by the pres-ence, *within* him, of other sodomitic texts that he had not written, like *A Rebours*. The omission of this dialogue is one of numerous gaps in his-tories of the trial that have obscured – until the recent appearance of the lost transcript – the case that Carson sought to make out against Wilde as a sexual actor of specifically "sodomitical" texts.

Although the judge ruled that Wilde could not be interrogated about the content of a sodomitic novel that was "in his mind," Carson was never-theless successful in linking Wilde with other texts he had not written and, through them, with what Carson continued to refer to in this portion of the trial as the "posing" of sodomy. The recently published transcript provides a great deal of testimony – much more than previous accounts of the trial – about an issue of the Oxford undergraduate magazine *The Chameleon*, in which Wilde's "Phrases and Philosophies for the Young" appeared alongside a homoerotic story by J.F. Bloxam entitled "The Priest and the Acolyte" – a story, "is it not," asked Carson, "of a priest having fallen in love with the acolyte, the boy who attended him at the Mass?" When Wilde reluctantly agreed to this characterization of the story, Carson began to probe the implications of Wilde having contributed to the same magazine in which such a story appeared:

CARSON: I think you would admit, Mr. Wilde, that anyone who was connected with or who would allow himself publicly to approve of that article would be posing as a sodomite?
WILDE: No, would you repeat your question?

CARSON: Anyone who would allow himself to be connected with that article or who publicly approved of that article would be, at least, posing as a sodomite.

WILDE: No.

CARSON: You don't think so? ... I am asking you, supposing a person had been connected with the production or had approved of it in public, would you say he was posing as a sodomite?

WILDE: I should say he had very bad literary taste.[64]

A shortened and bowdlerized version of this exchange appears in Hyde's standard narrative of the trial. Hyde merely quotes Carson as saying, "I think you will admit that anyone who would approve of such a story would pose as guilty of improper practices" – a misquotation that dilutes Carson's charge to the effect that Wilde's secondhand association with "The Priest and the Acolyte" made him an actor of its specifically sodomitic content.[65]

In one notable instance Wilde was represented as an actor of so-called "indecent" texts, as opposed to "sodomitic" ones, a potentially useful strategy because Queensberry's plea of justification had repeatedly accused Wilde of gross indecency, and in doing so, laid the foundation for the criminal trials to come. The allegedly indecent texts were letters written by Wilde himself to Lord Alfred Douglas, but in the first trial Carson treated them cautiously, focusing on whether they were "proper" and, as Wilde claimed, "beautiful" works of art. But in the decisive third trial in which Wilde was convicted of gross indecency, the prosecutor, Solicitor-General Sir Frank Lockwood, refocused Carson's argument about Wilde's letters in order to sexualize them as acts of indecency in textual form, violating an implied script for the performance of masculinity, a persistent subtext of all three trials. Lockwood read aloud a letter by Wilde to Douglas beginning "My own Boy" – a letter that the previous two trials had already made notorious – and questioned Wilde closely about its supposed indecency:

LOCKWOOD: Was it decent? ... Do you think that this was a decent way for a man of your age to address a young man of his?

WILDE: ... Decency does not enter into it.

LOCKWOOD: Doesn't it? Do you understand the meaning of the word?

WILDE: Yes.

LOCKWOOD: "It is a marvel that those rose-leaf lips of yours should have been made no less for music of song than for madness of kisses." And do you consider that decent?

WILDE: It was an attempt to write a prose poem in beautiful phraseology.

LOCKWOOD: Do you consider it decent phraseology?

WILDE: Oh, yes, yes.

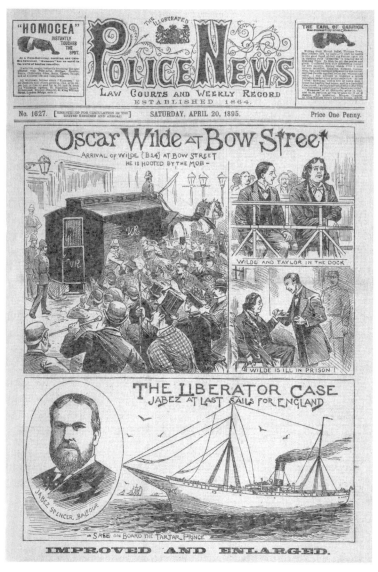

Figure 9. Wilde's carefully modeled celebrity persona was shattered by his courtroom trials and imprisonment. The *Police News* drew him on its front page of April 20, 1895, as a besieged and chastened man. (British Library)

LOCKWOOD: Then do you consider that a decent mode of addressing a young man?

WILDE: I can only give you the same answer ...[66]

The Solicitor-General's interrogation makes clear that Wilde was, in effect, accused of desecrating an implied script for what a "man" was supposed to say. In the context of the trials, therefore, one could not determine who or what Wilde was without framing him textually, both in terms of cultural directives for men and in terms of material texts that Wilde had actually written or was associated with in the courtroom proceedings. Textual issues were more prevalent in the first trial – unsurprisingly, since it was an action for libel – than in the criminal trials, but textuality remained a vital issue from beginning to end, informed by the unselfconscious assumption by Wilde's adversaries that what was at stake was not only sexual acts, but the text of masculinity itself and the performance of gendered identity for men. For example, in the first trial, Queensberry's lawyer Edward Carson quoted from another letter by Wilde to Douglas, insinuating that it implied indecent behavior through a use of language that was incompatible with true manhood. "You are the divine thing I want, the thing of grace and genius," Carson read aloud, then asked Wilde pointedly: "Is it the kind of letter that one man writes towards another man?"[67] The point of such courtroom exchanges was to show how texts produced or endorsed by Wilde were incompatible with the regulatory masculinity that the Criminal Law Amendment Act was designed to enforce.

In a crucial example of this textualizing of Wilde, and of gender itself, the prosecuting attorney in the second trial, Charles Gill, read from another text that Wilde had not written, the poem "Two Loves" by Lord Alfred Douglas, asking Wilde to explain the meaning of one line in the poem – "I am the Love that dare not speak its name." In his response Wilde indicated that whatever it was, it was not new. The love of men for other men and boys had flourished in many times and places, but tragically, as Wilde represented it here, the nineteenth century knew nothing about it. "The Love that dare not speak its name" had to be, if not invented, at least reinvented for his own time. But what *was* it? Although the question tethered Wilde once again to a text he had not written – the poem "Two Loves" – it could have provided a self-defining moment. Wilde's response, however, led him into a further repetition of his denials of sexuality and into the familiar trap of textuality. He said, to a mixture of applause and boos:

"The love that dare not speak its name" in this century is such a great affection of an elder for a younger man as there was between David and Jonathan, such as

Plato made the very basis of his philosophy, and such as you find in the sonnets of Michelangelo and Shakespeare. It is that deep, spiritual affection that is as pure as it is perfect. It dictates and pervades great works of art like those of Shakespeare and Michelangelo, and those two letters of mine, such as they are. It is in this century misunderstood, so much misunderstood that it may be described as the "Love that dare not speak its name", and on account of it I am placed where I am now. It is beautiful, It is fine. It is the noblest form of affection. There is nothing unnatural about it. It is intellectual, and it repeatedly exists between an elder and a younger man, when the elder has intellect, and the younger man has all the joy, hope, and glamour of life before him. The world mocks at it and sometimes puts one in the pillory for it.[68]

Wilde's explanation and defense of the type of manhood that had landed him "in the pillory" evaded the defining issue of sex with a blizzard of textual citations, referring his courtroom audience to the Bible, Plato, Shakespeare, Michelangelo, and Douglas's "Two Loves." At this crucial moment, one wishes that Wilde had been able to step outside of quotation marks, speak in his own voice, and in J.L. Austin's phrase of a half-century later, "make something happen" with performative speech.[69] The prosecutor's question – "what is 'the Love that dare not speak its name'?" – provided an opportunity to name himself into being, like the central character of his recent and most famous play, *The Importance of Being Earnest*. But unlike Jack Worthing, Wilde lacked the nerve, or the performative skill, to name himself in this defining moment. Instead, he kept off the subject in order to make a show of compliance with the sex and gender police who had brought him down. "The Love that dare not speak its name," he said, was "spiritual," it was "perfect"; above all, it was "*pure*" – that word again, celebrated by Josephine Butler as "the beautiful word of Purity," the favorite term in the rhetorical armory of Wilde's enemies. The idealizing terms and concepts that Wilde was now invoking and attaching himself to – and most especially the "beautiful word of Purity," as he was well aware – were the coded *text* of the *fin-de-siècle* reformers who had produced the new masculinity and law of gross indecency that were about to destroy him. His voice was not his own.[70]

It is also notable that Wilde's comments present a striking contrast to Michel Foucault's influential argument that a proliferation of sexualities in the late nineteenth century enabled the formation of homosexuality, producing a new kind of individual, a new "species." This new man would be "a personage, a past, a case history," as Foucault puts it in *The History of Sexuality*, and "nothing that went into his total composition was unaffected by his sexuality."[71] But Wilde's courtroom explanation of "the love that dare not speak its name" made it antiseptic and incorporeal. Instead of sexuality affecting everything in the new man's "total composition," as Foucault would have it, sexuality affected *nothing* in the spiritualized, disembodied personage characterized by Wilde in court. Describing a love that was above all "pure," Wilde's representation of men loving men was contaminated by what he most wanted to oppose – the *fin-de-siècle* "purity" that had put him in the pillory in the first place.

In attempting to bring alive "the Love that dare not speak its name" in a Victorian courtroom, Wilde found himself in the dilemma described by Jacques Derrida in his critique of J.L. Austin's conception of a performative language that creates something rather than referring to something existent. From Derrida's perspective, all speech and writing is cited, "put between quotation marks," and thus all language is characterized by a "general iterability" that makes every pronouncement not unlike the situation of an actor reciting lines on stage. Austin's classic examples of performative utterances – speech that is "the doing of an action," that makes, for example, a marriage or baptism happen – are viewed by Derrida as themselves ritualized expressions with a history and context that inevitably limit what the speaker can "do" with words. From this perspective, every utterance is "citational," and every speaker merely an actor rehearsing lines from a pre-existent script.[72] Whether universally true of people or not, this was the bind in which Wilde found himself in court, attempting to formulate an alternative masculinity under the rubric "the Love that dare not speak its name" – a phrase not of his own making, which he supplemented with a barrage of literary citations from Shakespeare to the Bible while saying little to the purpose in his own voice. Most egregiously, Wilde sabotaged all that he wanted to accomplish in this declamation by slipping, unconsciously perhaps, into the rhetoric of *fin-de-siècle* "purity" that had invented gross indecency in the first place and set him up as a puppet in what he would soon be calling his "hideous tragedy."

But even when the trials were obsessed with texts, they remained all about sex, reinventing Wilde as the sexual actor of "sodomotic" novels and "indecent" correspondence, of criminal texts he had written and others he had not. Trapped by texts, this courtroom incarnation of Oscar Wilde, "posing as a sodomite," also *became* a text. He became, in his own person and against his will, the dramatic enactment of the sexually specific meaning and puritanical morality of gross indecency.

CHAPTER 6

# *Prison performativity*

Wilde was not the only one trapped by texts in the matter of his trials. A judge invariably "cites" the law he applies, as Judith Butler points out in *Bodies that Matter*, and it was this "citational legacy," as she calls it, that constrained the judge who pronounced sentence on Wilde after the jury returned a verdict of guilty in the third trial.[1] "It is the worst case I have ever tried," the judge, Sir Alfred Wills, remarked acidly; "I shall, under such circumstances, be expected to pass the severest sentence that the law allows. In my judgment it is totally inadequate."[2] Wilde seemed "dazed" and "ready to faint," notes the 1906 *Trial of Oscar Wilde: From the Shorthand Reports*, as Justice Wills grudgingly followed the script and sentenced him to two years in prison at hard labor, wanting but unable to make it more than the maximum penalty provided for gross indecency in the statute written ten years earlier by Henry Labouchere.[3]

In prison afterward, Wilde was oppressed by a sense of his own citational legacy. Looking back on the trials, he began to understand himself as an actor confined within a controlling narrative – one already scripted, whose action, character, and dialogue he was bound to enact against his will. "I thought life was going to be a brilliant comedy, and that you were to be one of the graceful figures in it," Wilde wrote to Lord Alfred Douglas in his long letter from prison entitled *De Profundis* ("*Epistola: In Carcere et Vinculus*"). "I found it to be a revolting and repellent tragedy, and that the sinister occasion of the great catastrophe … was yourself."[4] Like the agents of the attenuated performativity of Derrida, Wilde saw himself as an actor whose speech and actions were not fundamentally his own – "a puppet worked by some secret and unseen hand to bring terrible events to an issue," as he writes in his letter from prison. Having departed from the directives of masculinity that had brought about the Criminal Law Amendment Act in the first place, Wilde was now facing the question that Judith Butler would pose a century later in *Bodies That Matter*: who is the "I" or "we" who stands behind the social script and enforces

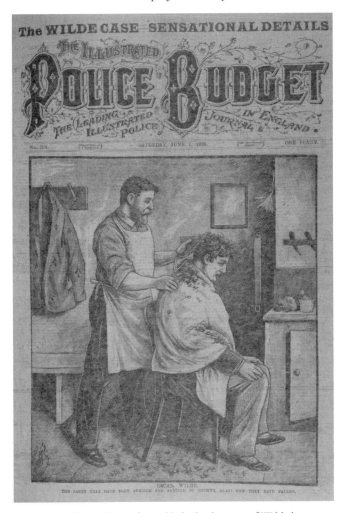

Figure 10. The *Police Budget* published a drawing of Wilde having his hair cut by the prison barber in its edition of June 1, 1895, thus capturing a moment in which institutional discipline interrupted, and disrupted, Wilde's theatrical self-presentation. (British Library)

its performance? Wilde's reference in *De Profundis* to "some secret and unseen hand" – a subject without a face – controlling the narrative of his life was an attempt to answer that question. His response prefigures Butler's own idea of a selfhood arising from a matrix of relations that form the subject, rather than from any single agency, person or persons, or other singly identifiable source. "There is no power that acts," as Butler suggests, "but only a reiterated acting that is power."⁵ It was not Douglas alone who determined his catastrophe, but the faceless and impersonal agency that Wilde now called "Society," whose puppet, lamentably, he had become.

As Wilde now saw it, however, it might be possible to reconceive himself in the wreckage of his life. Incarcerated, as he writes in *De Profundis*, "I was merely the figure and letter of a little cell in a long gallery, one of a thousand lifeless numbers, as of a thousand lifeless lives." As prisoner "C.3.3," a man with no name, Wilde had everything stripped from him – possessions, children, home, career – and on this blank surface he now hoped to rewrite himself, treating life as a fictional text in which he could inhabit and control protean identities. To become the author of his own life, however, he would have to look upon his past and put the burden of his doom "on my own shoulders," not on Douglas, notwithstanding the numerous and bitter condemnations of his lover in this long letter, and not on the law that brought him to prison. "I must say to myself that I ruined myself," Wilde writes; "and terrible as was what the world did to me, what I did to myself was more terrible still." He traces his fall to his own willful abdication of what he had once been: the lord of language and of himself – "a man who stood in symbolic relation to the art and culture of my age."

I became the spendthrift of my own genius, and to waste an eternal youth gave me a curious joy. Tired of being on the heights, I deliberately went to the depths in the search for new sensation … Desire, at the end, was a malady, or a madness, or both. I grew careless of the lives of others. I took pleasure where it pleased me, and passed on. I forgot that every little action of the common day makes or unmakes character, and that therefore what one has done in the secret chamber one has some day to cry aloud on the house-tops. I ceased to be lord over myself. I was no longer the captain of my soul, and did not know it. I allowed pleasure to dominate me. I ended in horrible disgrace. There is only one thing for me now, absolute humility.⁶

In this striking passage, after having spent many pages denouncing Douglas and others, Wilde joins the chorus of his accusers, the voices of the judges and lawyers who assailed him through three courtroom trials. He becomes now a willing actor in the ugly tragedy whose narrative he could not control – except perhaps in this way, realizing his position in the spectacle and embracing it, "the plank bed, the loathsome food, the hard ropes shredded into oakum till one's fingers grow dull with pain."⁷

Although denouncing himself in echo of the agents of "purity" who brought him down, Wilde finds a hidden potential in this subjection and in his position as the actor of a role forced upon him: "puppets themselves have passions. They will bring a new plot into what they are presenting, and twist the ordered issue of vicissitude to suit some whim or appetite of their own. To be entirely free, and at the same time entirely dominated by law, is the eternal paradox of human life that we realize at every moment ..."[8]

Although the script composed by a "secret and unseen hand" weighs heavily upon us, it still does not negate entirely the intentionality of the "puppets" that play their parts in it. Trapped within roles they have not chosen, they may yet, as Wilde imagines here, give vent to their own passions, alter the plot of the performance, and within strict limits satisfy some "whim or appetite of their own." It was this space for performative freedom that Wilde was striving to discover in his debased puppet-drama while serving two years at hard labor in prison. Paradoxically, however, the first step toward becoming the author of himself was "to absorb into my nature all that has been done to me, to make it part of me, to accept it without complaint, fear, or reluctance." To accept his role in the "repellent and revolting tragedy" had become for Wilde the precondition for breaking out of it.

Wilde found in incarceration the possibility of the free performativity that he now consciously sought. To turn his sorrow into gain, to accept it and yet move on to a new life – or rather, *lives* – Wilde turns to Christ as a model of the performative virtuosity to which he aspires. Indeed, Christ's life, seen in this light, becomes "the most wonderful of poems" and the purest imaginable instance of what J.L. Austin many years later would call performative speech.[9] The textuality of the Wildean Christ was utterly different from Wilde's own – Christ was a wonderful poem, a noble tragedy, whereas Wilde was diminished in a degraded puppet-show, the embodiment of "sodomitical" fiction and the word-made-flesh of Labouchere's statute on gross indecency. Christ was the author of himself, possessing an imaginative sympathy that allowed him to inhabit the lives of others, breaking through the barriers of his own personality and even obliterating the distinction between God and Man. "He calls himself the Son of the one or the Son of the other, according to his mood," Wilde observes in *De Profundis*, and out of this virtuosity arose the poem of Christ's life, a poem which is at the same time the noblest of dramas:

For "pity and terror" there is nothing in the entire cycle of Greek tragedy to touch it. The absolute purity of the protagonist raises the entire scheme to a height of romantic art from which the sufferings of Thebes and Pelops' line are by their very horror excluded, and shows how wrong Aristotle was when he said in his treatise on the drama that it would be impossible to bear the spectacle of one blameless in pain. Nor in Aeschylus or Dante, those stern masters of tenderness, in Shakespeare, the most purely human of all the great artists, in the whole of Celtic myth and legend, where the loveliness of the world is shown through a mist of tears, and the life of a man is no more than the life of a flower, is there anything that, for sheer simplicity of pathos wedded and made one with sublimity of tragic effect, can be said to equal or even approach the last act of Christ's passion.[10]

Stripped of his wealth and "all acquired culture," even his name, Wilde felt, in his sudden turn to Christ, that he had finally reached "my soul in its ultimate essence." Inhabiting this core of authentic selfhood, this "soul," Wilde proposes that his dispossession can become possession – of himself – now that everything external has been lost. Like his abrupt new affiliation with Christ, this decision to accept everything that has been done to him in order to discover a true, "buried self," as Matthew Arnold called it a half-century earlier, runs against the grain of nearly all Wilde's previous thought and writing. It marks the moment in *De Profundis* when Wilde becomes less the precursor of Derrida, and more conventionally Victorian, by embracing the idea of an autonomous individual with an "own self" who can bend the conditions of life to his will. To express this idea, he expands and deepens Emerson's axiom that "Nothing is more rare in any man than an act of his own." Eloquently, Wilde writes: "Most people are other people. Their thoughts are someone else's opinions, their lives a mimicry, their passions a quotation."[11]

In this striking formulation, Wilde uses the vocabulary and concepts that would be invoked a century later in articulating postmodern concepts of subjectivity. His assertion that the identity of most of us is contingent, a "mimicry" and "quotation" of other people, points in the direction of a similar idea expressed by Derrida that places every utterance within quotation marks, even performative ones that are said to make something "happen." In this instance, as in many others, Terry Eagleton is borne out in his judgment that modern literary theory, "for all its air of novelty, represents in some ways little advance on the fin-de-siècle," on Wilde in particular.[12] However, Wilde actually imagines in this prison interlude of nostalgic Victorianism that he is or can become one of the few who ever "possess their own souls," realizing himself through suffering and identification with Christ.

From Christ, or at least this version of Christ, Wilde learned that disgrace, imprisonment, and sorrow need not embitter or destroy him, but could be the means to self-enlargement with the grand potential of uniting humanity. As Wilde now understands him, while Christ did not say to men, "Live for others", he pointed out that there was no difference at all between the lives of others and one's own life. By this means he gave to man an extended, a Titan personality. Since his coming the history of each separate individual is, or can be made, the history of the world.[13]

The great importance of the Wildean Christ lay in this: he showed how to perform a self-transformation that would unify oneself with all others of the human race, the ugly and stupid as well as the brilliant and beautiful. But Christ was also the "True Man" of the social reformers who had conceived the law on gross indecency that landed Wilde in prison, a new masculinity marked by sexual purity, self-control, and an intense earnestness that demanded one "live for others."[14] Wilde's embrace of Christ in *De Profundis* is a rejection and reformulation of the Christ of the social-purity movement, and an effort to break out of the quotation marks that had contained him through his three disastrous trials. Wilde's Christ-like identification with the wretched of the Earth is not a gesture of self-sacrifice but a drama of self-expansion, incorporating everyone, great and small, into his own protean, radically individualist identity. But even in this self-enhancing identification with the poor and outcast, how very far Wilde has come, at this moment, from the state of mind he expressed a few years before in *The Picture of Dorian Gray*. The "divine" actress Sybil Vane performing in an East End theatre in his novel of 1891 is a kind of female Christ from Wilde's prison perspective, shattering the barriers that isolate one person from another in her audience of "common, rough people, with their coarse faces and brutal gestures." As Dorian Gray puts it, "She spiritualizes them, and one feels that they are of the same flesh and blood as oneself." But Lord Henry Wotton, the most Wildean of characters, shudders at this prospect: "The same flesh and blood as oneself! Oh, I hope not!" he exclaims, surveying the sordid gallery through his opera glasses.[15]

Christ's place may be among the dramatic tragedians, but in one important respect he is different from them, and as a matter of course from Wilde. "To the artist," as Wilde writes, "expression is the only mode under which he can conceive life at all. To him what is dumb is dead." The poet "conceives" life through words or other media, sympathizing with what has found a voice already, but with Christ it was gloriously different:

With a width and wonder of imagination that fills one almost with awe, he took the entire world of the inarticulate, its voiceless world of pain, as his kingdom, and made of himself its external mouthpiece. Those of whom I have spoken, who are dumb under oppression and "whose silence is heard only of God", he chose as his brothers. He sought to become eyes to the blind, ears to the deaf, and a cry in the lips of those whose tongues had been tied.

To artists, such as Wilde himself, people of this sort did not really exist at all because they had not fulfilled the condition of human life – the possession of an articulate voice. They had not been spoken into being. That artist of life, Lord Henry Wotton, dismisses the inarticulate masses in Sybil Vane's playhouse with a contemptuous aside, but Christ uniquely heard their silence, gave them a voice and a cry, and became "a very trumpet through which they might call to heaven." In so doing, Christ gave the poor a life and identity, making them his own brothers – more than his brothers, part of himself.[16]

Wilde himself, no more a poet, had become one of these dispossessed and inarticulate people – with no name, confined in a prison "of a thousand lifeless numbers, as of a thousand lifeless lives." Christ, however, knew how to fashion himself and others into being, for "out of his own imagination entirely did Jesus of Nazareth create himself" and became the mouthpiece through which unrealized individuals could express a being of their own.[17] Christ is Wilde's mouthpiece in *De Profundis*, and the long letter to Douglas, or rather a significant part of it, is Wilde's attempt to re-create himself in and through Christ. *De Profundis* was therefore Wilde's "attempt to write a gospel of his own," as Stephen Arata has insightfully written in a different context.[18] Wilde sought not only to be like Christ, but to *be* Christ, in the sense that matters most here – to partake of Christ's autonomous, divine performativity, the ability to become who and what he willed and transform the lives of those around him as well.

This performance, Wilde-as-Christ, seemed to offer the promise of radical self-fashioning, transforming his ordeal into a latter-day crucifixion that would be followed by transfiguration. But the pure agency that Wilde sought to achieve in this self-enactment would be extremely difficult, if possible at all, in a social world where people live inside quotation marks, the trap in which Wilde himself was caught, by his own admission, in the trials. After the exhilaration of imagining a Christ in whose presence "one becomes something," Wilde's mood suddenly darkens in *De Profundis* as he begins to realize that he has been unable, or has failed, to disentangle himself from the regulatory institutions and rituals that he wanted to transcend. For this reason the drama of Christ's life, in the end, was really hopelessly at odds with his own. Christ's tragedy was sublime, acted on his own terms, "but everything about my tragedy," Wilde reflects bitterly, "has been hideous, mean, repellent, lacking in style." Christ was the supreme individualist, but Wilde shrank from the individualism to which he aspired, allowing himself to appeal to "Society" in the form of an action for libel – an act that hopelessly compromised his aims, "the one disgraceful, unpardonable, and to all time contemptible action of my life." Wilde's "posing" of an unconventional identity had been filtered and screened, with his complicity, by the very social forces that he had hoped to resist and triumph over.[19]

The trials had given Wilde an opportunity to name himself into being as a different man from the one defined in the charge of gross indecency – an opportunity not only to remake himself, but to define and exalt "the Love that dare not speak its name." But as Wilde himself recognized, he was speaking in court with a voice not his own, for his unimaginative lies and evasions were denials of himself, and of what he aspired to be. This self-betrayal was, as he wrote in prison, a "loathsome" memory to him. "Instead of making beautiful coloured magical things such as *Salomé* and the *Florentine Tragedy* and *La Sainte Courtisane*, I forced myself to send long lawyer's letters and was constrained to appeal to the very things against which I had always protested." His trials were a story of surrender and pre-emption rather than self-definition. "This is where I found myself," he reproaches himself in *De Profundis* – "right in the centre of Philistia … I had come forward as the champion of respectability in conduct, of puritanism in life, and of morality in art. *Voilà où mènent les mauvais chemins.*"[20]

Indeed, the drama of Wilde's life had become, prophetically, the "social drama" of postmodern performativity. As Victor Turner points out in *The Anthropology of Performance*, social life is inherently dramatic, composed of complex sequences of symbolic acts – trials and legal processes, for example, as well as the scripted ways in which we present ourselves to the world, in dress, gesture, and speech – and the purpose served by these rituals is pre-eminently to enact the values and meanings that enforce order in a community. A transgressive figure who, like Wilde, breaks his role and asserts his own will against the man-made meaning that social performance celebrates will be called to account and, if possible, reattached to his assigned role.[21]

By contrast with Turner's idea of social life as a kind of puppet-drama, Christ had come to represent for Wilde a free, self-transforming performativity – but it is all but forgotten in the closing pages of his prison letter. Nearing the end, with scarcely a transitional phrase, he renews his attacks on Douglas for a variety of sins – for drawing him into his quarrel with his father, Queensberry, not writing to him in prison, not bringing him something to drink when he was ill, and in general for being out of his sphere, playing Rosencrantz and Guildenstern to Wilde's Hamlet. With Wilde-as-Christ put aside in the renewal of bitter recriminations against Douglas, this self-identification with Hamlet reminds us that, as *De Profundis* draws to a close, Wilde is still searching – flailing about, really – for a role and a script that would release him from the "hideous tragedy" in which he is imprisoned, literally and figuratively. It also reminds us that Wilde was defined by texts in his trials and imprisonment, both by his adversaries and by himself. In the trials he was portrayed as the sexual actor of "sodomitic" and "indecent" texts he had written, and of other texts, not his own, that were inscribed "in his mind." In the course of the trials he became the living specification of Labouchere's notoriously unspecific statute on gross indecency, while his own attempt to realize in language and thought "the Love that dare not speak its name" broke up into scattered citations of yet other texts.

Unlike Christ – "for out of his own imagination entirely did Jesus of Nazareth create himself" – Wilde was a puppet rather than an autonomous actor; he shrank from defining himself in the trials, and would not or could not define in any way that mattered the counter-normative community vaguely imagined in the phrase "the Love that dare not speak its name." This Wilde, the Wilde of real life, was not the "St. Oscar" of Terry Eagleton's memorable phrase.[22] His life had become, not a revolt against "Society's" structures of sex and gender, but a capitulation, and to no one was this failure more apparent than Wilde himself. Trapped by texts, ambushed by sex, Wilde took up the role that "Society" had prepared for him in the theatre of his trials – a sorrowful clown, a puppet, the failed hero of a tragedy that was, in every way, as he says in *De Profundis*, "hideous, mean, repellent, lacking in style."

# Epilogue
## Wilde and modern drama

The genesis of what we still call "modern drama" is usually traced to the rise of realism and naturalism in the theatre at the end of the nineteenth century. A blueprint for the revolution was Emile Zola's *Naturalism in the Theatre* (1878) with its insistence that playwrights learn to depict "real life on stage," providing a "detailed reproduction" of both character and environment in contemporary life. The new drama would embrace reality and renounce illusion, Zola proclaimed, and to do so it would have to turn away from the "ridiculous untruths" of previous modes of theatre, especially tragedy with its artificial rules and authoritarian principles. It would shift the focus from metaphysical concerns such as the soul or "being" of its characters and represent what were perceived to be the material, physiological foundations of human beings and the world they inhabit.[1] August Strindberg's *Miss Julie* (1888), as the playwright explains in his memorable preface, is an attempt to "modernize" drama along these naturalistic lines by tying its story of social ascendancy and decline to what he imagines to be "real life." Strindberg wants to tell his story with scientific detachment, tracing the fall of Julie and rise of Jean without moral preachment or supernaturalism – simply a laboratory demonstration of the old nobility of "honor" giving way now to the new nobility of brains and talent.

Raymond Williams has called this turn to realism in the theatre one of the great developments in art and thought – "to confront the human drama in its immediate setting, without reference to 'outside' forces and powers." Although scarcely mentioning Oscar Wilde at all in *Drama from Ibsen to Brecht*, Williams brilliantly expounds a theatrical naturalism that comes in many shapes and styles, flexible enough to take in nearly everything of note from Strindberg to Samuel Beckett. On one side, for example, Henrik Ibsen peels away layers of illusion to create a character such as Hedda Gabler, a "real" person, not merely a type, alienated from her womanly identity as understood in the 1890s and distracted by contradictory aims and conflicted motivations. Yet, as Williams points out, Ibsen's naturalism is not always congruent with so-called real life, despite the powerful verisimilitude with which he uncovers hidden and disturbing truth. His characters predictably explain themselves to the audience in the mode of older drama, and his plots proceed as relentlessly toward climax as does classical tragedy. The naturalism of Chekhov, by comparison, is focused on an alienated group more than upon a single person, as in *The Cherry Orchard*, and dispensing with soliloquies and asides the Russian playwright captures the pace of actual experience by showing people eating, walking about aimlessly, and talking randomly. To the leading Ibsen critic and translator, William Archer, Chekhov's realism was "empty and formless time-wasting" as compared to Ibsen's. Nevertheless, what binds these diverse realisms into a new kind of theatre, in style if not in substance, is the over-all reproduction on stage of lifelike behavior, speech, and environment.[2]

It was Oscar Wilde's perceived failure to achieve this representational fidelity that led many critics to perceive his plays as belonging to an outmoded past rather than an emergent modern drama. Wilde once remarked that no other dramatist of his time "has ever in the smallest degree influenced me," yet his plays from the beginning were thought to be shameless imitations of the work of French dramatists in particular – Victorien Sardou, Alexandre Dumas, Emile Augier, Eugène Brieux, and many others.[3] Critics then and now also noted Wilde's indebtedness to contemporaneous melodrama such as the perennially popular *East Lynne* and a host of more ephemeral specimens like Arthur Shirley's *Saved* and Sydney Grundy's *Glass of Fashion*.[4] Indeed, Sydney Grundy complained in an interview in 1892 that he could scarcely consider launching a revival of his highly successful *Glass of Fashion* "because Mr. Oscar Wilde did so, under the title of *Lady Windermere's Fan*."[5] From this not wholly inaccurate perspective, Wilde was seen, and to a large extent still is, as a playwright who rewrote the past rather than anticipated the future.

The closest thing to an English Ibsen – Bernard Shaw – was particularly contemptuous of *The Importance of Being Earnest*, whose first performance he reviewed under the heading "The Farcical Comedy Outbreak." Shaw could find no interest or merit in *Earnest* at all, relegating it to a pack of farces that in his view desecrated the reality principle and produced laughter in the audience through brute "galvanism." Although he had admired *An Ideal Husband* for its defiance of contemporary puritan morality, Shaw considered that in *Earnest* Wilde had not written a modern drama at all, but gone two decades backward to find his plot and characters in "farcical comedies dating from the seventies." In fact, Shaw wickedly suggested, Wilde probably wrote the play many years ago and only recently and lightly revised it before putting it on stage at the St. James's Theatre. "On the whole," Shaw wrote, "I must decline to accept *The Importance of Being Earnest* as a day less than ten years old." Above all, what made *Earnest* so appallingly anti-modern from Shaw's perspective was Wilde's lack of realism in characterization; Jack, Algernon, and the rest lacked any sense of "being" – no solid core of identity, in other words – and consequently could never instill "belief in the humanity of the play."[6] It was beyond Shaw's comprehension that in rejecting a characterological core for his dramatis personae Wilde might have been anticipating the theatre of the future rather than retreating into the theatre of the past.

Wilde's own view of the matter, like Harold Bloom's many decades later, was that all literature, including certainly his own, was a fratricidal assault on the past, not a complacent reiteration of it. *"Dans la littérature,"* as he once instructed the artist Will Rothenstein, *"il faut toujours tuer son père."*[7] Killing the father in this sense was precisely what Wilde imagined he had done in his career, looking back on it in prison clothes; he had been, in his own estimation, a man who not only defined his age but redefined its art and culture, in particular its drama. "I took the drama," as he explains in *De Profundis*, "the most objective form known to art, and made it as personal a mode of expression as the lyric or sonnet; at the same time I widened its range and enriched its characterisation."[8] This claim by Wilde that he had fundamentally changed the way plays were written – by making them self-expressive – builds on his earlier assertion in *The Critic as Artist*, audacious in itself, that all great characters in great plays are self-dramatizations of the poets who imagined them, "not as they thought they were, but as they thought they were not."[9] But these authorial self-enactments had been unpremeditated in earlier drama, the effect of the imaginative power of a great playwright unconsciously subverting the accepted need for drama to "hold the mirror up to Nature." Wilde, by his own estimation, had done something radically different – he had altered the course of drama by strategically abandoning its age-old mimetic basis, seeking not to imitate life but to create new worlds and perform new selves in a way that (as he says in *De Profundis*) "showed that the false and the true are merely forms of intellectual existence" and reconstituted both the poet and the world. "I treated art as the supreme reality," as Wilde sums up in *De Profundis*, "and life as a mere mode of fiction."[10]

Wilde refused to be dominated by the observable surface of life, or even to acknowledge that the surface was real, yet his work as a playwright was defined by the "structure of feeling" that Raymond Williams has argued is the distinctive core of modern drama. It was not the mere reproduction of contemporary, lifelike characters and environment on stage that changed the direction of drama and made it "modern," Williams asserts, but rather the discovery that there is something alienating and destroying in this so-called world that makes us yearn for a different one. The essence of modern drama, then, is its expression of the dramatic tension "between what men feel themselves capable of becoming, and a thwarting, directly present environment."[11] While naturalism in the theatre appeared to be setting a new agenda for drama, with a representational style implying a stable, manageable, even comfortable reality, it was Wilde who struck the distinctively modern note that the point of drama was no longer the imitation of action and character in life, but their making and unmaking – a search for some means of discovering or performing a humanity that could be lived beyond the limits of the regulated behavior and carefully ordered spaces of daily existence. This is the deeply personal, self-expressive modern drama that Wilde's comedies inaugurate, culminating with the dizzying if not wholly successful assaults on both objective reality and realism itself in *The Importance of Being Earnest*.

Writing many years before Antonin Artaud's convulsive manifesto urging a new kind of modern drama, Wilde anticipated in a far different register the repudiation of realism that lies at the heart of *The Theatre and Its Double*. Although Wilde would not have been at home amid the madhouse turbulence of a "theatre of cruelty," he would have found much to agree with in Artaud's denunciation of a passively mimetic drama in which the audience is shown only "a mirror of itself," an untimely, not really modern drama that seeks only to "bring life on the stage, plausible but detached beings, with the spectacle on one side, the public on the other."[12] Like Artaud, Wilde traced this error in part to Shakespeare, asserting in *The Decay of Lying*, tongue-in-cheek, that "that hackneyed passage about Art holding the mirror up to Nature ... is deliberately said by Hamlet in order to convince the bystanders of his absolute insanity in all art-matters."[13] And like Artaud, Wilde believed in, and meant to implement, a drama that was lyrical, personal, and transformative; life was, for him, a continuum of performance that occurred on both sides of the curtain, except that the theatre (at least when it worked properly) was "so much more real than life." Wilde's refusal to draw a straight line separating life from dramatic spectacle not only marks him off as a forerunner of late-twentieth-century

drama and cultural theory, but also helps to explain his own deeply theatrical experience of life – whether "posing" in America as a revolutionary
aesthete, performing (or trying to) a new script of gendered identity while
on trial for gross indecency, or aspiring in the close quarters of his prison
cell to what he thought of as the unlimited and liberating performativity
of Christ.

To be "acting Wilde," whether in plays or life, was to perform outside
the directives of surface reality; it was, or was meant to be, a transforma-
tional and revolutionary drama of Being and Becoming – for the cast of
characters, the public, and Wilde himself. This is the historic impulse
that divides Wilde from late-Victorian realism and connects him with
Artaud's theatre of cruelty and a great deal of our own contemporary
drama so different in style from his – for example, Tony Kushner's *Angels
in America*, or Sarah Kane's *Blasted*. A century before Kushner and Kane,
Wilde would have had no difficulty understanding what it meant when
the Angel plummets through the ceiling of Walter Prior's sickroom with
the intent of cracking history "wide open," or what to make of it when a
bomb blows a gaping hole in the wall of Kate and Ian's prison-like "real"
world, with terrible but possibly regenerative consequences. After Wilde,
the door stood open to a distinctively modern drama, not copied from
the surfaces of life, but exposing those surfaces as an illusion peopled with
characters of tenuous reality who, like Beckett's homeless men in *Waiting
for Godot*, experience the need to be constantly creating and recreating
themselves and the insubstantial world they live in. *The Importance of
Being Earnest*, with its hero who has to confess and act on the recognition that "I don't actually know who I am," is an early instance of this
modern drama of Being and Becoming, one that makes clear the limits
and opportunities of the performativity through which Jack Worthing
attempts to reinvent himself.

It has been vigorously argued in recent times that human society is
itself a constructed performance that establishes meaning and regulates
behavior by providing scripted directives of right and wrong, true and
false, and inflicts severe punishments for the suspension of "normative
role-playing."[14] Opposing this regulatory fiction with a mode of acting
that would be "so much more real than life," Wilde aspired in his plays
and in his rebelliously theatrical life to reorder the prescribed "realities" of
gendered and personal identity and the systems of authorized belief constructed to enforce them. That he experienced failures of nerve, fell short
of his goal, and was remorselessly disciplined by the guardians of social
order is appalling but not really surprising. In the process, however, Wilde

set the agenda for modern drama, not by putting visible reality on stage, but by undermining it with a yearning to discover through performance a humanity that (as memorably expressed by Raymond Williams) could not be realized in the alienating, ordered rooms of naturalist theatre or, for that matter, in "any available life."[15]

# Notes

1　Oscar Wilde, *The Picture of Dorian Gray* (1891), in *The Complete Works of Oscar Wilde*, vol. 3, ed. Joseph Bristow (Oxford: Oxford University Press, 2005), p. 237.

2　Oscar Wilde, *De Profundis ("Epistola: In Carcere et Vinculis")*, in *The Complete Works of Oscar Wilde*, vol. 2, ed. Ian Small (Oxford: Oxford University Press, 2005), p. 62.

3　Recently, for example, Jeff Nunakowa and Shelton Waldrep have written appreciatively and usefully on Wilde's attempts at "self-invention," although without situating them, as the present study attempts to do, in a matrix of theatre and theatrical practice as well as pivotal developments in late-Victorian sexuality and gender, social reform, and law. See Nunakowa, *Tame Passions of Wilde: The Styles of Manageable Desire* (Princeton, NJ: Princeton University Press, 2003, and Waldrep, *The Aesthetics of Self-Invention: Oscar Wilde to David Bowie* (Minneapolis, MN: University of Minnesota Press, 2004).

4　See Sos Eltis, *Revising Wilde: Society and Subversion in the Plays of Oscar Wilde* (Oxford: Clarendon Press, 1996).

5　Matthew Arnold, "The Buried Life," in *Matthew Arnold*, eds. Miriam Allott and R.H. Super (Oxford: Oxford University Press, 1986), pp. 153–55.

6　Nina Auerbach, *Private Theatricals: The Lives of the Victorians* (Cambridge, MA: Harvard University Press, 1990), p. 114. Auerbach has further discussed this dread of the theatre, and theatre's alarming contiguity with so-called reality, in "Before the Curtain," in *Cambridge Companion to Victorian and Edwardian Theatre*, ed. Kerry Powell (Cambridge: Cambridge University Press, 2004), pp. 3–14. The Victorian cultural panic over the theatre, insofar as it was organized around acting and actresses, is discussed at length in my book *Women and Victorian Theatre* (Cambridge: Cambridge University Press, 1997).

7　Lynn M. Voskuil, *Acting Naturally: Victorian Theatricality and Authenticity* (Charlottesville, VA: University of Virginia Press, 2004), p. 2.

8　Wilde, *The Picture of Dorian Gray*, ed. Bristow, p. 254.

9　James Eli Adams, *Dandies and Desert Saints: Styles of Victorian Masculinity* (Ithaca, NY: Cornell University Press, 1995), pp. 10–15.

10 Herbert Sussman, *Victorian Masculinities: Manhood and Masculine Poetics in Early Victorian Literature and Art* (Cambridge: Cambridge University Press, 1995), pp. 13–15.
11 Richard Dellamora, "Traversing the Feminine in Oscar Wilde's Salomé," in *Victorian Sages and Cultural Discourse: Renegotiating Gender and Power*, ed. Thais E. Morgan (New Brunswick: Rutgers University Press, 1990), p. 248.
12 *Illustrated Church News*, April 27, 1893, quoted from a clipping in the Clark Library.
13 Wilde, *De Profundis*, ed. Small, pp. 62–64.
14 Judith Butler, *Bodies That Matter* (New York: Routledge, 1993), p. 9.
15 Antonin Artaud, *The Theatre and Its Double*, trans. Mary Caroline Richards (New York: Grove, 1958), p. 79.

## CHAPTER I    POSING AND DIS-POSING: OSCAR WILDE IN AMERICA AND BEYOND

1 *New York Sun*, January 3, 1882, p. 1; *New York Times*, January 3, 1882, p. 5.
2 "The Theories of a Poet. An Interview with Oscar Wilde," *New York Daily Tribune*, January 8, 1882, p. 7.
3 *New York Daily Tribune*, September 23, 1881, p. 3.
4 "The Theories of a Poet. An Interview with Oscar Wilde," *New York Daily Tribune*, January 8, 1882, p. 7.
5 *New York Herald*, January 10, 1882, p. 5.
6 *New York Sun*, January 10, 1882.
7 *New York Times*, January 10, 1882, p. 5.
8 *New York Daily Tribune*, January 10, 1882, p. 2.
9 *New York Daily Tribune*, November 5, 1882, p. 3.
10 *New York Sun*, January 10, 1882.
11 *New York World*, January 10, 1882, p. 2.
12 *New York World*, January 10, 1882, p. 2.
13 *New York Sun*, January 10, 1882, p. 5.
14 *New York Herald*, January 10, 1882, p. 5.
15 "Oscar Wilde Sees 'Patience'," *New York Daily Tribune*, January 6, 1882, p. 5.
16 See Ben L. Bassham, *The Theatrical Photographs of Napoleon Sarony* (Kent, OH: Kent State University Press, 1978). Bassham provides a useful account of Sarony's methods as a photographer.
17 "Sarony as Seen by His Contemporaries," in *Photographic Journal of America*, 1897, p. 74.
18 "Sarony as Seen by His Contemporaries, p. 74.
19 Mitch Tuchman, *Smithsonian*, May 2004, pp. 17–18.
20 *New York Herald*, January 10, 1882, p. 5.
21 "Brief and Points for Plaintiff in Error," *Burrow-Giles* v. *Sarony*, Library of Congress microform, pp. 11–12.
22 "Did Sarony Invent Oscar Wilde?" *New York Times*, December 14, 1883, p. 4.

23 *Burrow-Giles* v. *Sarony*, 111 U.S. 53–61 (1883).

24 A rare exception to the disregard of *Burrow-Giles* v. *Sarony* in literary stud-ies is Jane M. Gaines's well-informed and useful discussion of the case in her book *Contested Culture: The Image, the Voice, and the Law* (Chapel Hill, NC: University of North Carolina Press, 1991); see chapter 2, "Photography 'Surprises' the Law: The Portrait of Oscar Wilde."

25 Doug Lichtman, "Copyright as a Rule of Evidence," Berkeley Olin Program in Law & Economics, Working Paper Series, Paper 52 (2003), especially pp. 10–16. In a legal context, the case confirmed a pre-existing law, Rev. Stat. 4952, that says photography is eligible for copyright "so far as the photograph is a representation of original intellectual conceptions."

26 *Burrow-Giles* v. *Sarony*, 111 U.S. 53 (1883).

27 Walter Benjamin, "The Work of Art in the Age of Mechanical Reproduction," in *Selected Writings / Walter Benjamin*, vol. 3, ed. Marcus Bullock and Michael W. Jennings (Cambridge, MA: Belknap Press, 1996), pp. 101–33.

28 Oscar Wilde, "The Relation of Dress to Art," in *The Artist as Critic: Critical Writings of Oscar Wilde*, ed. Richard Ellmann (Chicago, IL: University of Chicago Press, 1969), pp. 18–19.

29 Oscar Wilde, "Mr. Whistler's Ten O'Clock," in *The Artist as Critic*, ed. Ellmann, pp. 14–15.

30 Oscar Wilde, "London Models," in *The Artist as Critic*, ed. Ellmann, pp. 109–15.

31 Oscar Wilde, "The Portrait of Mr. W.H.," in *The Artist as Critic*, ed. Ellmann, pp. 169, 182–84.

32 Wilde, "The Portrait of Mr. W.H.," p. 152.

33 Wilde, "The Portrait of Mr. W.H.," p. 220.

34 Walter Benjamin, "The Work of Art in the Age of Mechanical Reproduction," pp. 101–33.

35 Alan Sinfield, *The Wilde Century: Effeminacy, Oscar Wilde, and the Queer Moment* (New York: Columbia University Press, 1994), pp. 17–21.

36 William A. Cohen, *Sex Scandal: The Private Parts of Victorian Fiction* (Durham, NC: Duke University Press, 1996), pp. 196–97.

37 Moe Meyer, "Under the Sign of Wilde: An Archeology of Posing," in *The Politics and Poetics of Camp* (London: Routledge, 1994), pp. 75–109.

38 Oscar Wilde, "The Critic as Artist," in *The Artist as Critic*, ed. Ellmann, p. 359.

39 Wilde, "The Critic as Artist," in *The Artist as Critic*, ed. Ellmann, p. 360.

40 Oscar Wilde, "The Artist as Critic," in *The Artist as Critic*, ed. Ellmann, pp. 363–64.

41 Wilde, "The Artist as Critic," in *The Artist as Critic*, ed. Ellmann, p. 368.

42 Wilde, "The Artist as Critic," in *The Artist as Critic*, ed. Ellmann, pp. 366–67.

43 Wilde, "The Artist as Critic," in *The Artist as Critic*, ed. Ellmann, p. 389.

44 Wilde, "The Critic as Artist," in *The Artist as Critic*, ed. Ellmann, pp. 385–86.

45 Wilde, *The Picture of Dorian Gray* (1891), in *The Complete Works of Oscar Wilde*, vol. 3, ed. Joseph Bristow (Oxford: Oxford University Press, 2005), p. 189.

46 *Dorian Gray*, Wilde, p. 189.

47  Wilde, *Dorian Gray* Wilde, pp. 188–89.
48  J.L. Austin, *How to Do Things with Words*, 2nd edn. (Oxford: Clarendon, 1975), especially Lectures 1–2, pp. 1–24.
49  Wilde, *Dorian Gray*, Wilde, p. 357.
50  Matt Cook, *London and the Culture of Homosexuality, 1885–1914* (Cambridge: Cambridge University Press, 2003), p. 111.

CHAPTER 2   PURE WILDE: FEMINISM
AND MASCULINITY

 1  The manuscript at the Ransom Humanities Research Center at the University of Texas, for example, has barely a mark on it – virtually no cross-outs or changes of wording. Few of Wilde's holograph manuscripts are so clean, regardless of whether they occurred early or late in the stream of revision of a particular play.
 2  Oscar Wilde, "The Critic as Artist," in *The Artist as Critic: Critical Writings of Oscar Wilde*, ed. Richard Ellmann (Chicago, IL: University of Chicago Press, 1969), pp. 385–86.
 3  See Barbara Caine's *Victorian Feminists* (Oxford: Oxford University Press, 1992), especially pp. 238–59, the chapter on the 1890s.
 4  Joan Rivière, "Womanliness as a Masquerade," in *Formations of Fantasy*, eds. Victor Burgin, James Donald, and Cora Kaplan (London: Methuen, 1986), p. 38.
 5  Given this common thread of purpose in the Criminal Law Amendment Act, it is entirely inaccurate to maintain, as some have, that "Section 11 dealt with an entirely different subject matter to the other sections of the Act, and had no nexus with them" (quoted from Jean Graham Hall and Gordon D. Smith, *Oscar Wilde: The Tragedy of Being Earnest* [Chichester: Barry Rose Law Publishers, 2001]).
 6  Charles Terrot, *The Maiden Tribute: A Study of the White Slave Traffic of the Nineteenth Century* (London: Frederick Muller, 1959), pp. 184–85.
 7  Frederic Whyte, *The Life of W.T. Stead*, vol. 1 (London: Jonathan Cape, 1925), p. 61.
 8  William T. Stead, *Josephine Butler: A Life Sketch* (London: Morgan and Scott, 1887).
 9  "Women's Protest," quoted by Josephine Butler, *Personal Reminiscences of a Great Crusade* (London: Marshall, 1896), p. 18.
10  Butler, *Personal Reminiscences*, p. 73.
11  Judith Walkowitz, *Prostitution and Victorian Society: Women, Class, and the State* (Cambridge: Cambridge University Press, 1980).
12  Stead, *Josephine Butler*, pp. 20–21.
13  Ellice Hopkins, *A Homely Talk on the New Law for the Protection of Girls: Addressed to Fathers* (London: Hatcherds, 1886), p. 4.
14  Hopkins, *A Homely Talk*, p. 4.
15  Stead, *Josephine Butler*, pp. 23–24, 36.

16  Millicent Fawcett and E.M. Turner, *Josephine Butler: Her Work and Principles and Their Meaning for the Twentieth Century* (London: Association for Moral & Social Hygiene, 1927), p. 1.

17  For a notable example of this persistent theme, see Josephine Butler, *Sursum Corda: Annual Address to the Ladies' National Association* (London: Purity Department of the Women's Christian Temperance Union, 1871).

18  Josephine Butler, "Letter to the Members of the Ladies' National Association," quoted by Caine, *Victorian Feminists*, p. 182.

19  Butler, *Personal Reminiscences*, p. 79.

20  Josephine Butler, *The Hour before the Dawn: An Appeal to Men*, 2nd edn. (London: Trubner, 1882), pp. 63–65, 71.

21  Josephine Butler, *Sursum Corda*, p. 18. She makes a similar point using similar language in *Social Purity: An Address Given to Students at Cambridge*, 2nd edn. (London: Dwyer, 1881), p. 20. One of W.E.H. Lecky's most widely read books, with many editions in the late nineteenth and early twentieth centuries, was *A History of European Morals from Augustus to Charlemagne* (London: Longmans, Green, 1869).

22  Judith Butler, *Gender Trouble: Feminism and the Subversion of Identity* (New York: Routledge, 1990), p. 136.

23  Josephine Butler, *Truth Before Everything* (London: Dyer, n.d.), p. 20.

24  Butler, *Truth before Everything*, p. 22.

25  Sarah Grand, *The Heavenly Twins* (New York: Cassell, 1893) and "The New Aspect of the Woman Question," *North American Review*, 158 (March 1894), pp. 170–76.

26  Sydney Grundy, *The New Woman: An Original Comedy, in Four Acts* (London: Chiswick, 1894), Act I, p. 28.

27  Victoria Cross, *The Woman Who Didn't* (London: Lane, 1895); Grant Allen, *The Woman Who Did* (Boston: Roberts, 1895).

28  Millicent Fawcett, "Woman's Suffrage," *Woman's World*, II (1889), pp. 9–12.

29  Frederick Dolman, "Lady Sandhurst at Home," *Woman's World*, III (1890), pp. 227–29.

30  Wilde's review of D.G. Ritchie's *Darwinism and Politics* (London: Sonnenschein, 1889) is reprinted in *The First Collected Edition of the Works of Oscar Wilde*, vol. 13, ed. Robert Ross (London: Methuen, 1908–22), pp. 486–88.

31  "Women and Politics," by Josephine E. Butler. Extract from a speech at a meeting of the Portsmouth Women's Liberal Association, 1888.

32  Oscar Wilde, *Play*, early holograph manuscript in the British Library, pp. 7–8, 21.

33  Wilde, *Play*, pp. 47, 50, 60.

34  For the final version, see the first edition (1893), the text used by Ian Small in his Mermaid edition of the play: *Lady Windermere's Fan*, 2nd edn. (New York: Norton, 2002), pp. 41–48.

35  *Pall Mall Budget*, February 25, 1892, p. 293.

36  Wilde, *Play*, p. 86.

37 The relatively late manuscript, in French, at the Ransom Humanities Research Center at the University of Texas has almost no corrections or strike-throughs, and the earlier manuscript at the Rosenbach Library, Philadelphia, has some emendations, mostly not in Wilde's hand and mostly unincorporated into the published version of the play. As has been pointed out, however, the possibility of missing, earlier manuscripts of the play cannot be discounted (see William Tydeman and Steven Price, *Wilde: Salome* [Cambridge: Cambridge University Press, 1996], pp. 17–19).

38 See Kerry Powell, *Oscar Wilde and the Theatre of the 1890s* (Cambridge: Cambridge University Press, 1990), pp. 33–54, for an analysis of Wilde's possible reasons for writing *Salomé* in French rather than English.

39 Walter Pater, *The Renaissance*, ed. Lawrence Evans (Chicago: Academy, 1977; reprinted from the Macmillan edition of 1910), p. 235.

40 Morley is quoted by David Womersley in a 2006 online review of a performance of Samuel Beckett's *Waiting for Godot* in the Oxford Playhouse production at New Ambassadors Theatre, London, October 10–November 18, 2006. www.socialaffairsunit.org.uk/blog/archives/001184.php.

41 Rupert Hart-Davis, ed., *Max Beerbohm's Letters to Reggie Turner* (Philadelphia, PA: Lippincott, 1965), p. 53.

42 Philippe Jullian, *Oscar Wilde* (London: Constable, 1969), p. 247.

43 Richard Dellamora, "Traversing the Feminine in Oscar Wilde's *Salomé*," in *Victorian Sages and Cultural Discourse: Renegotiating Gender and Power*, ed. Thais E. Morgan (New Brunswick, NJ: Rutgers University Press, 1990), p. 248.

44 Linda Dowling, "The Decadent and the New Woman in the 1890s," *Nineteenth Century Fiction*, 33 (1979), pp. 434–53.

45 William Archer, review of *Salomé* for *Black and White*, May 11, 1893, reprinted in Karl Beckson, ed., *Oscar Wilde: The Critical Heritage* (New York: Barnes and Noble, 1970), pp. 141–42.

46 Oscar Wilde, *Salomé*, in *Oscar Wilde: "The Importance of Being Earnest" and Other Plays*, ed. Peter Raby (Oxford: Oxford University Press, 1995), p. 81.

47 Wilde, *Salomé*, in *Oscar Wilde*, ed. Raby, p. 72.

48 Wilde, *Salomé*, in *Oscar Wilde*, ed. Raby, p. 87.

49 Wilde, *Salomé*, in *Oscar Wilde*, ed. Raby, p. 91.

50 Oscar Wilde, *A Woman of No Importance*, ed. Ian Small, 2nd edn. (New York: Norton, 1993), p. 45.

51 Butler, *An Appeal to Men*, p. 64.

52 Butler, *Sursum Corda*, p. 28.

53 This social-purity rhetoric was written into the first surviving draft of the play, now in the British Library, but was deleted in later versions, including the first edition – one of many significant alterations of this kind.

54 Wilde, *A Woman of No Importance*, ed. Small, p. 47.

55 Butler, *The Hour Before the Dawn*, pp. 8–10.

56 Wilde, *A Woman of No Importance*, ed. Small, p. 80.

57 Josephine Butler, "Women and Politics: Extract from a Speech at a Meeting of the Portsmouth Women's Liberal Association, 1888," a pamphlet among the Butler Papers in the Women's Library, London.

58 Josephine Butler, *The Hour Before the Dawn*, p. 64.
59 Quoted from Wilde's early autograph manuscript in the British Library, entitled *Mrs. Arbuthnot*, and from Jackson's 1993 edition of the play, p. 53.
60 Josephine Butler, *An Appeal to Men*, pp. 26–27.
61 Letter from Josephine Butler to Stanley Butler, June 4, 1895, MS, Women's Library, London.
62 "It is better to be beautiful than good" was deleted from the published play.
63 Quoted from Wilde's early autograph manuscript in the British Library, entitled *Mrs. Arbuthnot*, Act 1, p. 18.
64 Quoted from Wilde's early autograph manuscript in the British Library, entitled *Mrs. Arbuthnot*, Act 1, p. 41.
65 Quoted from the licensing manuscript of *A Woman of No Importance* in the British Library, dated April 15, 1893. Substantially the same speech occurs in an earlier typescript entitled *Mrs. Arbuthnot* in the Clark Library, UCLA, where it is inserted as an afterthought in handwriting on the verso of page 7 of the typescript.
66 Josephine Butler, *Personal Reminiscences*, pp. 31–32.
67 Wilde inserted this speech in his own handwriting on the verso of page 3, Act 3, in an early typed draft of the play in the British Library. The typescript was apparently derived from the earliest-known manuscript of the play.
68 Wilde, *A Woman of No Importance*, licensing manuscript in the Lord Chamberlain's Collection, British Library, dated April 15, 1893, pp. 43–44.
69 Wilde, *A Woman of No Importance*, ed. Small, p. 67.
70 This remark is crossed out in a typescript entitled *Mrs. Arbuthnot*, in the Clark Library at UCLA, which appears to mark an intermediate stage of the composition of the play, falling somewhere between the early autograph manuscript in the British Library and the licensing version that immediately preceded the first production.
71 Wilde, *Mrs. Arbuthnot*, closing scene of Act 3 in the autograph manuscript in the British Library.
72 These lines are crossed out in the typescript *Mrs. Arbuthnot* in the Clark Library, UCLA.
73 Quoted from the Clark Library typescript of *Mrs. Arbuthnot*.
74 Quoted from the Clark Library typescript of *Mrs. Arbuthnot*. In the first edition Wilde adds a few additional words, but preserves the subdued reaction by Lord Illingworth.
75 Quoted from a review of *A Woman of No Importance* in *Gentlewoman* magazine from a file of press clippings in the Clark Library.
76 These lines are quoted from the first edition. See *A Woman of No Importance*, ed. Small, p. 86.
77 *Westminster Budget*, April 28, 1893, p. 17.
78 *A Woman of No Importance*, ed. Small, p. 67.
79 *Illustrated Church News*, April 27, 1893, quoted from a clipping in the Clark Library.
80 Quoted from a clipping from the *Westminster Budget* in the Clark Library.

CHAPTER 3  PERFORMANCE ANXIETY
IN *AN IDEAL HUSBAND*

1   Jacques Derrida, "Signature Event Context," in *Margins of Philosophy*, trans. Alan Bass (Chicago, IL: University of Chicago Press, 1982), pp. 312–20.

2   The terminology is Josephine Butler's, from her *Personal Reminiscences of a Great Crusade* (London: Marshall, 1896), p. 320.

3   Oscar Wilde, *An Ideal Husband*, ed. Russell Jackson, 2nd edn. (London: Black, 1993), p. 84.

4   Wilde, *An Ideal Husband*, ed. Jackson, p. 33.

5   Wilde, *An Ideal Husband*, ed. Jackson, p. 84.

6   R.W. Burnie, Barrister-at-Law, *The Criminal Law Amendment Act, 1885: with Introduction, Commentary, and Forms of Indictments* (London: Waterlow & Sons, 1885), pp. 5–6.

7   I. Playfair [J.H. Wilson], *Gentle Criticisms on British Justice* (n.p.: privately printed, 1895), p. 3.

8   "C.G." [Charles Grolleau], *The Trial of Oscar Wilde, from the Shorthand Reports* (Paris: privately printed, 1906), pp. 52–53.

9   I. Playfair [J.H. Wilson], *Gentle Criticisms on British Justice*, p. 8.

10  Lord Alfred Douglas, "Oscar Wilde," trans. Christopher Millard, typescript in the Clark Library, UCLA, pp. 7–8.

11  Michael Foldy makes a strong case for the relationship between Rosebery and Drumlanrig influencing the conviction of Wilde. See *The Trials of Oscar Wilde: Deviance, Morality, and Late-Victorian Society* (New Haven, CT: Yale University Press, 1997), pp. 22–24.

12  Douglas, "Oscar Wilde," p. 9.

13  Wilde, *An Ideal Husband*, ed. Jackson, p. 51.

14  I. Playfair [J.H. Wilson], *Gentle Criticisms on British Justice*, pp. 3, 8.

15  Wilde, *An Ideal Husband*, ed. Jackson, p. 35.

16  Millicent Fawcett, "Women's Suffrage," *Woman's World*, II (1889), pp. 9–12.

17  W.T. Stead, *Josephine Butler: A Life Sketch* (London: Morgan and Scott, 1887), quoting Butler, p. 44; Ellice Hopkins, *The Power of Womanhood; or Mothers and Sons* (London: Wells Gardner, Darton, 1899), p. 180.

18  Wilde, *An Ideal Husband*, ed. Jackson, p. 46.

19  Wilde, *An Ideal Husband*, ed. Jackson, p. 85.

20  Wilde, *An Ideal Husband*, ed. Jackson, p. 89.

21  Oscar Wilde, *An Ideal Husband*, first draft in manuscript, undated, unpaged, Clark Library, UCLA.

22  Oscar Wilde, *An Ideal Husband*, licensing manuscript produced for the censor in the Lord Chamberlain's office, dated January 2, 1895, the day before the first production, p. 7.

23  Wilde, *An Ideal Husband*, ed. Jackson, p. 21.

24  Wilde, *An Ideal Husband*, ed. Jackson, p. 144.

25  Quoted from Wilde's autograph manuscript, undated, in the British Library.

26  Wilde, *An Ideal Husband*, ed. Jackson, p. 16.

27 Cited from Wilde's manuscript in the Clark Library, UCLA, the undated, unpaginated first draft of the play.

28 Cited from Wilde's manuscript in the Clark Library, UCLA.

29 Quoted from the manuscript/typescript, Act 4, p. 1, in the Clark Library, UCLA. About half the manuscript is in Wilde's hand, and the rest typed.

30 Quoted from the first draft of *An Ideal Husband*, which bears no page numbers or act markers. The manuscript is in the Clark Library, UCLA.

31 Quoted from the first draft of *An Ideal Husband*, Clark Library, UCLA.

32 Quoted from the first draft of *An Ideal Husband*, Clark Library, UCLA.

33 Quoted from Wilde's autograph manuscript, undated, in the British Library, Act 3, p. 17. In the final version, after having earlier tried deleting the ambiguous phrase "I want you," Wilde makes the note say: "I want you. I trust you. I am coming to you. Gertrude" (*An Ideal Husband*, ed. Jackson, p. 89).

34 The licensing manuscript of the play is in the Lord Chamberlain's Collection at the British Library. Act 3, p. 2, is quoted here.

35 Wilde, *An Ideal Husband*, ed. Jackson, p. 89.

36 Wilde, *An Ideal Husband*, ed. Jackson, p. 128.

37 Typescript of the play in the Clark Library, Act 4, p. 4. It is Act 4 that is dated March 1894; other acts bear different dates.

38 Wilde, *An Ideal Husband*, ed. Jackson, p. 87.

39 Wilde, *An Ideal Husband*, ed. Jackson, pp. 35–36.

40 Wilde, *An Ideal Husband*, ed. Jackson, p. 17.

41 Wilde, *An Ideal Husband*, ed. Jackson, p. 16.

42 This phrasing appears in Act 1 of an apparent prompt book, containing some revisions in Wilde's hand, in the Harvard Theater Collection.

43 Judith Butler, "Performative Acts and Gender Constitution," in *Performing Feminisms: Feminist Critical Theory and Theatre*, ed. Sue-Ellen Case (Baltimore, MD: Johns Hopkins, 1990), pp. 270–71.

44 Quoted from the typescript dated February 1894, in the Clark Library, UCLA, Act 1, p. 8.

45 Quoted from the autograph manuscript of the play in the British Library, Act 1, p. 51.

46 Quoted from a typescript dated 1894 in the Clark Library, UCLA, Act 1, p. 28.

47 Josephine Butler, "Women and Politics," a speech delivered to the Portsmouth Women's Liberal Association, 1888, in the collection of the Women's Library, London.

48 Wilde, *An Ideal Husband*, ed. Jackson, p. 62. Lady Chiltern's list of "delightful things" discussed at the meeting of the Women's Liberal Association is an echo of feminist and Liberal Party concerns in the early 1890s.

49 Late typescript/manuscript draft of *An Ideal Husband*, Act 2, p. 7 (verso) in Special Collections at Texas Christian University. The document is undated, part of a wide-ranging archive of rare books and manuscripts that previously belonged to the American collector W.L. Lewis. Also part of the Lewis archive is a presentation copy of the printed version of *An Ideal Husband*, given by

Wilde to Lewis Waller – suggesting that Wilde may have returned to Waller the revised typescript of the play along with the presentation copy of the book when it was published.

50　Wilde, *An Ideal Husband*, ed. Jackson, p. 84.

51　Wilde, *An Ideal Husband*, ed. Jackson, p. 101.

52　This conversation between Goring and Lady Chiltern is quoted from the over-looked 1894 typescript of Act 4 in the Clark Library, UCLA, p. 16. Similar but not identical versions of this conversation appear in the autograph manu-script in the British Library, Act 4, p. 60, and in the licensing manuscript in the British Library, Act 4, p. 16, before Wilde deleted this exchange altogether in the final revision.

53　Wilde, *An Ideal Husband*, ed. Jackson, pp. 137–39.

54　*An Ideal Husband*, ed. Jackson, pp. 137–39.

55　Richard Dellamora, "Oscar Wilde, Social Purity, and *An Ideal Husband*," *Modern Drama*, 37 (1994), p. 135.

56　Jacques Derrida, "Signature Event Context," in *Margins of Philosophy*, especially pp. 312–20.

57　Wilde, *An Ideal Husband*, ed. Jackson, p. 44.

58　Jacques Derrida, "Signature Event Context," in *Margins of Philosophy*, especially pp. 312–20.

CHAPTER 4　PERFORMATIVITY AND HISTORY: OSCAR WILDE AND *THE IMPORTANCE OF BEING EARNEST*

1　George Bernard Shaw, *Our Theatre in the Nineties*, in *Collected Works of Bernard Shaw*, vol. 23 (London: Constable, 1930–38), pp. 43–46.

2　These identifying marks of performativity are usefully elaborated by Eve Kosofsky Sedgwick in *Touching Feeling: Affect, Pedagogy, Performativity* (Durham, NC: Duke University Press, 2003), pp. 3–7. Although this thumb-nail sketch oversimplifies many complexities and nuances, as Sedgwick acknowledges, it nevertheless captures and positions the linguistic performa-tivity originated by J.L. Austin in *How to Do Things with Words*, 2nd edn. (Oxford: Clarendon, 1975) in relation to the performativity of deconstruction and gender studies with its theatrical anti-essentialism.

3　Oscar Wilde, *The Importance of Being Earnest: A Trivial Comedy for Serious People*, ed. Russell Jackson (New York: Norton, 2001), pp. 31–32, based on the 1899 first edition as revised by Wilde.

4　Barbara Meyerhoff, "Rites of Passage; Process and Paradox," in *Celebration: Studies in Festivity and Ritual*, ed. Victor Turner (Washington, DC: Smithsonian, 1982), pp. 109–35, especially pp. 115, 131.

5　Wilde, *The Importance of Being Earnest*, ed. Jackson, p. 30.

6　Victor Turner, *The Anthropology of Performance* (New York: PAJ, 1986), p. 81.

7　Sally F. Moore and Barbara G. Meyerhoff, "Introduction: Secular Ritual: Forms and Meanings," in *Secular Ritual*, eds. Moore and Meyerhoff (Assen, The Netherlands: Van Gorcum, 1977), pp. 16–17.

8  Wilde, *The Importance of Being Earnest*, ed. Jackson, p. 32.

9  The earlier version of the "parcel" scene appears in an early manuscript draft in the New York Public Library, and in a typescript of the four-act version of the play dating from October 1894, also in the New York Public Library. In the final version, the first edition of the play (1899), Jack is less assertive not only with Lady Bracknell, but in the ensuing scene in which he complains about her to Algernon. The original version also appeared in the licensing typescript submitted in January 1895 for the censor's approval.

10  Turner, *The Anthropology of Performance*, p. 94.

11  Quoted from an unpaginated notebook of dialogue [1893?] in the Clark Library, UCLA. Lady Bracknell's name was Lady Brancaster in early drafts; Algernon Moncrieff was Algernon Montford; *Lady Lancing*, the title of the play in some manuscript and typescript versions, names someone who never appears in any draft of *Earnest*. See Peter Raby, "The Origins of *The Importance of Being Earnest*," *Modern Drama*, Spring 1994.

12  Peter Raby, "The Making of *The Importance of Being Earnest*: An Unpublished Letter from Oscar Wilde," *Times Literary Supplement*, December 20, 1991, p. 13.

13  Anne Clark Amor, *Mrs. Oscar Wilde: A Woman of Some Importance* (London: Sidgwick and Jackson, 1983), p. 75. In late revisions, *An Ideal Husband* contains significant references to the Women's Liberal Association as the feminist organization with which Lady Chiltern is affiliated. Although the word "earnest" never occurs in *An Ideal Husband*, it is Lady Chiltern's insistence that her husband be an earnest man of "purity" that forms the crux of the play.

14  Frederick Dolman, "Lady Sandhurst at Home," *Woman's World*, III (1890), pp. 227–29.

15  Dolman, "Lady Sandhurst at Home."

16  Josephine Butler, "Letter to the Members of the Ladies' National Association," quoted by Barabara Caine, *Victorian Feminists* (New York: Oxford University Press, 1992), p. 182.

17  Josephine Butler, *Government by Police* (London: Dyer, 1879); W.T. Stead, *Josephine Butler: A Life Sketch* (London: Morgan and Scott, 1887), p. 36.

18  As her use of the term "crusade" suggests, the rhetorical practices of Josephine Butler and her allies were those of people who understood themselves to be engaged in a "holy war" – another phrase she was fond of and used often. See her memoir, *Personal Reminiscences of a Great Crusade* (London: Marshall, 1896).

19  Josephine Butler, *The Hour Before the Dawn: An Appeal to Men*, 2nd edn (London: Trubner, 1882), pp. 26, 63.

20  I am grateful to the professional staff of the Women's Library for their generous help in identifying little-known documents in the archive that form part of the contextual conditions of Wildean self-performance.

21  "Women and Politics," a pamphlet in the Woman's Library, London, reporting Josephine Butler's speech to the Portsmouth branch of the Women's Liberal Association, 1888.

22  Wilde, *The Importance of Being Earnest*, ed. Jackson, p. 67.

23 Quoted from Act 4, p. 130, of the early, but undated autograph manuscript in the British Library. In the final version of *Earnest*, there is no Act 4.

24 Josephine Butler, *Sursam Corda: Annual Address to the Ladies National Association* (London: Purity Department of the Women's Christian Temperance Union, 1871), p. 18.

25 *A Letter of Earnest Appeal and Warning from Josephine Butler to the Members of the British, Continental, and General Federation for the Abolition of the State Regulation of Prostitution* (London: Pewtress, 1895), a pamphlet in the collection of the Woman's Library, London. Butler's mention of W.T. Stead refers to the journalist's series of articles in the *Pall Mall Gazette*, beginning in July 1885, documenting child prostitution and creating an upheaval in public opinion that led quickly to the enactment of the Criminal Law Amendment Bill with its "section 11" forbidding gross indecency between men. Josephine Butler, Millicent Fawcett and many others in the feminist and social purity movements actively assisted and supported Stead in his reporting on child prostitution, and in the uproar that ensued, when Stead was imprisoned for purchasing a thirteen-year-old girl for £5 to document the sexual traffic in children in London. Among the witnesses who appeared in Stead's defense in court were Henry Labouchere, the Liberal politician who wrote the "gross indecency" amendment to the Criminal Law Amendment Bill. Oscar Wilde knew both Labouchere and Stead personally, and in the mid-1880s, shortly after Stead's sensational exposure of child prostitution and the enactment of the new law against gross indecency, Wilde wrote numerous book reviews for the *Pall Mall Gazette*, of which Stead was editor.

26 W. Davenport Adams, introduction to *A Book of Earnest Lives*, 7th edn. (London: Sonnenschein, 1894).

27 Ellice Hopkins, *The Power of Womanhood; or Mothers and Sons* (London: Wells Gardner, Darton, 1899), pp. 6–7. This campaign to reconstitute masculinity and put an end to the double standard by raising the moral bar for men was not limited, however, to the activists who campaigned with Josephine Butler and Ellice Hopkins. For example, Millicent Fawcett, best remembered today for her advocacy of political and educational rights for women, was a prominent member of the National Vigilance Association, the leading social-purity organization, and addressed its national meeting in 1895, a few months after the trial and imprisonment of Oscar Wilde for gross indecency. In her speech to the NVA, Fawcett was cheered loudly when she spoke of the need for "the rescue of fallen men," urging her audience to "make it clear to all that we seek in this matter, not to level down but to level up." From Fawcett's point of view in 1895, "the social evils and immoralities of our society emanate almost entirely from men," whose untamed passions are "like rampant wild beasts" (as quoted in *The Vigilance Record*, August 1895, pp. 18–19).

28 Wilde, *The Importance of Being Earnest*, ed. Jackson, p. 97.

29 For example, the *Oxford English Dictionary* cites one such reference to the word "uranist" in volume 33 of the *Journal of Comparative Neurology* (1895).

30 J.G.F. Nicholson, *Love in Earnest: Sonnets, Ballades, and Lyrics* (London: Stock, 1892), pp. 61, 131. Nicholson and his poetry were rediscovered by

Timothy D'Arch Smith, who places him within a tradition of "uranian" poetry in the late nineteenth and early twentieth centuries; see Smith, *Love in Earnest: Some Notes on the Lives and Writings of English "Uranian" Poets from 1889 to 1930* (London: Routledge and Kegan Paul, 1970).

31 Alan Sinfield, *The Wilde Century: Effeminacy, Oscar Wilde, and the Queer Moment* (New York: Columbia University Press, 1994), p. 37.

32 Matt Cook, *London and the Culture of Homosexuality, 1885–1914* (Cambridge: Cambridge University Press, 2003), pp. 7–8, 22–33.

33 Austin, *How to Do Things with Words*, p. 22.

34 Jacques Derrida, "Signature Event Context," in *Margins of Philosophy*, trans. Alan Bass (Chicago, IL: University of Chicago Press, 1982), especially pp. 325–27.

35 Wilde, *The Importance of Being Earnest*, ed. Jackson, p. 24.

36 Nicholson, *Love in Earnest*, p. 61.

37 Judith Butler, *Bodies That Matter: On the Discursive Limits of Sex* (New York: Routledge, 1993), p. 12.

38 Butler, *Bodies That Matter*, p. 9.

39 See Judith Butler, *Gender Trouble: Feminism and the Subversion of Identity* (New York: Routledge, 1990). These ideas are neatly summarized in Butler's essay "Performative Acts and Gender Constitution," in *Performing Feminisms: Feminist Critical Theory and Theatre*, ed. Sue-Ellen Case (Baltimore, MD: Johns Hopkins University Press, 1990), pp. 270–82.

40 Wilde, *De Profundis; "Epistola: In Carcere et Vinculis,"* in *The Complete Works of Oscar Wilde*, vol. 2, ed. Ian Small (Oxford: Oxford University Press, 2005), p. 62.

41 Derrida, "Signature Event Context," p. 326.

42 Wilde, *The Importance of Being Earnest*, ed. Jackson, p. 101.

43 Josephine Butler, *Social Purity: An Address Given to Students at Cambridge*, 2nd edn. (London: Dwyer, 1881), p. 5.

44 Wilde, *The Importance of Being Earnest*, ed. Jackson, p. 98.

45 Quoted from the licensing manuscript of the play, dated January 30, 1895 and entitled *Lady Lancing*, Act 2, pp. 14–15. This typescript is in the Lord Chamberlain's collection at the British Library.

46 Wilde, *De Profundis*, ed. Small, p. 95.

47 This scene occurs in the autograph manuscript in the British Library.

48 Wilde, *The Importance of Being Earnest*, ed. Jackson, p. 104.

49 Wilde, *The Importance of Being Earnest*, ed. Jackson, p. 104.

50 Wilde, *De Profundis*, ed. Small, p. 153.

CHAPTER 5   THE "LOST" TRANSCRIPT, SEXUAL ACTING, AND THE MEANING OF WILDE'S TRIALS

1 Wilde uses the phrase "hideous tragedy" in his letter from prison, *De Profundis ("Epistola in Carcere et Vinculis")*, in *The Complete Works of Oscar Wilde*, vol. 2, ed. Ian Small (Oxford: Oxford University Press, 2005), p. 71, in the context of accusing Lord Alfred Douglas of being the "true author" of

the spectacle, a view of his lover that he moderates and changes as the letter proceeds. But the view that his life has become a "hideous tragedy" remains to the end, as the question of its authorship becomes more subtle and complicated. Terry Eagleton characterizes Wilde as an "Irish Roland Barthes" in "Saint Oscar: A Foreword," *New Left Review*, 177 (September–October 1989).

2 Michel Foucault, *The History of Sexuality*, trans. Robert Hurley, vol. 1 (New York: Vintage, 1980), pp. 42–43.

3 Ed Cohen, *Talk on the Wilde Side: Toward a Genealogy of a Discourse on Male Sexualities* (New York: Routledge, 1993), pp. 99, 128–31, 172.

4 Stephen Arata, *Fictions of Loss in the Victorian Fin de Siècle* (Cambridge: Cambridge University Press, 1996), pp. 54–55.

5 See William T. Stead, "The Maiden Tribute of Modern Babylon," *Pall Mall Gazette*, July 6–10, 1885. The Criminal Law Amendment Bill was passed only a few days after the conclusion of Stead's series of articles.

6 H. Montgomery Hyde, *The Cleveland Street Scandal* (New York: Coward, McCann, Geoghegan, 1976), pp. 44–45; Colin Simpson, Lewis Chester, and David Leitch, *The Cleveland Street Affair* (Boston: Little, Brown, 1976), p. 6.

7 Hyde, *The Cleveland Street Scandal*, pp. 110–12.

8 Sean Brady, *Masculinity and Male Homosexuality in Britain, 1861–1913* (New York: Palgrave Macmillan, 2005), p. 82.

9 H.G. Cocks, *Nameless Offences: Homosexual Desire in the Nineteenth Century* (London: Tauris, 2003), pp. 78–79, 155–65.

10 Jeffrey Weeks, *Sex, Politics and Society: The Regulation of Sexuality Since 1800*, 2nd edn. (London: Longman, 1989), p. 103.

11 Eve Kosofky Sedgwick, *Epistemology of the Closet* (Berkeley, CA: University of California Press, 1990), p. 132.

12 Alan Sinfield, *The Wilde Century: Effeminacy, Oscar Wilde, and the Queer Moment* (New York: Columbia University Press, 1994), pp. 121–24.

13 Moe Meyer, "Under the Sign of Wilde: An Archeology of Posing," in *The Politics and Poetics of Camp*, ed. Moe Meyer (London: Routledge, 1994), pp. 75–109.

14 Cocks, *Nameless Offences*, pp. 105–15.

15 Matt Cook, *London and the Culture of Homosexuality, 1885–1914* (Cambridge: Cambridge Unversity Press, 2003), pp. 42–43.

16 Joseph Bristow, *Effeminate England: Homoerotic Writing after 1885* (New York: Columbia University Press, 1995), p. 2.

17 Mary Poovey, *Uneven Developments: The Ideological Work of Gender in Mid-Victorian Britain* (Chicago, IL: University of Chicago Press, 1988), p. 3.

18 Leslie J. Moran, *The Homosexual(ity) of Law* (London: Routledge, 1996), p. 33, quoting chapter 10 in Sir Edward Coke, *The Third Part of The Institutes of the Laws of England*.

19 See Jean Graham Hall and Gordon D. Smith, *Oscar Wilde: The Tragedy of Being Earnest* (Chichester: Barry Rose Law Publishers, 2001), p. 201. As to criminal libel in the late-Victorian period, the authors note: "A person who was seriously libeled, whether by publication to himself or to third parties,

could himself take criminal proceedings against the libeler; alternatively he could invite the police or the Director of Public Prosecutions to do so ... However, for an action of civil libel to succeed it had to be published to a third person" (p. 12). The Libel Act of 1843 had provided a new statutory defense to the charge of criminal libel – namely, that what was written was true and that it was written for the public good. Queensberry's counsel used this defense repeatedly in court.

20 My sources for information on the donor of the transcript, although anonymous, are unimpeachable.

21 *Central Criminal Court Sessions Papers*, vol. 121 (1895), pp. 531–32.

22 The phrase is Ed Cohen's, in *Talk on the Wilde Side*, p. 166.

23 The lost transcript of the libel trial – produced by stenographers of the London firm of Cherer, Bennett, and Davis – was first noted by Merlin Holland, then edited and published by him as *The Real Trial of Oscar Wilde: The First Uncensored Transcript of the Trial of Oscar Wilde vs. John Douglas (Marquess of Queensberry), 1895* (New York: Fourth Estate, 2003). It was published in Great Britain as *Irish Peacock and Scarlet Marquess: The Real Trial of Oscar Wilde*. The "standard" account of the trials has long been H. Montgomery Hyde, *The Trials of Oscar Wilde*, which originally appeared in 1948 as a very discreet and, consequently, inaccurate narration of the trials, a fault that later editions only partially remedied. The second edition of Hyde's book is widely available in a reprint by Dover (1973), which is the version quoted in this chapter.

24 R.W. Burnie, Barrister-at-Law, *The Criminal Law Amendment Act, 1885: with Introduction, Commentary, and Forms of Indictments* (London: Waterlow & Sons, 1885), pp. 5–6.

25 Josephine Butler, *A Letter of Earnest Appeal and Warning from Josephine Butler to the Members of the British, Continental, and General Fedration for the Abolition of the State Regulation of Prostitution* (London: Pewtress, 1895), p. 3.

26 Josephine Butler, *Truth Before Everything* (London: Dyer, n.d.), p. 22.

27 Frederick Mead and A.H. Bodkin, *The Criminal Law Amendment Act, 1885*, 2nd edn. (London: Shaw & Sons, 1890), pp. 67–68.

28 Sir James Fitzjames Stephen, *A Digest of the Criminal Law*, 4th edn. (London: Macmillan, 1887), p. 114.

29 Henry Labouchere's commentary on the Wilde verdict in *Truth*, May 30, 1895, p. 1331. Labouchere does, however, identify his source in writing the law: "I took the clause *mutatis mutandis* from the French code." In reality, however, the French penal code outlawed sexual assault instead of acts of "gross indecency" and did not penalize homosexual behavior between consenting adults in private. It must have been by conscious choice that Labouchere framed his amendment so vaguely as compared to the language of his self-described source, while departing from the French code as well by making his statute applicable to private conduct. For a discussion of the French law on homosexual behaviors, see Michael David Sibalis, "The Regulation of Male Homosexuality in Revolutionary and Napoleonic France, 1795–1815," and William A. Peniston, "Love and Death in Gay Paris: Homosexuality and

Criminality in the 1870s," in *Homosexuality in Modern France*, eds. Jeffrey Merrick and Bryant T. Ragan, Jr. (New York: Oxford University Press, 1996), pp. 30–53, 128–45.

30 Burnie, *The Criminal Law Amendment Act, 1885*, p. 33.

31 Mead, *The Criminal Law Amendment Act, 1885*, p. 67.

32 Mead, *The Criminal Law Amendment Act, 1885*, pp. 66–68.

33 *R. v. Willis* (1975). 1 All ER 620. 60 nCr App. Rep 146; *R. v. Spiers* and another. Court of Appeal (Criminal) (no date in original source); *M'Laughlan* v. *Boyd*. High Court of Justiciary. 1934 SC (JC) 19. November 2, 1933.

34 *King* v. *Bentley*. (In the Court of Criminal Appeal.) (1923) 1 KB 403. November 27, 1922.

35 *R. v. Hunt* (1950) 34 Crim. AR 135.

36 *Thompson* v. *Director of Public Prosecutions*. House of Lords. (1918–19) All ER Rep 521. December 3–4, 1917, January 24, 1918.

37 Cocks, *Nameless Offences*, p. 32.

38 Labouchere, *Truth*, May 30, 1895, p. 1331.

39 Cook, *London and the Culture of Homosexuality*, p. 151.

40 Indictment against the Marquess of Queensberry, in *The Real Trial of Oscar Wilde* (PRO ref. CRIM 4/1118), in *The Real Trial of Oscar Wilde*, ed. Holland, Appendix A, pp. 284–85.

41 Plea of Justification filed by the Defendant in *Regina (Wilde)* v. *Queensberry* (PRO ref. CRIM 4/1118), in Holland, *The Real Trial of Oscar Wilde*, pp. 286–91.

42 Holland, *The Real Trial of Oscar Wilde*, Holland, pp. 117–18. On several occasions, Carson accused Wilde of having sex with males at his home on Tite Street, Chelsea, when his wife Constance and their children were away.

43 Holland, *The Real Trial of Oscar Wilde*, p. 199.

44 Holland, *The Real Trial of Oscar Wilde*, pp. 206–09.

45 Holland, *The Real Trial of Oscar Wilde*, pp. 276–77.

46 Holland, *The Real Trial of Oscar Wilde*, pp. 281–82.

47 *The Trial of Oscar Wilde: From the Shorthand Reports* (Paris: privately printed, 1906) was edited by Charles Grolleau, who also translated some of Wilde's work into French, and deals only with the second and third trials, the criminal actions in which Wilde was accused of gross indecency. *Shorthand Reports* is a combination of narration and quoted testimony, and may have been based on shorthand notes taken down in the courtroom proceedings of the two criminal trials, although the shorthand notes themselves have since disappeared.

48 See Ed Cohen, *Talk on the Wilde Side*, p. 215. Since *Shorthand Reports* has been so rarely cited, it is worth noting that in addition to mischaracterizing it as deriving from "compilations" of press reports of the trail, Cohen also cites the title inaccurately: it is *The Trial of Oscar Wilde: From the Shorthand Reports*, not *The Trials of Oscar Wilde: From the Shorthand Reports*. Although Michael Foldy does not mention the book at all, his *Trials of Oscar Wilde: Deviance, Morality, and Late-Victorian Society* (New Haven, CT: Yale

University Press, 1997) provides a useful historical frame for Wilde's trials, and in particular a well-informed discussion of the social-purity movement.

49 Grolleau, *The Trial of Oscar Wilde* , pp. 23–24. This passage is directly echoed in Hyde's own revised account in *The Trials of Oscar Wilde*, 2nd edn. (New York: Dover, 1973), p. 171. This edition of Hyde's narrative is a widely available reprint of the enlarged second edition published by Penguin in 1962.

50 Hyde, *The Trials of Oscar Wilde*, p. 172; Grolleau, *The Trial of Oscar Wilde*, pp. 23–24.

51 Hyde, *The Trials of Oscar Wilde*, p. 181; Grolleau, *The Trial of Oscar Wilde*, p. 29.

52 Grolleau, *The Trial of Oscar Wilde*, pp. 87–88.

53 Grolleau, *The Trial of Oscar Wilde*, pp. 39–40; Hyde, *The Trials of Oscar Wilde*, pp. 181, 252.

54 Stephen, *A Digest of the Criminal Law*, p. 117.

55 Grolleau, *The Trial of Oscar Wilde*, p. 94.

56 Grolleau, *The Trial of Oscar Wilde*, pp. 18–19.

57 For the abbreviated but standard narrative of the trial's concern with *Dorian Gray*, see Hyde, *The Trials of Oscar Wilde*, pp. 109–15. The more explicit and complete account of the role *Dorian Gray* played in the libel trial is in Holland's *The Real Trial of Oscar Wilde*, pp. 77–103.

58 Holland, *The Real Trial of Oscar Wilde*, pp. 78–79.

59 *The Real Trial of Oscar Wilde*, ed. Holland, pp. 86–92.

60 Hyde, *The Trials of Oscar Wilde*, p. 113.

61 Holland, *The Real Trial of Oscar Wilde*, pp. 93–94.

62 Holland, *The Real Trial of Oscar Wilde*, pp. 96–98.

63 Holland, *The Real Trial of Oscar Wilde*, pp. 98–100.

64 Holland, *The Real Trial of Oscar Wilde*, pp. 69–73.

65 Hyde, *The Trials of Oscar Wilde*, pp. 106–08.

66 Hyde, *The Trials of Oscar Wilde*, p. 245.

67 Holland, *The Real Trial of Oscar Wilde*, p. 110.

68 Hyde, *The Trials of Oscar Wilde*, p. 201.

69 J.L. Austin, *How To Do Things with Words*, 2nd edn. (Oxford: Clarendon 1975), pp. 1–7.

70 It is true, on the other hand, that Wilde's mention of Plato in his courtroom explication of "the love that dare not speak its name" evokes faint echoes of an ideal of chaste and spiritual boy-love in some Greek writing, an ideal realized in practice by Socrates when he resisted desire for the young Alcibiades and "slept like a father with him under the same cloak." Wilde had made this case for a chaste and spiritual boy-love previously, most notably in "The Portrait of Mr. W.H." But the Greek ideal of *sophrosune* was not what Wilde's life and trials were about, and there was not the faintest echo of it in his relations with the blackmailers and prostitutes who were turning evidence against him in the Central Criminal Court.

71 Foucault, *The History of Sexuality*, vol. 1, p. 43.

72 Derrida, "Signature Event Context," in *Margins of Philosophy*, trans. Alan Bass (Chicago, IL: University of Chicago Press, 1982), pp. 326–27.

6 PRISON PERFORMATIVITY

1 Judith Butler, *Bodies that Matter: On the Discursive Limits of Sex* (New York: Routledge, 1993), p. 225.
2 H. Montgomery Hyde, *The Trials of Oscar Wilde*, 2nd edn. (New York: Dover, 1973), p. 272. Hyde's recital of the sentencing speech is similar to other surviving accounts. Others besides the judge in Wilde's case felt a need to exceed the sentencing limits for gross indecency. The author of an anonymous, unpublished letter in the files of the Public Record Office threatens to shoot Wilde, and hundreds of men, the writer asserts, would gladly do the same. (Included in a file of correspondence in the Public Record Office, this letter became the subject of a police report.) The Marquess of Queensberry, in a letter to his son, had already threatened to shoot Wilde "at sight," but Henry Labouchere, who knew both Queensberry and Wilde, urged forbearance, suggesting that Queensberry could give Wilde "a sound horsewhipping" instead, "for public opinion would be with him." Even Labouchere was frustrated by the limits that the law on gross indecency placed on the punishment of offenders, complaining in his article for *Truth* (May 30, 1895, p. 1331) of "the insufficiency of the severest sentence that the law allows." Although he wrote the law himself, he was not unconstrained in doing so. "As I had drafted it," Labouchere explained in his article, "the maximum sentence was seven years," but "the then Home Secretary and Attorney-General, both most experienced men ... suggested to me that it would be better were the maximum to be two years."
3 Grolleau, ed., *The Trial of Oscar Wilde: From the Shorthand Reports* (Paris: privately printed, 1906), p. 107.
4 Oscar Wilde, *De Profundis* (*"Epistola: In Carcere et Vinculis"*), in *The Complete Works of Oscar Wilde*, vol. 2, ed. Ian Small (Oxford: Oxford University Press, 2005), pp. 62–64.
5 Butler, *Bodies That Matter*, p. 9.
6 Wilde, *De Profundis*, ed. Small, pp. 95–96.
7 Wilde, *De Profundis*, ed. Small, p. 99.
8 Wilde, *De Profundis*, ed. Small, p. 62.
9 Wilde, *De Profundis*, ed. Small, pp. 109–11.
10 Wilde, *De Profundis*, ed. Small, p. 111.
11 Wilde, *De Profundis*, ed. Small, p. 113.
12 Terry Eagleton, "Saint Oscar: A Foreword," *New Left Review*, 177 (September–October 1989), pp. 125–28.
13 Wilde, *De Profundis*, ed. Small, p. 114.
14 See, for example, Ellice Hopkins, *The Power of Womanhood; or Mothers and Sons* (London: Wells Gardner, Darton, 1889), pp. 6–7; W. Davenport Adams, *A Book of Earnest Lives* (London: Sonnenschein, 1894), *passim*; and Thomas Hughes, *The Manliness of Christ* (Boston, MA: Houghton, Osgood, 1880), p. 67, where the author notes "Christ's whole life on earth was the assertion and example of true manliness."

15 Oscar Wilde, *The Picture of Dorian Gray* (1891), in *The Complete Works of Oscar Wilde*, vol. 3, ed. Joseph Bristow (Oxford: Oxford University Press, 2005), p. 238.
16 Wilde, *De Profundis*, ed. Small, pp. 114–15.
17 Wilde, *De Profundis*, ed. Small, p. 117.
18 Stephen Arata, "Oscar Wilde and Jesus Christ," in *Wilde Writings: Contextual Conditions*, ed. Joseph Bristow (Toronto: University of Toronto Press, 2004), p. 268. Arata suggests here that a "secular 'apostolic' community quickly formed around the figure of the suffering and martyred Wilde, a body of readers who found and continue to find in Wilde's texts and in his life the occasion for a communal guilt and redemption."
19 Wilde, *De Profundis*, ed. Small, pp. 123, 127, 129.
20 Wilde, *De Profundis*, ed. Small, pp. 130–31.
21 Victor Turner, *The Anthropology of Performance* (New York: PAJ, 1986), especially pp. 91–93.
22 Terry Eagleton, "Saint Oscar: A Foreword," *New Left Review*, September–October 1989.

### EPILOGUE

1 Emile Zola, "Naturalism in the Theatre," in *The Experimental Novel and Other Essays*, trans. Belle M. Sherman (New York: Haskell House, 1964), pp. 109–57.
2 Raymond Williams, *Drama from Ibsen to Brecht* (New York: Oxford University Press, 1969), especially the "Conclusion," pp. 331–47.
3 Wilde's assertion of originality was quoted in an interview published in the *St. James's Gazette* of January 18, 1895, pp. 4–5.
4 For a comprehensive and skeptical account of Wilde's supposed domination by his sources, see Kerry Powell, *Oscar Wilde and the Theatre of the 1890s* (Cambridge: Cambridge University Press, 1990).
5 "A Gossip with Sydney Grundy," *Era*, October 8, 1892, p. 11.
6 George Bernard Shaw, "Our Theatre in the Nineties," in *Collected Works of Bernard Shaw*, vol. 23 (London: Constable, 1930–38), pp. 43–46.
7 Will Rothenstein, *Men and Memories: A History of the Arts 1872–1922*, vol. 1 (New York: Tudor, n.d.), p. 132.
8 Wilde, *De Profundis ("Epistola: In Carcere et Vinculis")*, in *The Complete Works of Oscar Wilde*, vol. 2, ed. Ian Small (Oxford: Oxford University Press, 2005), p. 95.
9 "The Critic as Artist," in *The Artist as Critic: Critical Writings of Oscar Wilde*, ed. Richard Ellmann (Chicago, IL: University of Chicago Press, 1969), p. 389.
10 Wilde, *De Profundis*, ed. Small, p. 95.
11 Williams, *Drama from Ibsen to Brecht*, p. 335.
12 Antonin Artaud, "No More Masterpieces," in *The Theatre and Its Double*, trans. Mary Caroline Richards (New York: Grove, 1958), p. 76.

13 Wilde, "The Decay of Lying," in *The Artist as Critic*, ed. Richard Ellmann, p. 306.
14 Victor Turner, *The Anthropology of Performance* (New York: PAJ, 1986), p. 72–98.
15 Williams, *Drama from Ibsen to Brecht*, p. 338.

# *Bibliography*

## MANUSCRIPT SOURCES

### THE TRIALS OF OSCAR WILDE

*Regina (Oscar Wilde)* v. *John Douglas, Marquess of Queensberry, before R.M. Newton, Esquire (Magistrate).* Notes of Proceedings, March 9, 1895, Police Court, Great Marlborough Street. "From the Shorthand notes of Messrs. Cherer Bennett & Davies." Manuscript on loan at the British Library.

*The Queen (on the prosecution of Oscar Wilde)* v. *The Marquess of Queensberry, before Mr. Justice Collins and a Jury.* Notes of Proceedings, April 3–5, 1895, Central Criminal Court. "From the Shorthand Notes of Messrs. Cherer Bennett, and Davies." Manuscript on loan at the British Library.

### *LADY WINDERMERE'S FAN* (LISTED IN SUPPOSED CHRONOLOGICAL ORDER)

First manuscript draft, entitled *Play*. British Library.

Manuscript draft, *Lady Windermere's Fan*. William Andrews Clark Memorial Library. University of California at Los Angeles.

Typescript, entitled *A Good Woman*. Clark Library, UCLA.

Typescript entitled *Lady Windermere's Fan*. Clark Library, UCLA.

Typescript entitled *A Good Woman*. Harry Ransom Humanities Research Center, University of Texas at Austin.

Licensing typescript, *Lady Windermere's Fan*. Dated February 15, 1892. Lord Chamblerlain's Collection, British Library.

### *A WOMAN OF NO IMPORTANCE* (LISTED IN SUPPOSED CHRONOLOGICAL ORDER)

Manuscript draft, entitled *Mrs. Arbuthnot*. British Library.

Typescript with revisions in manuscript, entitled *Mrs. Arbuthnot*. British Library.

Another typescript with manuscript revisions, entitled *Mrs. Arbuthnot*. British Library.

Typescript with manuscript revisions, entitled *Mrs. Arbuthnot*. Clark Library, UCLA.

Typescript with manuscript revisions, entitled *Mrs. Arbuthnot*. Humanities Research Center, University of Texas.

Licensing typescript, entitled *A Woman of No Importance*. Dated April 15, 1893, Lord Chamberlain's Collection, British Library.

*AN IDEAL HUSBAND* (LISTED IN SUPPOSED CHRONOLOGICAL ORDER)

Fragmentary early manuscript, *An Ideal Husband*. Dated June 1893, Clark Library, UCLA.

Fragmentary manuscript/typescript, Act 4, *An Ideal Husband*. Clark Library, UCLA.

Manuscript draft, *An Ideal Husband*. British Library.

Typescript with manuscript revisions, *An Ideal Husband*. Dated January–March 1894, Clark Library, UCLA.

Typescript with manuscript revisions, *An Ideal Husband*. Dated March 1894, British Library.

Licensing typescript, *An Ideal Husband*. Dated January 2, 1895, Lord Chamberlain's Collection, British Library.

Typescript draft with revisions, *An Ideal Husband*. Texas Christian University.

*THE IMPORTANCE OF BEING EARNEST* (LISTED IN SUPPOSED CHRONOLOGICAL ORDER)

Manuscript fragments, *The Guardian*. Clark Library, UCLA.

Manuscript draft, Acts 1–2, *A Serious Comedy for Trivial People*. New York Public Library.

Manuscript draft, Acts 3–4, *Lady Lancing*. British Library.

Typescript, Acts 1, 3, 4, *Lady Lancing: A Serious Comedy for Trivial People*. Dated September 19 and November 1, 1894. New York Public Library.

Typescript, Acts 1–4, *The Importance of Being Earnest*. Dated October 31, 1894. New York Public Library at Lincoln Center.

Licensing typescript, *Lady Lancing: A Serious Comedy for Trivial People*. Dated January 30, 1895. British Library.

OTHER MANUSCRIPT SOURCES

Doulgas, Lord Alfred. "Oscar Wilde," trans. Christopher Millard, typescript in the Clark Library, UCLA.

BOOKS AND OTHER PUBLISHED WRITING BY WILDE

*The Artist as Critic: Critical Writings of Oscar Wilde*, ed. Richard Ellmann (Chicago, IL: University of Chicago Press, 1969).

*The Complete Letters of Oscar Wilde*, ed. Merlin Holland and Rupert Hart-Davis (News York: Holt, 2000).
*De Profundis ("Epistola: In Carcere et Vinculis")*, in *The Complete Works of Oscar Wilde*, vol. 2, ed. Ian Small (Oxford: Oxford University Press, 2005).
*An Ideal Husband*, ed. Russell Jackson, 2nd edn. (London: Black, 1993; New York: Norton, 1993).
*The Importance of Being Earnest: A Trivial Comedy for Serious People*, ed. Russell Jackson (New York: Norton, 2001).
*Lady Windermere's Fan*, 2nd edn. ed. Russell Jackson (New York: Norton, 2002).
*The Picture of Dorian Gray*, in *The Complete Works of Oscar Wilde*, vol. 3, ed. Joseph Bristow (Oxford: Oxford University Press, 2005).
*Salomé*, in *Oscar Wilde: "The Importance of Being Earnest" and other Plays*, ed. Peter Raby (Oxford: Oxford University Press, 1995).
*A Woman of No Importance*, ed. Ian Small, 2nd edn. (New York: Norton, 1993).

## CRITICISM AND CONTEXTS

Adams, James Eli. *Dandies and Desert Saints: Styles of Victorian Masculinity* (Ithaca, NY: Cornell University Press, 1995).
Adams, W. Davenport. *A Book of Earnest Lives*, 7th edn. (London: Sonnenschein, 1894).
Allen, Grant. *The Woman Who Did* (Boston, MA: Roberts, 1895).
Arata, Stephen. *Fictions of Loss in the Victorian Fin de Siècle* (Cambridge: Cambridge University Press, 1996).
  "Oscar Wilde and Jesus Christ," in *Wilde Writings: Contextual Conditions*, ed. Joseph Bristow (Toronto: University of Toronto Press, 2004), p. 268.
Arnold, Matthew. "The Buried Life," in *Matthew Arnold*, eds. Miriam Allott and R.H. Super (Oxford: Oxford University Press, 1986).
Artaud, Antonin. *The Theatre and Its Double*, trans. Mary Caroline Richards (New York: Grove, 1958).
Auerbach, Nina. *Private Theatricals: The Lives of the Victorians* (Cambridge, MA: Harvard University Press, 1990).
Austin, J.L. *How to Do Things with Words*, 2nd edn. (Oxford: Clarendon, 1975).
Bassham, Ben L. *The Theatrical Photographs of Napoleon Sarony* (Kent, OH: Kent State University Press, 1978).
Beckson, Karl, ed. *Oscar Wilde: The Critical Heritage* (New York: Barnes and Noble, 1970).
Benjamin, Walter. "The Work of Art in the Age of Mechanical Reproduction," in *Selected Writings /Walter Benjamin*, vol. 3, ed. Marcus Bullock and Michael W. Jennings (Cambridge, MA: Belknap Press, 1996), pp. 101–33.
Brady, Sean. *Masculinity and Male Homosexuality in Britain, 1861–1913* (New York: Palgrave Macmillan, 2005).
Bristow, Joseph, *Effeminate England: Homoerotic Writing After 1885* (New York: Columbia University Press, 1995).

ed. *Wilde Writings: Contextual Conditions* (Toronto: University of Toronto Press, 2004).

Burnie, R. W. *The Criminal Law Amendment Act, 1885: with Introduction, Commentary, and Forms of Indictments* (London: Waterlow & Sons, 1885).

Butler, Josephine. *Sursam Corda: Annual Address to the Ladies' National Association* (London: Purity Department of the Women's Christian Temperance Union, 1871).

*Government by Police* (London: Dyer, 1879).

*Social Purity: An Address Given to Students at Cambridge*, 2nd edn. (London: Dwyer, 1881).

*The Hour before the Dawn: An Appeal to Men*, 2nd edn. (London: Trubner, 1882).

"Women and Politics: Extract from a Speech at a Meeting of the Portsmouth Women's Liberal Association" (pamphlet, 1888).

*A Letter of Earnest Appeal and Warning from Josephine Butler to the Members of the British, Continental, and General Federation for the Abolition of the State Regulation of Prostitution* (London: Pewtress, 1895).

*Personal Reminiscences of a Great Crusade* (London: Marshall, 1896).

*Truth Before Everything* (London: Dyer, n.d).

Butler, Judith. *Gender Trouble: Feminism and the Subversion of Identity* (New York: Routledge, 1990).

"Performative Acts and Gender Constitution," in *Performing Feminisms: Feminist Critical Theory and Theatre*, ed. Sue-Ellen Case (Baltimore, MD: Johns Hopkins University Press, 1990), pp. 270–82.

*Bodies That Matter: On the Discursive Limits of Sex* (New York: Routledge, 1993).

Caine, Barbara. *Victorian Feminists* (New York: Oxford University Press, 1992).

Clark Amor, Anne. *Mrs. Oscar Wilde: A Woman of Some Importance* (London: Sidgwick and Jackson, 1983).

Cocks, H. G. *Nameless Offences: Homosexual Desire in the Nineteenth Century* (London: Tauris, 2003).

Cohen, Ed. *Talk on the Wilde Side: Toward a Genealogy of a Discourse on Male Sexualities* (New York: Routledge, 1993).

Cohen, William A. *Sex Scandal: The Private Parts of Victorian Fiction* (Durham, NC: Duke University Press, 1996).

Cook, Matt. *London and the Culture of Homosexuality, 1885–1914* (Cambridge: Cambridge University Press, 2003).

Cross, Victoria. *The Woman Who Didn't* (London: Lane, 1895).

D'Arch Smith, Timothy. *Love in Earnest: Some Notes on the Lives and Writings of English "Uranian" Poets from 1889 to 1930* (London: Routledge and Kegan Paul, 1970).

Dellamora, Richard. "Traversing the Feminine in Oscar Wilde's *Salomé*," in *Victorian Sages and Cultural Discourse: Renegotiating Gender and Power*, ed. Thais E. Morgan (New Brunswick, NJ: Rutgers University Press, 1990), pp. 247–61.

"Oscar Wilde, Social Purity, and *An Ideal Husband*," *Modern Drama*, 37 (1994), pp. 120–38.

Derrida, Jacques. *Derrida, Margins of Philosophy*, trans. Alan Bass (Chicago, IL: University of Chicago Press, 1982).

Dolman, Frederick. "Lady Sandhurst at Home," *Woman's World*, III (1890), pp. 227-29.

Dowling, Linda. "The Decadent and the New Woman in the 1890s," *Nineteenth Century Fiction*, 33 (1979), pp. 434-53.

Eagleton, Terry. "*Saint Oscar*: A Foreword." *New Left Review*, 177 (September–October 1989), pp. 125–28.

Ellmann, Richard. *Oscar Wilde* (New York: Knopf, 1988).

Eltis, Sos. *Revising Wilde: Society and Subversion in the Plays of Oscar Wilde* (Oxford: Clarendon, 1996).

Fawcett, Millicent. "Woman's Suffrage," *Woman's World*, II (1889), pp. 9-12.

Fawcett, Millicent and Turner, E. M. *Josephine Butler: Her Work and Principles and Their Meaning for the Twentieth Century* (London: Association for Moral & Social Hygiene, 1927).

Foldy, Michael. *The Trials of Oscar Wilde: Deviance, Morality, and Late-Victorian Society* (New Haven, CT: Yale University Press, 1997).

Foucault, Michel. *The History of Sexuality*, trans. Robert Hurley, vol. 1 (New York: Vintage, 1980).

Gaines, Jane M. *Contested Culture: The Image, the Voice, and the Law* (Chapel Hill, NC: University of North Carolina Press, 1991).

Grand, Sarah. *The Heavenly Twins* (New York: Cassell, 1893).

"The New Aspect of the Woman Question," in *North American Review*, 158 (March 1894), pp. 170-76.

Grolleau, Charles ["C.G."]. "C.G." *The Trial of Oscar Wilde, from the Shorthand Reports* (Paris: privately printed, 1906).

Grundy, Sydney. *The New Woman: An Original Comedy, in Four Acts* (London: Chiswick, 1894).

Hall, Jean Graham and Smith, Gordon D. *Oscar Wilde: The Tragedy of Being Earnest* (Chichester: Barry Rose Law Publishers, 2001).

Hart-Davis, Rupert. *Max Beerbohm's Letters to Reggie Turner* (Philadelphia, PA: Lippincott).

Hind, R. J. *Henry Labouchere and the Empire, 1880–1905* (London: Athlone, 1972).

Holland, Merlin. *The Real Trial of Oscar Wilde: The First Uncensored Transcript of the Trial of Oscar Wilde vs. John Douglas (Marquess of Queensberry), 1895* (New York: Fourth Estate, 2003).

Hopkins, Ellice. *A Homely Talk on the New Law for the Protection of Girls: Addressed to Fathers* (London: Hatcherds, 1886).

*The Power of Womanhood; or Mothers and Sons* (London: Wells Gardner, Darton, 1899).

Hughes, Thomas. *The Manliness of Christ* (Boston, MA: Houghton, Osgood, 1880).

Hyde, H. Montgomery. *The Power of Womanhood; or Mothers and Sons* (London: Wells Gardner, Darton, 1899).

*The Trials of Oscar Wilde*. 2nd edn. (New York: Dover, 1973).

*The Cleveland Street Scandal* (New York: Coward, McCann, Geoghegan, 1976).

Jullian, Philippe. *Oscar Wilde* (London: Constable, 1969).

Mead, Frederick, and Bodkin, A.H. *The Criminal Law Amendment Act, 1885*, 2nd edn. (London: Shaw & Sons, 1890).

Merrick, Jeffrey, and Ragan, Bryant T. eds. *Homosexuality in Modern France* (New York: Oxford University Press, 1996).

Meyer, Moe. "Under the Sign of Wilde: An Archeology of Posing," in *The Politics and Poetics of Camp*, ed. Moe Meyer (London: Routledge, 1994), pp. 75–109.

Meyerhoff, Barbara. "Rites of Passage: Process and Paradox," in *Celebration: Studies in Festivity and Ritual*, ed. Victor Turner (Washington, DC: Smithsonian, 1982), pp. 109-35.

Moore, Sally F., and Meyerhoff, Barbara G. eds. *Secular Ritual* (Assen, The Netherlands: Van Gorcum, 1977).

Moran, Leslie J. *The Homosexual(ity) of Law* (London: Routledge, 1996).

Nicholson, J. G. F. *Love in Earnest: Sonnets, Ballades, and Lyrics* (London: Stock, 1892).

Nunakowa, Jeff. *Tame Passions of Wilde: The Styles of Manageable Desire* (Princeton, NJ: Princeton University Press, 2003).

Pater, Walter. *The Renaissance*, ed. Lawrence Evans (Chicago: Academy, 1977).

Peniston, William A. "Love and Death in Gay Paris: Homosexuality and Criminality in the 1870s," in *Homosexuality in Modern France*, eds. Jeffrey Merrick and Bryant T. Ragan, Jr. (New York: Oxford University Press, 1996), pp. 128–45.

'Playfair, I.' [J. H. Wilson]. *Gentle Criticisms on British Justice* (n.p.: privately printed, 1895).

Poovey, Mary. *Uneven Developments: The Ideological Work of Gender in Mid-Victorian Britain* (Chicago, IL: University of Chicago Press, 1988).

Powell, Kerry. *Oscar Wilde and the Theatre of the 1890s* (Cambridge: Cambridge University Press, 1990).

*Women and Victorian Theatre* (Cambridge: Cambridge University Press, 1997).

*Cambridge Companion to Victorian and Edwardian Theatre* (Cambridge: Cambridge University Press, 2004).

Raby, Peter. *Oscar Wilde* (Cambridge: Cambridge University Press, 1988).

"The Making of *The Importance of Being Earnest*: An Unpublished Letter from Oscar Wilde," *Times Literary Supplement*, December 20, 1991, p. 13.

*The Cambridge Companion to Oscar Wilde* (Cambridge: Cambridge University Press, 1997).

Ritchie, D. G. *Darwinism and Politics* (London: Sonnenschein, 1889).

Rivière, Joan. "Womanliness as a Masquerade," in *Formations of Fantasy*, eds. Victor Burgin, James Donald, and Cora Kaplan (London: Methuen, 1986), pp. 35–44.

Ross, Robert, ed. *The First Collected Edition of the Works of Oscar Wilde*, vol. 13 (London, Methuen, 1908–22)

Rothenstein, Will. *Men and Memories: A History of the Arts 1872–1922*, vol. 1 (New York: Tudor, n.d.).

Sedgwick, Eve Kosofsky. *Epistemology of the Closet* (Berkeley, CA: University of California Press, 1990).

*Touching Feeling: Affect, Pedagogy, Performativity* (Durham, NC: Duke University Press, 2003).

Shaw, George Bernard. *Our Theatre in the Nineties, in Collected Works of Bernard Shaw*, vol. 23 (London: Constable, 1930–38).

Sibalis, Michael David. "The Regulation of Male Homosexuality in Revolutionary and Napoleonic France, 1795–1815," in *Homosexuality in Modern France*, eds. Jeffrey Merrick and Bryant T. Ragan, Jr. (New York: Oxford University Press, 1996), pp. 30–53.

Simpson, Colin, Chester Lewis, and Leitch, David. *The Cleveland Street Affair* (Boston, MA: Little, Brown, 1976).

Sinfield, Alan. *The Wilde Century: Effeminacy, Oscar Wilde, and the Queer Moment* (New York: Columbia University Press, 1994).

Small, Ian and Guy, Josephine. *Oscar Wilde's Profession: Writing and the Culture Industry in the Late Nineteenth Century* (Oxford: Oxford University Press, 2000).

Stead, William T. *Josephine Butler: A Life Sketch* (London: Morgan and Scott, 1887).

Stephen, Sir James Fitzjames. *A Digest of the Criminal Law*, 4th ed. (London: Macmillan, 1887).

Sussman, Herbert. *Victorian Masculinities: Manhood and Masculine Poetics in Early Victorian Literature and Art* (Cambridge: Cambridge University Press, 1995).

Terrot, Charles. *The Maiden Tribute: A Study of the White Slave Traffic of the Nineteenth Century* (London: Frederick Muller, 1959).

Turner, Victor, ed. *Celebration: Studies in Festivity and Ritual* (Washington, DC: Smithsonian, 1982).

*The Anthropology of Performance* (New York: PAJ, 1986).

Tydeman, William and Price, Steven. *Wilde: Salome* (Cambridge: Cambridge University Press, 1996).

Voskuil, Lynn M. *Acting Naturally: Victorian Theatricality and Authenticity* (Charlottesville, VA: University of Virginia Press, 2004).

Waldrep, Shelton. *The Aesthetics of Self-Invention: Oscar Wilde to David Bowie* (Minneapolis, MN: University of Minnesota Press, 2004).

Walkowitz, Judith. *Prostitution and Victorian Society: Women, Class, and the State* (Cambridge: Cambridge University Press, 1980).

Weeks, Jeffrey. *Sex, Politics and Society: The Regulation of Sexuality Since 1800*, 2nd edn. (London: Longman, 1989).

Whyte, Frederic. *The Life of W.T. Stead*, vol. 1 (London: Jonathan Cape, 1925).

Williams, Raymond. *Drama from Ibsen to Brecht* (New York: Oxford University Press, 1969).

Zola, Emile. "Naturalism in the Theatre," in *The Experimental Novel and Other Essays*, trans. Belle M. Sherman (New York: Haskell House, 1964).

# Index